SHAKESPEARE'S GARDEN

SHAKESPEARE'S GARDEN

THE BIRTHPLACE, STRATFORD-ON-AVON

SHAKESPEARE'S GARDEN

*Being a Compendium of Quotations
and References
from the Bard to all Manner of Flower,
Tree, Bush, Vine, and Herb,
Arranged According to the Month in which
They Are Seen to Flourish.*

BY J. HARVEY BLOOM, M.A.

Rector of Whitchurch

With Four Illustrations

London: Methuen & Co., 1903
Republished by Tower Books, Book Tower, Detroit,
1971

Library of Congress Catalog Card Number 78–77000

THIS BOOK IS DEDICATED BY ITS AUTHOR

TO THE

RIGHT HON. ALGERNON BERTRAM
LORD REDESDALE

IN GRATEFUL MEMORY OF KINDLY

ENCOURAGEMENT

CONTENTS

		PAGE
PREFACE	- - - - - -	- ix
PRINCIPAL AUTHORITIES CONSULTED	- -	- xi
INTRODUCTION	- - - - -	- 1
APRIL	- - - - - -	- 9
MAY	- - - - - -	- 20
JUNE	- - - - - -	- 35
JULY	- - - - - -	- 58
AUGUST	- - - - - -	- 71
SEPTEMBER	- - - - - -	- 87
OCTOBER	- - - - - -	- 99
NOVEMBER	- - - - - -	- 113
DECEMBER	- - - - - -	- 120
JANUARY	- - - - - -	- 126
FEBRUARY	- - - - - -	- 138
MARCH	- - - - - -	- 147

APPENDIX

TABLE OF QUOTATIONS FROM THE PLAYS AND POEMS - 159

LIST OF ILLUSTRATIONS

	PAGE
THE BIRTHPLACE, STRATFORD-ON-AVON	*Frontispiece*
THE CEDARS, WARWICK CASTLE	29
SHAKESPEARE'S GARDEN AT NEW PLACE, STRATFORD-ON-AVON	*To face* 159
MULBERRY-TREES SAID TO HAVE BEEN PLANTED BY SHAKESPEARE, WINCOT	174

PREFACE

MORE than one author has written a treatise on Shakespeare's flowers, and more than one has achieved success. The small books with coloured illustrations, of which there are many more or less artistic, cannot be counted in this category. They are not meant to be aids to serious study. The first to attempt a volume of the latter kind was Sidney Beisley, who wrote "Shakespeare's Garden" in 1864. He was followed by a series of essays in the "Garden" by the Rev. Henry Ellacombe in 1876, and these were republished in book form in 1878 by Pollard, of Exeter, and reprinted in 1884 (Satshell and Co., London), and again in 1896 (Arnold, London), while in 1883 George H. Grindon's "Shakespeare Flora" appeared (Palmer and Howe, Manchester).

The present volume is cast in the form of a calendar, and, month by month, the trees, shrubs, and flowers coming to perfection at that particular time of the year are duly treated. As a rule, the time of flowering is considered the time of perfection also ; but certain exceptions are made in favour of well-known fruits, whether British or foreign. This

calendar commences in April, since that would be
the first month of the new year, Old Style, omitting
the last five days of March.

The second part of the work contains an Appendix,
in which every mention of plants and their direct
products occurring in the poet's plays and poems is
arranged as it occurs, thus giving at a glance the
number of plants and mode of allusion in each play,
and also avoiding repetition.   But the more beautiful
passages are also quoted in the body of the work, and
discussed by aid of various extracts from Elizabethan
herbalists ; nor is their current folk-lore, legends, or
botany neglected.

J. H. B.

PRINCIPAL AUTHORITIES CONSULTED

"The Secretes of the Reverende Mayster Alexis of Piemount, translated out of Frenche into Englishe by Willyam Warde," in three books. London, 1559-1563. Quoted as Alexis.

"The Herball or Generall Historie of Plantes." John Gerard. London, 1597.

"Maison Rustique, or the Countrie Farme," compiled in the French tongue by Charles Stevens and John Leeboult; translated into English by Richard Surfleet. London, 1600; 4to. Quoted as Stevens.

"Popular Names of British Plants." R. I. A. Prior, D.D. London, 1863. Quoted as Prior.

"Observations on the Popular Antiquities of Great Britain." John Brand, M.A. Bohn's series; 2 vols. London, 1849. Quoted as Brand.

"Student's Flora of the British Islands." Sir J. D. Hooker, K.C.S.I. London, 1878. Quoted as Hooker.

"Hortus Cantabrigiensis." James Donn. London, 1826.

"Hortus Kewensis." London, 1811.

"The Shakespeare Flora." Leo H. Grindon. Manchester, 1883. Quoted as Grindon.

"The Plant Lore and Garden Craft of Shakespeare." Henry N. Ellacombe, M.A. London and New York, 1896. Quoted as Ellacombe. (First edition in 1878.)

"The Lake Dwellings of Switzerland," etc. Frederick Keller. Translated by John Edward Lee. London, 1878; 2 vols.

SHAKESPEARE'S GARDEN

Yet nor the lays of birds nor the sweet smell
Of different flowers in odour and in hue
Could make me any summer's story tell,
Or from their proud lap pluck them where they grew.
Sonnets, xcviii.

An odorous chaplet of sweet summer buds.
Midsummer-Night's Dream, II. i. 110.

"Retired Leisure
That in trim gardens takes his pleasure."
MILTON : *Il Penseroso*.

THAT man who can witness unmoved the moods
and passions of Nature, whether seen in some
mighty cataclysm or in the pure calm of moonlit
landscape, must be very strangely composed ; but in
Nature's many varied colourings and harmonies what
more glorious than her lavish display of flower and
fruit, some long stretch of hillside sheeted with
golden gorse or dyed by the setting sun with a thousand purpling shades of ling and heather, where all
things—rock, foliage, and sky—speak alike the glory
of the Divine Father? What wonder, then, that flower
and fruit have played a not ignoble part in the civilization of the world, and have helped to soften many
a rugged nature and have brought precious solace to
many a broken heart !

1

When Europe and the West were far behind the East in social progress, much that we look upon with pride to-day in the twentieth century A.D. was known, utilized, and loved in the twentieth century B.C. The gardens of Babylon and Nineveh were grand in their beauty, while in Egypt the worship of the Ka itself was indissolubly bound up with that of the presiding goddess of trees, and we can look kindly on the imagination which conjured up, out of the shady depths of the sycamore or the slender glories of the palm, a Divine emanation. If we read the hieroglyphs aright, to deck their gardens the Egyptians exacted as tribute from distant regions rare and beautiful plants. Some, such as the anemone and bay-tree, were special favourites; and in the gardens of the wealthy the shrine of Khem rose amid her shady avenues, aromatic herbs, and variegated flowers, in much the same way as the "garden-house" of an Elizabethan garden did in Shakespeare's day.

While these nations were at their mightiest zenith of power and influence, Asiatic pressure forced the neolithic farmers and herdsmen of the Stone Age through Northern and Central Europe, bringing with them the knowledge of the cultivation of plants for food, medicine, and, perchance, even for decoration; and as tools improved and knowledge extended, so more and ever more horticulture and agriculture flourished side by side. In Roman Britain, although an extreme province of that mighty Empire, villas arose, modelled on the sumptuous edifices that decked the valleys of the Adriatic or the hills about Tivoli; and can we doubt that, as the Northern provincials copied hypocaust and pavement, so they copied the garden, with its dainty flowers and vines, its fountains and statues, its marble benches and rare trees? Indeed, if tradition speaks aright, we owe more than one of our wild plants to Roman influence. The Roman nettle is an example, the most virulent of all its order in these islands, a plant grown by them as a pot-herb, and still to be found here and there lingering on the old site.

In the savage life of the Northern barbarians there was but little time or space for floriculture, and many a flower died out, and even some of the more useful edible plants, under their rule, although in their own mythology the tree Yggdrasil took no insignificant place. With the Norman Conquest came the dawn of modern gardening: there is a pretty legend quoted by the talented author of "A History of English Gardening,"* telling how the Red King visited Romsey Abbey ostensibly to see the roses. Within the walls of the religious Houses gardening thus early found a home, and it was a matter of necessity to the community that the hortulanus should provide vegetables in plenty for the table, and herbs both for medicine and flavouring; and to these fruits were added, and flowers, also some brought, perchance, through the constant interchange of brethren and pilgrims both at home and abroad. And this importation increased yet more when once the great trading companies of the Hanseatic League and the Staple of Calais began to export and import their many wares. Yet we have very little left us either in illuminations or elsewhere to show how a medieval garden was arranged. Blomfield† gives a plate from Harl. MS. 4425 of a garden, which is drawn divided into two plots by a fence with a high gateway in the centre, and entirely surrounded by a wall with

* "A History of Gardening in England," by the Hon. Alicia Amherst. London, 1896.
† "The Formal Garden in England."

1—2

battlements.   In the middle of the left-hand plot
stands a fountain, apparently of metal and marble,
and in the right-hand plot are small lawns, in one of
which is an orange-tree enclosed by a circular low
railing, and at one end a fence of trellis overhung
with flowers, and here and there peacocks sunning
themselves.   The Wars of the Roses gave little time
for gardening ; but when matters were settled, and
the educational movements which marked the dawn
of the Renaissance began, the gardens once again,
after a break of more than a thousand years, went
back to classical models, as interpreted by the Italian
school of the time.   Thus, the gardens of the Palace
of Nonsuch, 1539, and Theobalds, 1560, showed all
the new ideas : flower-beds edged with low trellises ;
topiary work of cut box and yew, whereby the
natural growth of the trees was trained into figures
of birds and animals, and especially of peacocks ;
while here and there mounts were thrown up against
the orchard or garden wall, ascended by flights of
steps and crowned with arbours, while sometimes
the view obtained in this manner was deemed in-
sufficient, and trellised galleries extended the whole
length of the garden.   In 1575 the gardens of
Kenilworth, which Shakespeare almost certainly
visited, had a terrace walk twelve feet in width,
and raised ten feet above the garden, terminating
at either end in arbours redolent with sweetbriar
and flowers.   Beneath these, again, was a garden an
acre or more in size, divided into four quarters by
sanded walks, and having in the centre of each plot
an obelisk of red porphyry with a ball at the top.
These were planted with apple, pear, and cherry,
while in the centre was a fountain of white marble.*
But the Elizabethan garden was by no means strictly
conservative.   It adopted not only native customs,

* See Blomfield's " Formal Garden."

but introduced new methods from France, Italy, and Holland. The design was essentially architectural; he who designed the house designed the garden. The terraced walk has been mentioned; flights of steps led from it to sanded walks called forthrights, while these broader paths were intersected by others, parallel to the terrace, and the interstices filled up with grass plots, mazes, or knotted beds. The design carried out in these latter corresponded to the pierced pattern in the house parapet, and was edged with box, thrift, or tile. The general arrangement of a house of the size of Shakespeare's would be similar to that so carefully described in the "Maison Rustique, or Countrie Farme, of Charles Stevens and John Leebault, Doctors of Physicke, London, 1600." So exactly does this volume describe the manner of forming such a garden as Shakespeare's father may have had in Henley Street, or the poet himself at New Place, that we may be forgiven for reproducing it in its entirety. After describing the garden for vegetables he proceeds :

"THE GARDEN OF PLEASURE

shall be set about and compassed in with arbours made of jesamin, rosemarie, boxe, juniper, cypress-trees, savin, cedars, rose-trees, and other dainties first planted and pruned according as the nature of every one doth require, but after brought into some forme and order with willow or juniper poles, such as may serve for the making of arbours. The waies and alleyes must be covered and sowen with fine sand well bet or with the powder of the sawing of marble or else paved handsomely with good pit stone.

"This garden by means of a large path of the breadth of six feet, shall be divided into two equal parts ; the one shall containe the herbes and flowers used to make nosegaies and garlands of, as March violets, Provence gilloflowers, purple gilloflowers, Indian gilloflowers, small paunces, daisies, yellow and white gilloflowers, marigolds, lilly conually, daffodils, canterburie bels, purple velvet flowers, anemones, corne flag, mugwoort lilies and other such like, and it may be called the nosegaie garden.

" The other part shall have all other sweet smelling herbes, whether they be suche as beare no flowers, or if they beare any, yet they are not put in nosegaies alone but the whole herbe be with them, as Southern wood,' wormewood, pellitorie, rosemarie, jesamin, marierom, balme mints, peniroyall, costmarie, hyssop, lavander, basil, sage, savorie, rue, tansey, thyme, cammomill, mugwoort, bastard marierim, nept, sweet balme, all-good, anis, horehound, and others such like, and this may be called the garden for herbes of good smell. . . .

" These sweet herbes, and flowers for nosegaies shall be set in order upon beds and quarters, of such like length and breadth, as those of the kitchen garden, others in mazes made for the pleasing and recreating of the sight, and other some are set in proportions made of beds interlaced and drawen one within another or broken off with borders or without borders." *

Such was the garden in which the poet may have spent some at least of his summer hours half-buried in his arbours of woodbine and sweetbriar, the air quivering in the hum of insect-life. Nor need we trace the development of gardens any further. Yet to those who wish to do more we here add a brief list of authorities, looked upon in Shakespeare's time as such. They commence with " The Grete Herball " of Peter Treveris, which ran to six editions, and first appeared

* " Maison Rustique," p. 301.

in 1516. It was followed in 1523 by Fitzherbert's
"Husbandry," of which four versions were printed.
Then in 1525 came W(alter) C(ary's) "Herball" (three
editions), "Jerome of Brunswick-Andrew," a folio
printed in London in 1527 ; Macer's "Herbal," 1535.
The "Libellus" of William Turner appeared in 1548,
"The Names of Herbes" in 1548, and "New Herball"
in 1551, with a second part in 1562. In 1540 Andrew
Borde brought out "a Boke for to lerne a Man to be
Wyse in buylding of his House." In 1573 came Thomas
Tusser's "Five Hundred Points of Good Husbandry,"
and in 1563 Thomas Hill produced "A Most Brief and
Pleasaunt Treatyse teachynge how to Dress, Sowe and
Set a Garden," and in 1568 "The Profytable Arte of
Gardening," and he was possibly the author of "The
Gardener's Labyrinth," London, 1577. In 1578
Dodoens-Lyte published at Antwerp "A Newe
Herball," republished in 1586, 1595, and 1619. In
1579 William Langham produced "The Garden of
Health," and in 1592 John Wolf brought out a little
treatise (the unique property of Earl Crewe) entitled
"Short Instructions Very Profitable and Necessary
for all those that delight in Gardening." John
Gerard's "Catalogue of Trees," another unique book
now in the British Museum, is dated 1596, while his
"Herball" appeared in 1597. In 1599 Dubravius
published "A Newe Booke on Good Husbandry," and
Gardner's "Kitchen Garden" is said to have appeared
in the same year, but no copy is known. These
practically complete a list of the more important
books of the period dealing with gardening and
plants. Here it will be well to leave them. Elizabethan methods survived for some time, and it was
not, perhaps, until the eighteenth century that
"pleached alleys," mounds and knotted beds fell out
of favour. Nowadays there is an echo in the air of
better ways. Such gardens as those of Mr. Freeman-

Mitford at Batsford set before us the cultivation of flowers in Nature's methods, their native elegance unrestrained and unfettered by man. The leading idea is to copy Nature as near as may be, and discard the tiring, gaudy colouring and set lines of bedding plants, the straight rectangular walks and plots, and to have everywhere constant change of shape and colour, an orderly wilderness of bloom against a background of ever-varying green.

APRIL

When daisies pied and violets blue
And lady-smocks all silver-white
And cuckoo-buds of yellow hue
Do paint the meadows with delight.
Love's Labour's Lost, V. ii. 904.

WITH April the purple of the violets melts into the yellow of the primrose, the white of our Lady's smock, and the blue of the woodland scilla. If the winds be not chill and the sky palled in gray, Nature's beauties will fast respond to the spattering of April showers, and with the carols of the birds wake into life.

The flower of the month is undoubtedly the primrose. One quotation is worth giving :

Primrose, first-born child of Ver,
Merry spring-time's harbinger
With her bells dim.
Two Noble Kinsmen, Introd.

This reminds us of the German name for the flower, the *Schlüssel Blumen* (the key flower), the key with which our Lady unlocks the treasure-house of spring. Three times Shakespeare gives the flower the epithet of "pale," chiefly in the lines

Pale primroses,
That die unmarried, ere they can behold
Bright Phœbus in his strength.
Winter's Tale, IV. iv. 122.

[9]

And again :

> Thou shalt not lack
> The flower that's like thy face, pale primrose.
> *Cymbeline*, IV. ii. 220.

And once the word "pale" is replaced by "faint" :

> Where often you and I
> Upon faint primrose beds were wont to lie.
> *Midsummer-Night's Dream*, I. i. 214.

Twice the primrose-decked way is used as a synonym for easy dalliance : *Hamlet*, I. iii. 50, and *Macbeth*, II. iii. 21.

Certes Shakespeare dearly loved the primrose-decked banks of his native lanes, where they still flourish in wonted luxuriance.

But the flower has a more than romantic interest : it is so variable, so tending to cross with its near relatives, that it has ever been a botanical puzzle. It is the *Primula acaulis* of Linn., the *P. vulgaris* of Huds., and found throughout Europe as far south as North Africa. It has a very marked stalked variety and two hybrids, while crosses with the oxslip and cowslip are met with in a wild state. It is, moreover, the parent of all the numerous variegated polyanthus flowers of our old-fashioned cottage gardens.

Its name is as much a difficulty with the etymologist as the plant itself is to the botanist, and it has passed, so says Prior, from *flor di prima vera*, through the Italian *primaverola* to the French *prime-verole*, and thus through *primerole* to Spenser's "primrose," but was also used in the form "pryme-rose" for privet (Turner), and even Gerard calls privet "prim privet," and the Latin form *primula* seems to have been assigned by early writers to the daisy. There is little doubt Shakespeare stamped the name upon the flower now so called, and after his date it is rarely named by any other. Following the primrose, in flower towards the end of the month and well into May, is another old favourite, the cowslip, the *Primula veris* of Linn., the *P. officinalis* of Jacq., found, like its cousin, throughout Europe, Siberia, and reaching into Western Asia and North Africa. It is identical with the *Herba paralysis* of Brunfels, and with the *Verbasculum odoratum* of Fuchsius.

This plant was well known to, and beloved of, the poet. Witness the care of his descriptions:

> The freckled cowslip.—*Henry V.*, V. ii. 49.

> Cinque-spotted, like the crimson drops
> I' the bottom of a cowslip.—*Cymbeline*, II. ii. 37.

> The cowslips tall her pensioners be:
> In their gold coats spots you see;
> These be rubies, fairy favours.
> *Midsummer-Night's Dream*, II. i. 10.

And yet again the

> Yellow cowslip cheeks.—*Ibid.*, V. i. 339.

As in the case of the primrose and violet, the flower was used for household decoration. The poet says:

> The violets, cowslips, and the primroses
> Bear to my closet.—*Cymbeline*, I. v. 85.

In the Warwickshire country of to-day the very best of wines made in the homesteads is that from the dried blossoms—the "pips," so called; and in many villages quite a harvest is made by the women and children in the cowslip-picking season.

As with the primrose, so with the cowslip: there is much doubt, never really well explained, as to the derivation of its names, whether they be cowslip or paigle. It should not be forgotten that the "pensioners" of the passage were a guard of gentlemen with peculiarly sumptuous livery of gold and jewels, which Shakespeare doubtless saw first at Kenilworth.

In the meadows where the yellow cowslip best
loves to disport its drooping bells, there often grows
one of our most delicate of flowers, referred to once
only, viz., in the lines quoted as our chapter heading.
The plant is an interesting one, belonging to the
large edible order of Cruciferæ, and is called by
botanists *Cardamine pratensis*, L.*   It is found wild in
all the North temperate regions.   Its name is said to
be a word - picture of the sweetness, gentleness,
and purity of the Blessed Virgin Mary, who has
many flowers called after her, such as Lady's tresses†
—a white orchis of exceedingly delicate scent—
Lady's mantle, Lady's fingers vetch, Lady laces, and
Lady signet.   The local Warwickshire name is still
"smell smock."   The leaves of the plant produce in
autumn small bulbils, which fall off and help to pro-
pagate the species.

Another flower of the sylvan hedge bank this
month is the yellow dead-nettle, or archangel, which
Grindon considers the nettle of Ophelia's wreath;
but it is much more likely the ordinary stinging-
nettle would be the flower selected by the distraught
maiden in her phantasies.   Archangel is a very
handsome plant, with flowers of deep golden yellow.
It is the *Lamium galeobdolon* of science, and a by no
means uncommon plant in Warwickshire hedges.

The next plant to deal with is the cuckoo-flower,
mentioned but once in the poet's works, and then in
connection with many common hedgerow plants :

> Crowned with rank fumiter and furrow-weeds,
> With burdocks, hemlock, nettles, cuckoo-flowers,
> Darnel, and all the idle weeds that grow
> In our sustaining corn.—*King Lear*, IV. iv. 3.

---

* Other native species are, *C. hirsuta*, *C. amara*, and
C. impatiens.

† Some of these probably came through worship of Venus
and Freyja.

These weeds are all coarse and hardy denizens of badly-tilled cornfields, as well as of their boundary wastes. There is no doubt that the weed is that still called cuckoo - flower in the county, namely, the two commonest of the wild geraniums (*Geranium dissectum*, L., and *G. molle*, L.). It does not usually flower until May, but in sheltered spots it blossoms earlier. We have in all eleven wild geraniums, some of which are truly handsome plants, and not unknown in our gardens. The two mentioned are found throughout Europe, and in Western Asia and Northern Africa also. One of the wild geraniums, herb Robert, was a very popular plant among the herbalists. There have been many suggestions as to what plant Shakespeare meant by cuckoo-flower. Ellacombe suggests that cuckoo-flower and cuckoo-bud are identical, and quotes (p. 67) Mr. Swinfen Jervis as identifying the flower with the cowslip. Grindon suggests the corn bluebottle (*Centaurea cyanus*, L.), on account of a local name of cuckoo-wood still used in some localities ; but, after all, the use of the name for members of the Geraniaceæ in the neighbourhood of Stratford would seem to settle the question. With regard to " cuckoo-buds," the plants they are classed with grow in part in damp meadows, in part in the sheltered dingles adjoining. The lady-smocks would also grow near the water, and surely the most conspicuous flower by its banks would be the golden kingcup, the horse-blobs of the Warwickshire children. It could surely be as well associated with the lady-smock and daisy as the violet, and, apart from it, we can but fall back on the various species of ranunculus, which truly " paint the meadows with delight," but are hardly in flower with the lady-smock, the only early species. The starry celandine (*R. ficaria*) is a plant of copses and shady hedgebanks, although found in meadows

beneath the shade of trees. After some consideration, we think the marsh marigold, kingcups, or
horse-blobs, call it what you may, is the plant from
which the cuckoo-buds of the poet is derived. As
we have said, it is a conspicuous—nay, a wonderfully
handsome—plant, with broad, glossy leaves and stately
flowers of a rich golden colour, and is found throughout Arctic Europe, spreading into Asia and Africa.
It is prone to variation, in accordance with the dry-
ness or moisture of its situation. The only other
British species is the *Caltha radicans* of Forster, a
plant which Hooker says is now only known in
cultivation.

This month of April is with us a month of many
perplexities. There is a flower mentioned in *Venus
and Adonis*, line 1168, as

> A purple flower sprung up, chequered with white,
> Resembling well his pale cheeks and the blood
> Which in round drops upon their whiteness stood.

The legend is, of course, that of Adonis, son of
Cinyras, King of Cyprus, with whom Venus became
enamoured, thus arousing the jealousy of Mars, who
accomplished the death of Adonis while hunting a
wild boar. The unfortunate youth was, however,
changed by Venus into a flower, the anemone, and
his loss yearly bewailed. Ellacombe reasons ably
that Shakespeare had the anemone in view when he
wrote this passage, and no doubt scarlet anemones
flecked with white could be seen in the gardens of
his day; but Linnæus, however, gave the name
Adonis to another plant, a close ally of the anemone.

There is a plant naturalized in Suffolk and the
South of England representing the genus in our
islands. This beautiful little flower—the *Adonis
autumnalis*, L.—has graceful leaves very much divided,
and of a bright green. It has also a scarlet flower,

with deep black basal spot. Its popular name is
pheasant's-eye, but whether it be the classical flower
or not, the opinion of Linnæus is worth quoting.
On the other hand, Ellacombe quotes Golding's
translation of Ovid, 1567, and says that from it
Shakespeare possibly obtained his information.   The
lines run :

Of all one colour with the bloud, a flower she there did
    find,
Even like the flower of that same tree, whose fruit in tender
    rind
Have pleasant graines enclosede—howbeit the use of them is
    short,
For why, the leaves do hang so loose through lightnesse in
    such sort
As that the windes that all things pierce with everie little
    blast
Do shake them off and shed them so as long they cannot
    last.

This is all very well for the delicate white *Anemone
pulsatilla,* our wind-flower *par excellence ;* but species
such as *A. coronaria* and its allies are remarkably
sturdy plants, and Prior may be correct in thinking
the anemone of the Adonis legend the cistus.   It
is impossible to be certain one way or the other.

If we turn from the flowers of garden and hedge
bank to the forests of our land, we shall be able to
consider two of our stateliest native trees, both of
which, weather permitting, flower this month.   The
ash (*Fraxinus excelsior,* L.) is but once mentioned by
the poet, and then in metaphor :

> O Martius, Martius !
> Each word thou hast spoken hath weeded from my heart
> A root of ancient envy. . . .
>   Let me twine
> Mine arms about that body, where against
> My grainèd ash a hundred times hath broke
> And scared the moon with splinters.
>   *Coriolanus,* IV. v. 106.

The reference is to the ashen shafts of spears, such wood being that almost universally employed in their manufacture.

The beauty of the ash and its useful qualities were enhanced by traditions, carried to the very extreme in the Yggdrasil of Northern mythology, which is thus described in the Younger Edda :

" It is biggest and best of all trees ; its head reacheth unto the heavens. Three roots sustain the tree, and stand wide apart. The first is with the Asi ; the second is with the Hrimthusar ; and the third is over Niflheim. Under that root is Hvergelmer, but Nidhavger gnaws this root beneath : under the root that trendeth to the Hrimthusar is Mimer's spring where knowledge and wit are hidden. He that keeps the spring is called Mimer. He is full of wisdom for that he drinks of the spring from the horn Gioll. Thither came the Allfather and begged a drink of the spring, but he got it not before he had laid an eye in pledge. The first root of the ash standeth in Heaven, and under this root is a spring that is right holy, hight Urthr's spring. There hold the Gods their doomstead, riding their horses thither over Bifrost-bridge (the rainbow). The Nornir who dwell in the fair hall under the ash, and shape the lives of men, are named Urthr, Verthandi, and Skund. An eagle sits on the boughs ; he is wise, but between his eyes abides a hawk. The squirrel, Ratatoskr, runs up and down along the ash, and bears words of hate between the eagle and Nidhavger (the dragon). Four harts run amid the branches and bite the buds. The Nornir water the tree daily from Urthr's spring."

Such is the Northern legend, weird as it is. It reminds us of how great a part a sacred tree bore in ancient religions, whether it be the sacred pine-tree of the snake goddess of Ur Eridhu or its lineal descendant, the tree of good and evil of our Book

of Genesis. The ash, however, was not alone the
centre of mythical legends; it had medical qualities, perchance springing originally from mytho-
logical ones. A specimen from Alexis of Piedmont
must suffice. From him we learn that, if a serpent
bite a man, a few ash leaves, bruised and laid on the
wound, will effect a certain cure, or, failing this, a
drink containing the juice from the leaves will
suffice. The reason given is characteristic : "because
that the serpent is so great enemy unto the ashe
tree, that he would rather go thorow the fire, then
passe by an ashe" (Alexis, ii. 23 in d.).

The jet-black flower of the ash is to many pro-
phetical. A common Warwickshire saying is usually
given thus :

> When the ash flowers before the oak,
> We are sure to have a soak.

The tree is one of our loftiest and most elegant;
it reaches in favourable circumstances a height of
50 to 80 feet, and adds not a little to the beauty
of a well-wooded landscape. But it is far exceeded
by the national tree, the oak, grand at all times, even
in the depth of winter, but especially beautiful when
the first spring green clothes its rugged and gnarled
branches, in which dwell hosts of insects, serving to
add their own wonderful economies to its beauties.
Some roll the leaves into fairy dwellings, others
adhere closely to their under surface, while others,
again, cover its boughs with oak-apples, spangle,
and cherry-galls. We have but one native species of
oak, *Quercus robur*, L., whose mighty trunk reaches
from 60 to 100 feet, with a girth of 70 feet (at Cow-
thorpe in Yorkshire); it ranges from Syria and the
Taurus almost to the Arctic Circle. Shakespeare
loved the tree in all its phases. He noted it in his
Arden forest :

2

> He lay along
> Under an oak whose antique root peeps out
> Upon the brook that brawls along this wood.
> *As You Like It*, II. i. 30.

And, again, he calls to mind the ancient monarch of the forest :

> Under an oak, whose boughs were mossed with age,
> And high top bald with dry antiquity.
> *Ibid.*, IV. iii. 105.

Shakespeare knew, too, that the oak, king of trees, was fitly assigned to the King of Heaven :

> To the dread rattling thunder
> Have I given fire and rifted Jove's stout oak
> With his own bolt.—*Tempest*, V. i. 44.

How often is Herne's oak in the Great Park of Windsor the scene for mystery and adventure! One example must suffice :

> Till 'tis one o'clock
> Our dance of custom round about the oak
> Of Herne the Hunter let us not forget.
> *Merry Wives of Windsor*, V. v. 78.

There is also reference to the oaken crown of victory :

> He proved best man i' the field, and for his meed
> Was brow-bound with the oak.—*Coriolanus*, II. ii. 101.

This crown, the *corona civica*, was given to him who had saved the life of a Roman citizen. It was made of oak leaves, and bore the inscription, OB CIVEM SERVATUM. Under the Emperors it was bestowed by the Prince alone, and attended with special honours : the fortunate recipient wore it at the games, and sat next the Senate, and when he entered the audience rose as a mark of respect. Among the honours showered on Augustus by the

Senate was the right to suspend a civic crown on the top of his palace between two laurel branches, as the perpetual defender of his people, and it is thus represented on certain of his coins.

The other references in the poet to the civic crown are:

> To a cruel war I sent him, from whence he returned,
> His brows bound with oak.—*Coriolanus*, I. iii. 15.

> He comes the third time home with oaken garland.
> *Ibid.*, II. i. 137.

The fruit of the tree is also mentioned in several places. Thus,

> All their elves for fear
> Creep into acorn-cups* and hide them there.
> *Midsummer-Night's Dream*, II. i. 30.

The use of the acorns for food of swine is thus referred to in a passage from *Cymbeline* (II. v. 16):

> Like a full-acorned boar—a German one.

We might add much, did space permit, of Oak-apple Day and King Charles's adventures, of the many historical or magnificent oaks that still adorn our country, of their use in shipbuilding and architecture; but April days are passing, and much lies before us; hence we must leave the delicate sessile blossoms and peculiar green of the oak to its insect hosts—to the pretty but destructive little *Tortrix viridana* and the various cynips, aphides, and weevils that love its shady recesses.

---

* These cups are technically " glans," a word applied to fruits in which three layers are lignified, like the acorn and nut.

MAY

On a day—alack the day!—
Love, whose month is ever May,
Spied a blossom passing fair
Playing in the wanton air :
Through the velvet leaves the wind,
All unseen, can passage find ;
That the lover, sick to death,
Wish himself the heaven's breath.
Love's Labour's Lost, IV. iii. 101.

Up, then, I say, both young and old, both man and
  maid, a-maying,
With drums and guns that bounce aloud, and merry
  tabor playing.—*Knight of the Burning Pestle*, IV. v.

MAY, the month of Venus, consecrated to love
and joy, the month when at sunrise on its
dawning day Phœbus opens the gate of Spring ! In
theory the best of months, in practice very often a sadly
disappointing one ; but, nevertheless, poets welcome
it with unfeigned jubilation. We ourselves must
needs a-maying go with heart and soul. Its very
name calls up to us a hundred innocent pleasures :
"knots of flowers" ; the maypole, with its May
Queen ; country revels in which all played their part,
whether it were "under the greenwood tree" or in
the verdant flower-strewn meads or hawthorn glades.
England was "merrie England" then, and may be
so once again if the would-be educationalists would
cease, before they have expelled all originality of
thought and all idea of humour from our rustic

[20]

population and cast them as iron in a uniform mould. Let us first to the forest, where more than one tree awaits us in its wealth of flower. The delicate pendent catkins and silver bark of the birch will be certain to attract us, since it is one of the most grace-ful of trees. Our species is *Betula alba*, L., a tree known to reach, though rarely, the height of 80 feet, an inhabitant of Northern Europe, Asia, and North America. The bark is still used in tanning, while the wood is useful for many articles of carpentry ; moreover, it exudes a fragrant oil, and a wine is made from its sugary juices. From it canoes have been made by native tribes, and its bark is used by them for cordage, matting, and roofing ; while from the twigs beer is brewed, and the leaves form a substitute for tea. Its wood is used for sabots, its slender branches for brooms. As an instrument of punishment its fame is recorded by Shakespeare's contemporaries :

> And now the burchin tree doth bud, that makes the school-
> boy cry.
> > BEAUMONT AND FLETCHER :
> > *Knight of the Burning Pestle*, IV. v.

And, again, old Turner : " Howbeit it serveth for many good uses, and for none better than for betynge of stubborn boys, that either lye or will not learn." And so our poet himself :

> > fond fathers,
> Having bound up the threatening twigs of birch,
> Only to stick it in their children's sight
> For terror, not to use, in time the rod
> Becomes more mock'd than fear'd.
> > *Measure for Measure*, I. iii. 23.

Brooms, at this time made solely of its branches, are twice referred to :

> I am sent with broom before,
> To sweep the dust behind the door.
> > *Midsummer-Night's Dream*, V. i. 396.

They fell on : I made good my place; at length they came
to the broomstaff with me.—*Henry VIII.*, V. iv. 56.

Another woodland beauty, no less remarkable for
its palmate foliage than for its glossy red-brown fruit,
was probably introduced by the Romans. It is the
Castanea vulgaris of Linnæus, the sweet chestnut of
commerce. Not only is it good to eat, but its timber
is excellent and extremely durable. A good deal of
ancient timber-work ordinarily considered oak is
really of this tree. We have many fine specimens of
it·in our English deer-parks, not forgetting those at
Tortworth—old in the reign of King John. It is
referred to by the poet as an edible in—

> A sailor's wife had chestnuts in her lap,
> And munch'd, and munch'd, and munch'd.
> > *Macbeth*, I. iii. 4 ;

as bursting while roasting :

> And do you tell me of a woman's tongue,
> That gives not half so great a blow to hear
> As will a chestnut at a farmer's fire.
> > *Taming of the Shrew*, I. ii. 208 ;

and once as a colour :

> Chestnut was ever the only colour.
> > *As You Like It*, III. iv. 12.

The crab-tree is one of our greatest ornaments this
month in hedge and copse. And not only an ornament, for was it not under a crab that the poet is
said by a scandalous tradition to have fallen asleep
after a drinking-bout at the Falcon Inn in Bidford?
The crab apple (*Pyrus malus*, L.) is the native source
from which all our domesticated apples are derived.
And not only so, but its strong, tough wood was
employed in the manufacture of quarter-staves.
Hence we get :

> Fetch me a dozen crab-tree staves, and tough ones.
> > *Henry VIII.*, V. iv. 7.

Its fruit, roasted, was an ingredient in the spiced ale of the Christmas frolics:

> When roasted crabs hiss in the bowl,
> Then nightly sings the staring owl.
> > *Love's Labour's Lost*, V. ii. 935.

And, again, the mischievous Puck:

> And sometimes lurk I in a gossip's bowl,
> In very likeness of a roasted crab,
> And when she drinks, against her lips I bob.
> > *Midsummer-Night's Dream*, II. i. 47.

It was used also uncooked, and that not for want of better apples. From the juice verjuice was made, and the acidity of the crab is often mentioned in the poet's metaphors:

> She will taste as like this as a crab does to a crab.
> > *King Lear*, I. v. 18.

> *Pet.* Nay, come, Kate, come! you must not look so sour.
> *Kath.* It is my fashion, when I see a crab.
> *Pet.* Why, here's no crab; and therefore look not sour.
> > *Taming of the Shrew*, II. i. 228.

We may pass quickly by the various garden apples to which the poet refers. First comes the apple-john—probably, says Ellacombe, the Easter pippin of Maund. It is twice mentioned:

> I am withered like an old apple-john.
> > 1 *Henry IV.*, III. iii. 4.

> Mass! thou sayest true. The prince once set a dish of apple-johns before him, and told him there were five more Sir Johns, and, putting off his hat, said, "I will now take my leave of these six dry, round, old, withered knights."—
> > 2 *Henry IV.*, II. iv. 4.

The bitter-sweeting is once mentioned:

> Thy wit is a very bitter-sweeting; it is a most sharp sauce.
> > *Romeo and Juliet*, II. iv. 83.

The codling is a name applied at that time to any unripe apple. Thus,

> A codling when 'tis almost an apple.
> *Twelfth Night*, I. v. 167.

It does not mean the variety so called in our modern gardens.

Leathercoats, referred to in 2 *Henry IV.*, V. iii. 44, are brown russets.

The pippin, originally applied to any apple raised from pips, is now, and may have been in Elizabethan times, assigned specifically to bright-skinned apples with good keeping qualities. Thus, as an example, the apple is referred to as "last year's pippin" in 2 *Henry IV.*, V. iii, 2, and again in the *Merry Wives of Windsor*, I. ii. 13:

> There's pippins and cheese to come.

The pomewater cannot be identified ·with any certainty. Ellacombe suggests the modern Lord Suffield apple:

> The pomewater, who now hangeth like a jewel in the ear of caelo.—*Love's Labour's Lost*, IV. ii. 4.

There is also the costard, a coarse variety, used as a contemptuous epithet for an ignorant head in *King Richard III.*, I. iv. 159. Its name is of interest, since our word "costermonger" is derived from it.

Besides all these, we have a reference to a dish as popular then as it is to-day—apple tart:

> What's this? a sleeve?   'Tis like a demi-cannon:
> What! up and down, carved like an apple-tart?
> *Taming of the Shrew*, IV. iii. 88.

And, lastly, to the apple of the Garden of Eden,

which, by the way, was certainly not an apple, but probably the orange, citron, or quince :

How like Eve's apple doth thy beauty grow !
Sonnets, xciii.

A handsome tree is the sycamore (*Acer pseudoplatanus*, L.). A native of Middle Europe, but now well naturalized in our islands, few trees exceed it in beauty, and its shady branches rise to the height of 40 to 60 feet. Nor is it useful for sight alone. Its fine-grained wood is much used in turnery, and its sap is sufficiently sugary to serve for maple sugar. Our native species of the genus is a small tree, seldom exceeding 10 to 20 feet; but, small as it is, the wood is very finely and delicately grained.

This tree must not be confounded with the sycamore or zicamine of the Bible, which is a fig mulberry, and a native of Africa and Syria. In Scotland the sycamore bears the name of dool, or grief tree, and was used for feudal executions. The most celebrated is that at the Castle of Cassilis. Shakespeare mentions the " cool shade of a sycamore " in *Love's Labour's Lost*, V. ii. 89 ; " the grove of sycamore " in *Romeo and Juliet*, I. i. 128 ; and in *Othello*, IV. iii. 41,

The poor soul sat sighing by a sycamore-tree.

There is, however, a small tree which takes one of its names—" may "—from this month. It is also called the albespoine, hawthorn, hawthorn quickset or whitethorn, or simply thorn by the country people, and is the *Cratægus oxyacantha*, L. Its snowy blossoms, massed in profuse luxuriance on their setting of bright green leaves, serve to make a hawthorn glade one of the loveliest components of English scenery. And when the leaves are painted with their autumnal

dyes, and the bright red hips appear, it is almost
equally striking.

> Mark the faire blooming of the hawthorn-tree,
> Who, finely clothed in a robe of white,
> Fills full the wanton eye with May's delight.
> BROWNE : *Britannia's Pastorals*, ii. 2.*

It is said by Ellacombe seldom to flower till June,
except in Devonshire and Cornwall ; but even in
this year 1902, cold as it is, it is in full flower in
Warwickshire as I write (May 14), and some was
bound in our village maypole on the first of the
month. An old Suffolk custom, it appears, allowed
a dish of cream to those who brought a bough in full
blossom into the house on May Day ; but this in
Brand's time was discontinued. Sir John Mandeville,
in speaking of our Blessed Lord, says :

"Then was our Lord yled into a gardyn, and there
the Jewes scorned hym and maden hym a crowne of
the branches of the albiespyne, that is whitethorn,
which grew in the same gardyn, and setten yt upon
hys heved. And therefore hath the whitethorn
many virtues. For he that beareth a branch on
hym thereof, no thundre, ne no maner of tempest
may dere hym, ne in the house that it is ynne may
non evil ghost enter" (Ellacombe, p. 117).

Its uses in Shakespeare's phrases are various. As
an object on which Orlando hangs odes, it is found
in *As You Like It*, III. ii. 379 ; as a "tiring-house"
for the players in *Midsummer-Night's Dream*, III. i. 4.
Its buds are referred to in the same play (I. i. 184) :

> When wheat is green, when hawthorn buds appear;

and, again, as "lisping hawthorn buds" in *Merry
Wives of Windsor*, III. iii. 77, and compared, much

* Quoted by Ellacombe, p. 115.

to its advantage, with the royal canopy in the beautiful lines in *3 Henry VI.,* II. v. 42 :

> Gives not the hawthorn bush a sweeter shade
> To shepherds looking on their silly sheep,
> Than doth a rich embroider'd canopy
> To kings that fear their subjects' treachery ?
> O yes, it doth ; a thousandfold it doth.

Even in the winter, when leaves and fruit alike have gone, the poet notes it :

> Through the sharp hawthorn blows the cold wind.
> *King Lear,* III. iv. 48.

Its thorns are possibly referred to (*Midsummer-Night's Dream,* III. i. 61 and V. i. 136) under the term " bush-of-thorn," and possibly in *Romeo and Juliet,* I. iv. 25.

The thorn has a wide geographical range ; it is found throughout Europe and in North Africa, and as far into Asia as the confines of India. In the English hedges there are several well-marked varieties, viz., *oxyacanthoides, laciniata, kyrtostyla,* and *monogyna ;* and many beautiful forms, with double, single, and coloured flowers, adorn our gardens.

In the hedgerows there also grows the elder (*Sambucus nigra,* L.), a tree with strong scent, found throughout Europe to Northern Africa, and which tradition has assigned—no doubt from its brittle nature—as the tree on which the arch-traitor, Judas, hanged himself, as in *Love's Labour's Lost,* V. ii. 608, where Holofernes plays on the word with Biron :

> *Hol.* Begin, sir ; you are my elder.
> *Biron.* Well followed : Judas was hanged on
> an elder.

Sir John Mandeville was shown the identical tree in Jerusalem. He says :
" And faste by is zit, the Tree of Eldre that Judas

henge himsilf upon, for despeyr that he hadde, when
he solde and betrayed oure Lorde."

The elder had, however, many admirers, despite
its ill fame, while its scented flowers are used to-day
to soften hard water, for the complexion, and for
perfumes, while from its fruit wine is largely manu-
factured. One of Alexis of Piedmont's recipes may
be given as a specimen of the repute it was held in
by the Elizabethan herbalists:

"For to make a cleere voyce ye shall take the
floures of an elder tree, and drye them in the
sunne, but take heede they take no moysture or
wet, then make pouder of them, and drinke of
it with white wine every mornyng fasting" (Alexis,
ii. 17).

The hard external wood, the large space occupied
by the soft pith, are noticed by the poet in the
jeering, taunting speech of the Host (*Merry Wives,*
II. iii. 29):

What says Esculapius? my Galen? my heart of elder?

And its boyish use as a suitable material for pop-
guns is not forgotten, either:

That's a perilous shot out of an elder gun.
Henry V., IV. i. 209.

And, lastly, its strong scent:

And let the stinking elder, grief, untwine
His perishing root with the increasing vine.
Cymbeline, IV. ii. 59.

Turning from our English trees, let us survey
the stateliest of the old-world pines—the cedar of
Lebanon (*Cedrus libanus*), the impersonation of
majesty and grandeur. Ellacombe doubts if Shakespeare ever saw the tree, as it is not supposed to
have been introduced until it was planted at Bretby

THE CEDARS, WARWICK CASTLE

Park, in Derbyshire, in 1676 ; but it is worth mention that there is a tradition, but wholly unsupported by any evidence, that the famous cedars ot Warwick Castle (*see plate*), so cruelly destroyed in the gale of March 25, 1895, were planted there by the Crusaders. How well the words apply !—

> Let the mutinous winds
> Strike the proud cedars 'gainst the fiery sun.
> *Coriolanus*, V. iii. 59.

> And by the spurs plucked up
> The pine and cedar.
> *Tempest*, V. i. 47.

Many of the passages in which the poet names the cedar are very grand. Unfortunately, we have not here room for all ; but they will be found in their proper sequence by-and-by. One or two deserve special attention :

> But I was born so high,
> Our aery buildeth in the cedar's top,
> And dallies with the wind and scorns the sun.
> *Richard III.*, I. iii. 265.

> The cedar stoops not to the base shrub's foot,
> But low shrubs wither at the cedar's root.
> *Lucrece*, 664.

And lastly :

> He shall flourish,
> And, like a mountain cedar, reach his branches
> To all the plains about him.
> *Henry VIII.*, V. v. 253.

From our Eastern tree we turn to another garden ornament, a stately flower with elegant drooping bells of red or gold—the crown imperial, native of Persia, Afghanistan, and Cashmere (the *Fritillaria imperialis*, L.). As old Parkinson says, " it deserveth the first place in this our garden of delight," and none the less for its pretty legend.

In that saddest of gardens, Gethsemane, the crown imperial grew and lifted its snow-white flowers with lofty pride among its compeers; and as our Blessed Lord passed by in that dark night of sorrow, all other flowers bent low before Him, and worshipped in sorrowing reverence, but this proud lily held its head erect, until at length the sense of shame smote into its life, and a deep horror bade it crimson itself with blushes. While bending low its erst-proud head, it ever weeps deep tears of sorrow for its sin. These tears old Gerard describes thus:

"In the bottome of each of the bells there is placed six drops of most cleere shining water, in taste like sugar, resembling in shew faire orient pearles, the whiche drops, if you take away, there do immediately appeare the like; notwithstanding if they be suffered to stand still in the floure according to his owne nature, they wil never fall away."

It is only once referred to in the plays, viz., *Winter's Tale*, IV. iv. 125:

> Bold oxlips and
> The crown imperial.

Since we have mentioned oxlips, we may consider them next in order. This plant, allied so closely with both primrose and cowslip, is the *Primula elatior* of Jacquin. In England it is only found wild in Suffolk, Cambridge, and Essex, and on the Continent south of Gothland, excluding Greece and Turkey, and of course Siberia. It bears large primrose-like flowers on a central flower-stalk. Beside the passage already quoted, it is mentioned with thyme and violet on the "wild thyme" bank of *Midsummer-Night's Dream*, II. i. 249, and in *Two Noble Kinsmen*, "oxlips in their cradles growing." Compared to either the primrose or cowslip, it is a "bold" flower, though not, of course, rated with crown imperial. The force of Ellacombe's objection to calling Shakespeare's plant oxlip lies in which way we read the adjectives. The oxlip is the *Verbascum non-odoratum* of Fuchsius. Nothing seems known of the derivation of the name.

One of the showiest plants of our cottage gardens, and of those fortunate woods in which it is a native, is the curious columbine, or dove plant (*Aquilegia vulgaris*, L.), one of the members of the great order *Ranunculaceæ*), bearing little superficial resemblance to the typical plants of that group, owing to the irregularities of its corolla. It is a widely-spread plant, found in Europe, Morocco, the Canaries, and Asia, to the Western Himalaya. Under cultivation it has assumed an infinite variety of form and colour, some of the shapes and tints being as beautiful as those of irids or orchids ; but in a state of nature it is only found with blue or purple flowers. Twice the plant is named in the plays—once in *Love's Labour's Lost*, V. ii. 663, and, again, in *Hamlet*, IV. v. 180 :

> There's fennel for you and columbines.

Of our seven native fumitories, but one is referred to by the poet, *Fumaria officinalis*, L., a plant so delicate in foliage, with such slender bright pink flowers, that it seems at first as though the epithet "rank" twice applied to it (*King Lear*, IV. iv. 3, and *Henry V.*, V. ii. 45) were incorrect ; and yet it has a decidedly rank method of spreading itself over the surface of cultivated ground, and is not alone a trouble to the cultivator, but injurious to the crop. The name is said to be derived from the French *fume-terre*, Latin *fumus terræ*—i.e., earth smoke— from the belief that it sprang without seed, spontaneously engendered by vapours rising from the earth, which legend is credited not only by Peter

Treveris in the "Grete Herball," but in Dodoens-Lyte's "Newe Herball," 1586. The other species of fumaria are mostly rare; others of great beauty adorn our gardens, notably *Dicentra spectabilis*.

The plantain is hardly a flower, but must find a place here; yet it is a popular plant, and one of many names, such as waybroad (German *Wegebreit*), rib-wort, cocks, cockfighters, and waybread. Prior derives plantain from *plantago—i.e., planta*, the sole of the foot—from a fancied resemblance, but this seems hardly reasonable. Its scientific name, or rather, names, since there are three common plantains, are *Plantago lanceolata*, L., *P. major*, L., and *P. media*, L. It is said to have been used as a medicine in twenty-two different diseases, among others for tertian ague; and its leaves were pounded up with white of eggs and applied as a plaster to burns (Stevens). The method of application is given thus in Ellacombe (p. 228) : " If a man ache in half his head . . . delve up waybroad without iron ere the rising of the sun, bind the roots about the head with cross-wort by a red fillet; soon he will be well." These plants have a tendency to revert into teratological variations. As a flower, the most interesting is *Plantago media*, which has long purple filaments and white anthers, while *P. lanceolata*, the ribwort, has yellowish-white stamens, and *P. major* purple anthers. The dried seed spike of this last is much gathered for cage-birds, who are very fond of the black, rough seeds.

In the hedgerows keck or kecksies will be in full blossom, a coarse yet elegant plant of deep green tint, with slender umbels of snow-white flowers, a favourite resting-place of the orange-tip butterfly (*Anthocharis cardamines*), whose mimicry of mottled green and white decking its lower under-wings effectually protects it from observation. The plant

is not, as Ellacombe says, the hemlock, but the
chervil, which is still called keck in the Warwickshire
villages.   The name is applied to the living plant, and
not to the dead stems, although this may once have
been the case.   The book-name for the plants, since
two are common wild, is "beaked parsley" (*Anthriscus
vulgaris*, Pers., *A. sylvestris*, Hoffm., and the garden
escape, *A. cerefolium*, Hoffm.).   They are all natives of
Arctic Europe, and the first-named was once cultivated as a pot-herb.   The plant is but once referred
to by the poet, and that in company with those
plants usually found with it—docks, thistles and
burs (*Henry V.*, V. ii. 52).   Ellacombe quotes two
passages from early authors showing the use of "kex"
for dead stems, but Shakespeare certainly refers to a
living plant, not a dead one.

We have now to consider the mysterious flowers
which formed the wreath of the unhappy Ophelia :

> There with fantastic garlands did she come
> Of crow-flowers, nettles, daisies, and long purples.
> *Hamlet*, IV. vii. 169.

Before advancing any new opinion, let us see what
the authorities have to tell us.   Grindon gives them
as equivalent to the harebell, archangel, daisy,
and purple orchis, quoting for the first Turner's
" Herball " of 1551, wherein crow toes, crow fote and
crow tees are synonyms for *Scilla nutans ;* for the
second no reason is assigned except that Ophelia
would admire them ; for the last he argues the case
fully proven for *Orchis mascula*, " dead men's fingers,"
as the name given from its palmate root.   It is much
to be doubted if anyone in Shakespeare's age would
have noticed either the orchis or its root, in spite of
Dr. Lightfoot and the commentators.   Ellacombe is
inclined towards ragged-robin as the crow-flower, on
the strength of Gerard's remark that they serve

" for garlands and crowns and to deck the garden,"
but it is open to doubt whether Gerard's ragged-
robin is not some other lychnis, and not our *flos cuculi*,
which fades so rapidly it could never be suitable for
garlands, or, indeed, for decking a garden. "Nettles"
in the text he tacitly assumes to be the ordinary
stinging-nettles, and favours the *Orchis mascula* and
its allies for "long purples."

It is generally assumed that the flowers are those
of the meadow, and that a moist one. Why? It is
equally probable they are those of the shady hedge
bank, and that the crow-flowers are the poisonous,
rank *Ranunculus reptans*, L., and its allies, that the
nettles are the ordinary *Urtica dioica*, L., not neces-
sarily in flower ; or if this be objected to on account
of the stinging qualities, which the distraught
Ophelia might not be insensible to, its place could
be taken by the white dead-nettle (*Lamium album*, L.).
The daisies may be moon-daisies, and the long
purples *Arum maculatum*, L., another plant of baneful influence, with its mysterious dead-white spadix,
bearing no very far-fetched resemblance to a dead
man's finger wrapped in its green winding-sheet, and
whose grosser name, the cuckoo-pint, is ready at
hand. With this selection we have plants of the
same situation flowering at the same time, and all
more or less baneful in their attributes.

JUNE

Under the greenwood tree
Who loves to lie with me,
And turn his merry note
Unto the sweet bird's throat,
Come hither, come hither, come hither:
Here shall he see
No enemy
But winter and rough weather.
As You Like It, II. v. 1.

THIS is the month of summer glory, ere the full green of the trees has faded, and Nature fills the air with the murmuring hum of insects and the scent of flowers, when beneath the greenwood tree there is the coolness and joy of a summer rest. Shakespeare knew it, and loved it, we may be sure, and in the groves of Welcombe and Clopton and the parks of Fulbroke and Ettington may have often enjoyed his summer slumber.

June is the month for the queen of flowers, the rose, a favourite of man from the very earliest date, a flower remarkable for graceful habit, elegant and varied foliage, most fragrant and delicately tinted flowers and brilliant fruit. In Shakespeare's age it was a deserved favourite with florists, and Gerard grew several varieties in his London garden. There we should have found the Austrian briar (*R. lutea*, L.), the cinnamon-scented rose (*R. cinnamonea*, L.), the rose of Provence (*R. provincialis*, L.), the hundred leaved Dutch rose (*R. centifolia*, L.), the Damascene

3—2   [35]

rose (*R. damascena*, L.), the musk rose (*R. moschata*, L.), as well as *R. alba* and *R. gallica*, L.

But it is not alone the garden roses that Shakespeare mentions ; we must be prepared for the truth of the old proverb, "There is no rose without a thorn ;" and many of his quotations refer, obviously, to the wild and native species. Concerning these there is much difference of opinion among authors, some making the number of species small, some very large. The ninth edition of the "London Catalogue" gives the following as genuinely native : *R. pimpinellifolia*, L. ; *R. involuta*, Sm. ; *R. hibernica*, Sm., very rare ; *R. mollis*, Sm. ; *R. tomentosa*, Sm. ; *R. rubiginosa*, L. ; *R. micrantha*, Sm. ; *R. sepium*, Thuill ; *R. obtusifolia*, Desv. ; *R. canina*, L. ; *R. glauca*, Vill. ; *R. stylosa* (sp. collect.); *R. arvensis*, Huds. ; and several naturalized, viz., *rubella*, Sm.; *pomifera*, Herm. ; *gallica*, L. ; *lucida*, Ehrh. ; *cinnamonea*, L. ; *Dicksoni*, L., and *semper-virens*, L. Of all these, the poet probably is thinking chiefly of *R. canina*, the dog rose ; *R. arvensis*, the snow-white corn rose, bright with its yellow stamens; and the sweetbriar, *R. rubiginosa*.

We can hardly say when roses were introduced, but they came into heraldic repute at an early date, when they were usually represented conventionally as a flower of five petals and six sepals with a golden centre, or, as heralds say, a rose gules, barbed vert and seeded or. It appears to have been used as a badge by Edward I., who may have inherited it from his mother, Eleanor, the Rose of Provence. In 1340, the Great Seal has small roses in lieu of stops between the words of the inscription, but it was not a prominent badge until the Civil War. Why roses were assumed is not at all clear : the red may have been for the Lancastrian Honour of Richmond, while the white rose was used by Richard, Earl of

Cambridge, second son of Edward III. through
Maud, his wife, whose family used it in memory
of Fair Rosamund (Woodward, " Brit. and For. Her.,"
323, 324), whose epitaph ran:

> Hic jacet in tomba Rosamunda,
> Non Rosa Mundi,
> Non redolet, sed olet, quæ redolere solet.

To these York and Lancaster roses Shakespeare thus
refers :

In 1 *Henry VI.*, II. iv. 27, Richard Plantagenet
speaks:

> Let him that is a true-born gentleman
> And stands upon the honour of his birth,
> If he suppose that I have pleaded truth,
> From off this briar pluck a white rose with me ;

whereon the Earl of Somerset answers :

> Let him that is no coward nor no flatterer,
> But dare maintain the party of the truth,
> Pluck a red rose from off this thorn with me.

And in the memorable scene that ensues Warwick
declares his gage :

> I pluck this white rose with Plantagenet,

and Suffolk for Somerset. The full speeches of each
will be found at the end of the present volume,
hence I forbear to add them here, save only the
awful concluding words of the mighty King-maker :

> This brawl to-day,
> Grown to this faction in the Temple-garden,
> Shall send between the red rose and the white
> A thousand souls to death and deadly night.

Apart from its use as a badge, the flower was held
in much repute among herbalists as a scent with
preservative tendency ; one example from strange
old Alexis of Piedmont must suffice :

" Take the buddes of redde roses, and brase them in

a morter, as thoughe you woulde have the juyce out of
theym wyth Rose Water, and so water theym and
drye theym agayne often tymes, and thanne make
theim a poulder, the whyche you shal parfume wyth
the poulder of Cypre, as the other aforesayde, and
keepe it in a vyolle."

The recipe mentions another use, that of rose-
water, to which Shakespeare himself thus refers :

> Let one attend him with a silver basin*
> Full of rose-water and bestrewed with flowers.
> *Taming of the Shrew*, Induct. i. 55.

There is also a reference to " cakes of roses," made
of the dried leaves and sold by apothecaries for
much the same purposes as the pot-pourri of our
grandmothers (*Romeo and Juliet*, V. i. 47).

By many the rose is considered to be that flower
of Venus which Cupid consecrated to Harpocrates,
the God of Silence ; it was therefore a fit symbol of
discretion, and in ancient entertainments chaplets
of roses were worn, and secrets spoken thus *sub rosa*
were never revealed (Brand, ii. 345). Chaplets of
roses were also carried before the funerals of un
married women in many parts of England. They
were formed of white roses, and had a pair of kid
gloves attached, and were preserved in the church.
The line in *Hamlet* (V. i. 56) :

> Yet here she is allowed her virgin crants

is said by Brand to have reference to the custom.
Roses, too, were among the flowers anciently strewn
on graves—Paris had been strewing Juliet's " bridal
bed " when he fell in with Romeo and his death.

The many quotations in which we find the rose
mentioned, now as an object of Nature, anon in a

---

* These rose-water basins are some of the handsomest
pieces of plate of the great City companies.

figurative sense, will be found in the Appendix, but
one or two allusions are too beautiful to be missed,
as is Lysander's simile :

> Why is your cheek so pale ?
> How chance the roses that do fade so fast ?
> *Midsummer-Night's Dream*, I. i. 128.

Again :

> Fair ladies masked are roses in their bud ;
> Dismask'd, their damask sweet commixture shown,
> Are angels veiling clouds, or roses blown.
> *Love's Labour's Lost*, V. ii. 295.

It may be remarked that twice in *Hamlet* there are
expressions which may mislead. In *Hamlet*, Laertes
says (IV. v. 157) :

> O rose of May !
> Dear maid, kind sister, sweet Ophelia !

merely intending youthful womanhood. And, again,
in the same play (III. ii. 288), he speaks of

> Two Provincial roses on my razed shoes,

when ribbon rosettes are intended.

In the majority of passages where briars are
alluded to, it is to their unpleasant qualities, such as :

> Rude-growing briars.—*Titus Andronicus*, II. iii. 199.

> O how full of briars is this working-day world !
> *As You Like It*, I. iii. 12.

> I'll have thy beauty scratched with briars.
> *Winter's Tale*, IV. iv. 436.

And in the spirits' mischievous tricks they figure as
objects of punishment :

> through
> Toothed briars.—*Tempest*, IV. i. 178.

> Bedabbled with the dew, and torn with briars.
> *Midsummer-Night's Dream*, III. ii. 443.

So, too, in *Coriolanus*, III. iii. 52, the wounds
caused by briars are made objects of mirth in contradistinction to graver wounds :

> Scratches with briars,
> Scars to move laughter only.

When the poet turns to the wild plant growing in
its native luxuriance, he shows how familiar he is
with its varied forms.   Thus, for instance,

> What subtle hole is this,
> Whose mouth is covered with rude-growing briars.
> *Titus Andronicus*, II. iii. 198.

A sentence indicating one of its modes of growth as
well and as exactly as a botanist could describe it.

Its summer burst of leaves is set out in *All's Well*,
IV. iv. 31,

> The time will bring on summer,
> When briars shall have leaves as well as thorns,
> And be as sweet as sharp.

While in flower we have (*Midsummer-Night's Dream*,
III. i. 106),

> Of colour like the red rose on triumphant briar,

which also serves to portray the luxuriant shoots
conquering the host by which they have climbed to
sunshine and liberty.

In fruit (*Timon of Athens*, IV. iii. 422) :

> The oaks bear mast, the briars scarlet hips.

Two species of rose deserve more than a passing
thought ; both are conspicuous for their scent, both
were common in Elizabethan gardens, although one
was but a wilding.   To take this, the eglantine
(*R. rubiginosa*, L.), before the stranger, we have the
passage from *All's Well*, IV. iv., we have quoted
above, and it also occurs in *Cymbeline* as part of a

beautiful comparison of flowers with Imogen (*Cymbeline*, IV. ii. 222):

> No, nor
> The leaf of eglantine, whom, not to slander,
> Out-sweetened not thy breath ;

but chiefly in the beautiful " wild thyme bank " song in *Midsummer - Night's Dream*, II. i. 249, where ramped its scented shoot, a bower for the fair spot.

The foreign rose, native of North Africa (*R. moschata*, L.), is exclusively given over to Titania and her fairies. Here we learn, contrary to truth, it climbs upon her wild thyme bank with eglantine and honeysuckle :

> Quite overcanopied with luscious woodbine,
> With sweet musk-roses and with eglantine.

It is again referred to in the next scene, where the fairies are sent (*Midsummer-Night's Dream*, II. iii. 3):

> Some to kill cankers in the musk-rose buds.

The lily is most usually joined with the rose, companions in beauty, grace, and song, and they are none the less paired in Shakespeare. From the earliest times the lily has been the symbol of purity and holiness, fit image of our Lady's mind and virtues. Many a beautiful denizen of foreign lands has graced our gardens in the last century, many of the fairest in colour and form, but none that can compare in purity and grace with *Lilium candidum*, L., the Annunciation lily of the painters. It came to us originally from its native wilds in Turkey and Greece, but long before the time of Shakespeare it adorned the monastic garden and castle terrace of our English homes. Other species, too, were no doubt known to the poet ; and Gerard grew the showy orange lily, so bright an ornament in cottage gardens, the *Lilium croceum*, L., of botanists, native of the valleys of the

Pyrenees ; not only this, but *L. spectabile* also, and
the scarlet martagon (*L. chalcedonicum*, L.), brought
us from Western Asia, and the yellow-spotted lily of
the Pyrenees (*L. Pyrœnaicum*, L.), a martagon with
strangely fœtid smell. All these remain what they
were then—garden favourites. More than twenty
times over our poet mentions the lily, usually in
metaphor. One or two examples to show the method
of the master's treatment must perforce suffice us
here. Thus, in *Love's Labour's Lost*, V. ii. 351, the
Princess protests :

> Now by my maiden honour, yet as pure
>   As the unsullied lily ;

and in the superb benediction on the baby Elizabeth
the Archbishop ends :

> But she must die,
> She must, the saints must have her ; yet a virgin,
> A most unspotted lily shall she pass
> To the ground, and all the world shall mourn her.
>   *Henry VIII.*, V. v. 60.

Turning from the sublime to the ludicrous, we get
the Pyramus and Thisbe scene, where Thisbe
addresses Pyramus in these words :

> Dead, dead ? A tomb
> Must cover thy sweet eyes.
>   These lily lips,
>   This cherry nose,
> These yellow cowslip cheeks,
>   Are gone, are gone.
>   *Midsummer-Night's Dream*, V. i. 335.

Such other flowers as occur this month we may
take in alphabetical order, beginning with the
poisonous yet elegant aconite, a plant of stately
grace and curious anomalous flower structure, most
puzzling to the botanical tyro, who would never
dream it a near ally of the buttercup. So curious is
the flower that it gives to the plant more than one of

its popular names. The herb itself, so well known to the poisoners of the time, is the monk's-hood or wolf's-bane (*Aconitum napellus*, L.), a plant naturalized in England in shady places near streams, but truly wild through the greater part of Europe to the Himalaya region. Many other forms were known, and in Gerard's garden, besides that we have mentioned, the great yellow Swiss species, *A. lycoctonum*, L., and *A. pyramidale*, grew ("Herbal," 820-823). It is but once mentioned, and that in 2 *Henry IV.*, IV. iv. 47 :

> Though it do work as strong
> As aconitum or rash gunpowder.

But the poison of the apothecary in *Romeo and Juliet*, V. i., may be that extracted from this terribly deadly plant.

The flower we next consider is supposed to be referred to in the following lines :

He capers, he dances, he has eyes of youth, he writes verses, he speaks holiday, he smells April and May ; he will carry 't, he will carry 't, 'tis in his buttons; he will carry 't. —*Merry Wives*, II. ii. 67.

In the Elizabethan age more than one double flower was alluded to under the name of bachelor's-buttons, and supposed to have some mystic effect on lovers' affairs. Chief among them stands the double buttercup (*Ranunculus acris*, *fl. pl.*) and the double featherfew (*Matricaria parthenium*, *fl. pl.*), and even the daisy was included in this category. But by the Warwickshire peasantry of to-day the name is applied to the two caryophyllaceous plants whose flowers certainly resemble fairly well the linen buttons of the old-world rustics—the white and pink campion, *Lychnis alba*, Mill,* and *L. dioica*, L., so common in every shady hedge-bank. Of these, the pink form is

* The old *L. vespertina*, Sibth.

peculiarly liable to reduplication of its floral parts.
The white form is a cornfield plant, but in a lesser
degree than the cockle, a plant which is twice
referred to by the poet.   Thus,

> Sowed cockle, reaped no corn.
> *Love's Labour's Lost*, IV. iii. 383.

> We nourish against our senate
> The cockle of rebellion, insolence, sedition.
> *Coriolanus*, III. i. 69.

The weed in question is another species of the
genus we have just been considering, namely, *L.
githago*, Scop., and in places becomes a serious
nuisance.   It is not considered a genuine native, but
a colonist only.   It reaches throughout Europe to
Persia, and may at once be distinguished by its
peculiar purple flower, set in a calyx whose woolly
sepals far exceed the petals.   It is a close ally to a
garden plant of more interest—the ancient campion
of Apollo,* twined in the chaplets of the victors in
the Corinthian games.   Grindon quotes Drayton as
an authority for calling the cockle " the crimson
darnel flower," and says there was considerable confusion in the nomenclature of the cornfield weeds,
more than one species being considered under the
name of cockle.
We must now pass from the cornfield to the riverside, and admire the gorgeous gold of the yellow
flags drifting down the flooded waters or fast
anchored at the bankside.   The one expression may
be merely generic, and refer to any flat-leaved river
plant, but " flag " is a good old name applied to one
of our most beautiful natives, viz., the *Iris pseudo-
acorus*, L., which, together with the woodland plant
I. fœtidissima, L., whose scarlet berries are prized as
a winter decoration, are our only indigenous members

* *Lychnis coronaria*, L.

of one of the most beautiful orders of plants, which as seen in our gardens to-day are no mean rivals of the Orchidaceæ. But not only are they beautiful, not only is it

> The vagabond flag upon the stream
> (*Antony and Cleopatra*, I. iv. 45);

but the iris or flag, which you will, has been generally considered the prototype of the fleur-de-lis, to which Shakespeare makes frequent allusion. As a flower, it is one of those desired by Perdita (*Winter's Tale*, IV. iv. 125):

> Bold oxlips and
> The crown imperial; lilies of all kinds,
> The flower-de-luce being one! O, these I lack
> To make you garlands of.

Before we consider the heraldic quotations in which the poet speaks of the flower, it may be as well to see what species were known in the Elizabethan age, and, as usual, we turn to Gerard's garden, where we should have been able to gather the dwarf *I. pumila*, the beautiful *susiana*, *florentina*, *biflora*, *variegata*, and *germanica*, the foster-mother of our innumerable German irises, ranging in colour from snowy white to most lurid bronzes: *Sub-biflora*, *pallida*, *xiphioides*, *Lusitanica*, *graminea*, and *tuberosa*, all of which in a thousand interchanging shades are grown to-day.

Returning to the heraldry of the flower, we find such quotations as this in 1 *Henry VI.*, I. i. 80,

> Cropped are the flower-de-luces in your arms;
> Of England's coat one half is cast away,

in reference to the ruinous losses in France at the death of Henry V.

And again in the same play (I. ii. 99), speaking of

her sword-sheath embroidered with the royal arms,
Joan says :

> Here is my keen-edged sword,
> Decked with five flower-de-luces on each side ;

and yet again, 2 *Hen. VI.* (V. i. 8) :

> I cannot give due action to my words
> Except a sword or sceptre balance it :
> A sceptre it shall have, have I a soul,
> On which I'll toss the flower-de-luce of France.

The fleur-de-lis itself, so different from the birds
and animals of prey assumed by other Sovereigns, is
explained by the beautiful legend that it was brought
by an angel to Clovis, King of the Franks, at his
baptism, as a special grace from the Blessed Mary,
and this was even assigned as a title to precedence
by the French Bishops at the Council of Trent.   It
was probably little more than a rebus signifying
Fleur-de-Louis, the Kings of that name calling
themselves Loïs or Loys, and it first appears on the
coins of Louis VI. and VII.   The arms of France in
the form Azure, semée de lis, called by the heralds
France Ancient, was quartered by England after
1340 ; but in 1405 the modern coat of France
(Azure, three fleurs-de-lis) was substituted, and this
shield of England remained in use until the close of
the reign of Elizabeth.   The fleur-de-lis finally dis-
appeared from our national arms in 1801, on the
union with Ireland.

The plant to be considered next is once again
generic, and embraces in all probability members of
the two orders Cruciferæ and Caryophylleæ.   To the
former the "white and yellow gilloflowers" of
Stevens belong, and are represented by the plants
still called in Warwickshire gilliflowers and Whitsun
gillies, the one the beautifully variegated plant
which decks with its gorgeous colouring many a

shattered ruin, the *Cheiranthus cheiri* of botanists, the wallflower of commerce; the other *Hesperis matronalis*, L., the dame's violet.

But in Shakespeare's day the term "gilloflower" was applied to many of the pinks. Stevens mentions Provence gilloflowers and Indian gilloflowers, which may be closely allied to carnations. It will be advisable, perhaps, to consider them under the heading of the clove pink, *Dianthus caryophyllus*, L. This plant, which is found wild through Belgium and France, Italy, Hungary, and Greece, is only a naturalized plant in Great Britain, where it grows on old castle walls, but from it have descended the innumerable beautiful hybrids of our modern gardens.

Perdita apparently disliked flowers which had been produced merely by the skill of the gardener, and there is a good deal to be said for her objection; they rarely gain elegance of habit by man's improvement.

> Streaked gilly-flowers,
> Which some call nature's bastards : of that kind
> Our rustic garden's barren, and I care not
> To get slips of them.
>
> I'll not put
> The dibble in earth to set one slip of them.
> *Winter's Tale*, IV. iv. 81.

Turn from the garden to the sandy hedge bank and copse, and we may find a spotted plant of exceeding ill fame, verdant in its peculiar glaucous green and white dainty umbels. It is the *Conium maculatum* of Linnæus. In the two passages (*Henry V.*, V. ii. 45) it is classed with darnel and fumitory, and again in *King Lear*, IV. iv. 4, it appears in much the same company, and it is just the company in which the plant makes itself thoroughly at home.

It has long been held up to opprobrium as the poison by which Socrates was executed, and in Shakespeare's time was looked upon as only fit for a witch's broth, with such other plants of evil repute as henbane, nightshade, moonwort, and leopard's-bane.   The only other reference is in *Macbeth*, IV. i. 25, where to obtain the requisite strength we find :

> Root of hemlock, digged i' the dark.

From the unattractive hemlock it is a pleasant duty to re-enter once again Titania's bower, and rest with that dainty queen beneath the clustering masses of woodbine.   Everyone knows the honey-suckle, with its fragrant trumpet-shaped flowers, which the wild bees pierce at the base to plunder the nectary.   Only one species is truly native, the *L. periclymenum*, L., but two others are naturalized— *L. caprifolium*, L. (in Oxfordshire and Cambridge) ; *L. xylosteum*, L. (in Sussex and Herts) ; while in Gerard's garden the red species from Switzerland, *L. alpigena*, was growing in 1596.

The two English names for the plant are used to-gether by Titania :

> Sleep thou, and I will wind thee in my arms. . . .
> So doth the woodbine the sweet honeysuckle.
> > *Midsummer-Night's Dream*, IV. i. 44.

Hero speaks of

> the pleachèd bower,
> Where honeysuckles, ripened by the sun,
> Forbid the sun to enter.
> > *Much Ado about Nothing*, III. i. 7.

And later on, in the same play, we get :

> Beatrice, who even now
> Is couchèd in the woodbine coverture.
> > *Ibid.*, III. i. 29.

The name in Anglo-Saxon was " wide-winde," a
form it still retains in the country parlance of Warwickshire. Note also " waywind " for the small bind-
weed.

The remaining flower to be considered under this
month is one of those which are so doubtful that it
will probably never be satisfactorily settled, namely,
the pæony or peony. The verse runs :

> Thy banks with pioned and twilled brims,
> Which spongy April at thy hest betrims,
> To make cold nymphs chaste crowns.
> *Tempest*, IV. i. 65.

According to Grindon, the words " pioned and
twilled " are old words referring to the use of spade
and mattock. Ellacombe thinks, however, or assumes,
that the flower pæony is meant. But it is not an
English plant, nor a riverside one, either, and it would
seem but common-sense to paraphrase: the river with
its banks hollowed out as by the work of man, and
decked in April with greenery and kingcups, a fitting
crown for a chaste water-nymph.

If we turn from flowers to fruit, the fruit of the
month is the strawberry, the delicious pseudocarp of
Fragaria vesca, L., a native of the woodlands of Europe
and North Africa, reaching eastwards to the Himalaya. The fruit has been used by man from the
Bronze Age, and is found, or, rather, its achenes are
found, among the débris of Swiss lake-dwellings. It
should be remembered that the strawberry is technically an " etærio of achenes," and the edible part the
enlarged thalamus. There are three references to
the plant in the plays—to the excellence of the fruit
in the Bishop of Ely's garden (*Richard III.*, III. iv. 34) ;
to their native habit :

> The strawberry grows underneath the nettle
> (*Henry V.*, I. i. 60) ;

4

and last to their stain:

> Have you not sometimes seen a handkerchief
> Spotted with strawberries in your wife's hand?
> (*Othello*, III. iii. 434.)

The Elizabethan gardeners knew the wild strawberry, and grew it well, and they had also (*F. virginiana*) from North America the parent of our Scarlet, but not the Hautbois, Chilian or Carolina.

With regard to the name, "strawberry" is derived from the Anglo-Saxon "streowberrie," either, Prior says, from its straw-like haulms, or from their lying strewn (*i.e.*, strawed) on the ground. Some, he adds, derive the name from the custom of selling wild strawberries threaded on straws, but the name is used before this custom is at all likely to have originated.

A group of savoury herbs, denizens of the "garden of herbes of sweet savour," flower in this month, namely, balm, hyssop, parsley and rue. Of the former, at least two different plants are referred to: the greater number of references being to the balm of the apothecaries, the mysterious gum which Ellacombe says is exuded by the mastic, *Pistacia lentiscus*, L., or by the balm of Gilead, *Balsamodendron gileadense*; but Grindon says merely that it is derived from trees of the order Amyridaceæ, which he says

> Drop tears as fast as the Arabian trees
> Their medicinal gum.—*Othello*, V. ii. 350.

Perhaps the most interesting references are those in which Shakespeare alludes to balm as one of the constituents of the sacred coronation oil, as in *Richard II.*, III. ii. 54:

> Not all the water in the rough, rude sea
> Can wash the balm off from an anointed king.

Wickham Legg, the authority on all matters pertaining to the coronation rites, tells us that only four Kings had a right to be anointed and crowned—and that those of England and France were among them —and alone were entitled to the holy oil called " cream," which was made of a mixture of olive-oil and balm, and used in the Sacraments of Confirmation and Ordination, and in the consecration of Bishops. Richard II., to make stronger his slender right to the throne, invented a myth that the Blessed Mary had given St. Thomas of Canterbury the cream for anointing Kings, preserved in a golden eagle, but discovered by Divine revelation towards the close of his reign. Whereupon he desired to be anointed anew. At the coronation the King is anointed with holy oil on the hands, breast, between the shoulders, the elbows, and in the form of a cross upon the head; then, lastly, the holy cream is used in the same form and position as the last anointing with oil on the head, in the form of a cross (" The Sacring of English Kings," pp. 5-7).

But it is not only the foreign plant: we have naturalized in the South of England the bastard balm, *Melissa officinalis,* L., a native of the middle and South of Europe, with white corolla spotted with rose. It is perhaps alluded to in the *Merry Wives of Windsor,* V. v. 65 :

> The several chairs of order look you scour
> With juice of balm and every precious flower;

and again in *Antony and Cleopatra,* when the latter considers death " as sweet as balm."

A plant the reverse of sweet is the hyssop; yet a handsome plant, notwithstanding, with rich, deep purple flowers and, unfortunately, unpleasant smell. Like the balm, it is a labiate and native of the southern parts of Europe. It takes its specific name

4—2

from its drug-shop fame, *Hyssopus officinalis*, L. ;
it was growing in Gerard's garden.   It is used in the
poet's work in but one place (*Othello*, I. iii. 324), in a
curious description of bad gardening :

> If we will . . . set hyssop.

It was cultivated as early as 1548 (Turner's
" Names of Herbes ").

Parsley can hardly be called a savoury herb, but
it does not matter greatly if we find a place for its
pretty curled green foliage here.   It is a cultivated
scion from a plant, native of Sardinia, *Carum petrose-
linum*, Benth., which was growing in our English
gardens as early as 1551. It is only mentioned once,
and that as an ingredient in stuffing for a rabbit, pre-
sumably roast (*Taming of the Shrew*, IV. iv. 99).

There are many species closely allied to the garden
parsley found wild with us, including three of the
same genus, viz., *C. verticellatum*, a local plant found
chiefly in the West ; *C. segetum*, Benth., also local, but
found here and there in hedgebanks ; and *C. carui*
and *C. bulbo-castaneum*, which we mention elsewhere.
Garden parsley itself has a habit of escaping culture
and making itself at home on castle walls and waste
places.

We have now to deal with a plant represented in
no order inhabiting our islands, but one that has
been very long amongst us, and to which untold
virtues have at times been assigned, the rue, *Ruta
graveolens*, a native of the South of Europe, a plant
of a peculiarly beautiful glaucous foliage and an ex-
ceptionally evil smell.   Five times is it referred to in
the poet—now as " herb o' grace," now as the symbol
for sorrow, most pathetically, perhaps, in Ophelia's

There's rue for you, and there's some for me : we may call
it herb-grace o' Sundays : O, you must wear your rue with a
difference.—*Hamlet*, IV. v. 181.

And in the *Winter's Tale*, IV. iv. 74,

For you there's rosemary and rue.

Hooker says it is not known in a wild state. Among
the many medical purposes for which it was employed was its use as a plague remedy.   Two
versions of these remedies I give from curious old
Alexis :
    "Take whyte Dictanium, rounde Aristolochia,
Crodilium, called also Cardina or Cardua Verveyne,
Gentian seduaris, an herbe called in Latin *pes milui,*
of eche of them two unces, stampe all thys a lyttle
wyth a handfull of Rue ; than take a violle that
holdeth at the leaste three quartes, and fyll it wyth
the best wyne that you canne fynde, whereinto you
shall putte all the foresayde thinges, and leave it to
standynge in youre house : and in dangerous tymes
take everye mornynge before you goe out of your
house halfe a glasse-full of the sayd wyne, but you
must have taken fyrst a walnutte, a fygge and twoo
or three lytle braunches of Rue."
    Another against the plague :
    "Take the toppe of Rue, a garlicke head and half
a quarter of a walnutte and a corne of salte.   Eat
thys every mornynge, contynuing so a muneth
together and be merry and jocunde" (Alexis,
p. 38).
    It is not a long walk from the garden of " herbes
of sweet savour " to the vegetable-garden, and here
again certain species of plants, if the gardening be
neglected, will be found in blossom.   The first is the
cool salad plant, the lettuce, a member of the vast
order Compositæ, brought to us from the East at some
long-forgotten date, perchance by the Romans, who
certainly grew it.   All we know is it was grown in
1562.   It is the *Lactuca sativa* of Linnæus, and several
allied species are found wild with us, though three at

least—viz., *L. scariola*, L., *L. saligna*, L., and
L. muralis, Tresen—are rare ; the last-named, however, grows freely on the walls of Warwick Castle.
The other native species, *L. virosa*, L., is far from a
common plant.   The lettuce appears in Shakespeare
only in *Othello*, I. iii. 324, in connection with hyssop
and thyme as symbols of those pleasing qualities
self-culture produces.   The exact words are :

> If we will plant nettles or sow lettuce.
> *Othello*, I. iii. 325.

The name is derived from the Latin *lactuca ;*
Early English, *lettice ;* Old French, *lactuce*—a name
derived from its milky juice.

The bean (*Faba vulgaris*, Mch.), said by Dorme to
be a native of Egypt, is one of the most ancient and
best of the farinaceous foods of mankind.   It has
been found among other plants in the lake-dwellings
of Switzerland, which shows that three or four
thousand years ago it was a staple article of food,
and in no very great way different from the best
varieties of modern market-gardeners.   It may be
worth while to quote here the deduction of the
talented author of " Lake Dwellings," namely, that
" all plants which come in contact with man become
changed up to a certain point, and thus man
participates in the great transformations of Nature,
while the wild plants . . . do not exhibit the smallest
change " (p. 530).

Ellacombe quotes a Lincolnshire proverb, that you
must " sleep in a bean-field all night if you want to
have awful dreams or go crazy."

The most curious use to which beans have been
put is probably that of parish register.

At the baptistery of San Giovanni, Florence, the
baptismal church of that great city, the yearly

number baptized was calculated by means of beans dropped into a bag : for every boy a black one, for every girl a white (Murray's " Handbook of North Italy ").

In Shakespeare's day several kinds of beans were grown. Twice he refers to them, once as part of the food for horses. Mischievous Puck says :

> When I a fat and bean-fed horse beguile.
> *Midsummer-Night's Dream*, II. i. 45.

And secondly, in 1 *Henry IV.*, II. i. 9 :

> Peas and beans are as dank here as a dog.

Two species of the genus *Allium* flower this month, the garlick and onion, plants popular at that time not only as food, but as medicine, and much might be said of their reputed virtues. The garlic, *Allium sativum*, L., is a native of Southern Europe, but grows easily in our gardens. Stevens quaintly says :

" Garlicke taken fasting is the countrie man's treacle in the time of the plague and other dangerous diseases, as also against all manner of venom and poison."

He advises, to prevent the unpleasant smell, it is well to eat " a bean or ribbe of a beete or mallage or green parsley." There is no doubt its objectionable smell made it unpleasant to the refined palate, and Shakespeare only uses it when alluding to the coarse food of the lower orders. Thus, in *Midsummer-Night's Dream*, IV. ii. :

> And, most dear actors, eat no onions nor garlic, for we are to utter sweet breath ;

and again in 1 *Henry, IV.*, III. i. 161 :

> I had rather live
> With cheese and garlic in a windmill, far,
> Than feed on cates, and have him talk to me.

Yet another recipe may be inserted before we pass on to the next plant:

"A goodly and a pleasaunt secrete to heale the coughe, in rubbyng of the soales of the feete, and is a thynge very easy and certayne. Take two or three garlyke heades well mundified and made cleane, stampe them well, then put to them hogges sewot, and stampe them well anew: and at nyghte whenne you goe to bedde warme well the soales of youre feete, and annoynte them well with the sayd confection, and then warme them agayne as hote as you may endure, rubbynge them welle a preatye space: and beyng abedde, let youre feete be bounde with some warme lynnen cloathe, and rubbe also the smalle of your legges with the sayde oyntemente, by this meanes you shall be healed in three nyghtes (Alexis, p. 36).

The companion plant of the order and genus, the common onion, *Allium cepa*, L., apparently came originally from Spain, but, like the garlic, had long been cultivated, and was considered a most healthy and useful food. Stevens tells us that tender onions eaten in honey give health, that the juice is a remedy for baldness, that it is good for the complexion, and takes away white spots from the face, while, "mingled with hen's grease, it drieth up the kibes," and last, but not least, mixed with honey and salt, is a soveraigne remedy against the bite of a mad dog (p. 221).

Shakespeare uses it in very much the same way that he handles garlic in the advice to the players already quoted, but he also mentions the effect of its vapour on the sight:

And if the boy have not a woman's gift,
To rain a shower of commanded tears,
An onion will do well for such a shift.
                    Taming of the Shrew, Induct. i. 124 ;

and again in *Antony and Cleopatra*, I. ii. 176 :

Indeed, the tears live in an onion that should water this sorrow.

JULY

Here's flowers for you ;
Hot lavender, mints, savory, marjoram ;
The marigold, that goes to bed wi' the sun,
And with him rises weeping ; these are flowers
Of middle summer. . . .
                    bold oxlips, and
The crown imperial ; lilies of all kinds,
The flower-de-luce being one ! . . .
To make you garlands of.

Winter's Tale, IV. iii. 103.

COMPARED to the beautiful plants which deck
the month of June, as interesting in their lore
as they are beautiful in form and scent, those of the
early dog-days are far from attractive, and yet one
is the most rich and gorgeous of our native wild
flowers, and another decks our garden trellises with
a profusion of golden blossoms.

Who does not know the scarlet of poppy land
when the *Papaver rhœas* of Linnæus has been allowed
to grow too freely amongst the fields of corn and
pease ? It is more brilliant far than the daisy trimmed
meads, or those which the buttercup has "painted
with delight"; and yet it is an evil weed, notwithstanding, found only too commonly, the agricul-
turist would say, throughout Europe to India. The
poppy of Shakespeare is that known as the opium
poppy (*Papaver somniferum*, L.), a plant with handsome glaucous foliage and large white flower of
four petals marked with a bold cross of dark purple.

[58]

It is found wild over the whole of Europe and Asia and in Western Africa, and its countless varieties, single, semi-double, and double, ranging from snowy white to purplish-black, are a great ornament in an old-world garden. Only once is the plant mentioned, and then the reference is to the strong narcotic juice, which has been used as a drug by man since the Bronze Age, and has done more than any other decoction to debase the minds of its votaries. It is not truly wild in our islands, though a not uncommon escape. It is mentioned in connection with mandrakes in *Othello*, III. iii. 330.

England has several species of pinks habiting its fields, woods, and pastures, but it is hardly likely that the poet refers to any of these, sweet and dainty as they are. He thinks of the garden, of the carnation and gilliflower, of the many "pied" varieties the Elizabethan gardeners produced, apart from hybrids. Gerard grew the sweet william, still a great favourite, and deservedly so, called by scientists *Dianthus barbatus*, L., a native of Central Europe. It has hybridized into a hundred forms, now white, now all but black, and another several shades of pink and white in one cyme. The old name sops-in-wine, or sops, used for carnations, suggests the modern use of sweet herbs, such as woodruff, in the mingled wines called by the Rhenish peasants "bola." It seems to have been specially used to flavour the bridal wine. See *Taming of the Shrew*, III. ii. 174 :

> Quaffed off the muscadel,
> And threw the sops all in the sexton's face.

The word "carnation" is said by Prior to be derived from Coronaria, and represents the *Vetonica coronaria* of early herbalists, because its flowers were used in chaplets, and he quotes in illustration Spenser's " Shepherd's Calendar " :

> Bring coronations and sops-in-wine
> Worn of paramours.

We have already pointed out under June that the source of our garden carnations is the semi-wild *Dianthus caryophyllus*, L. It may be worth while noting that the popular white and pink pinks of our garden are of far later introduction.

The flax, although a useful plant, and as such, perhaps, unfitted for a position among the flowers, whether of field or garden, yet is none the less an object of beauty, since its dazzling blue is of the sky's own tint. Few plants are more useful to man, few better deserve their specific names. *Linum usitatissimum*, L., is not a native; it is, however, Hooker says, naturalized wherever flax is cultivated for oil or fibre. Such cultivation began exceedingly early. The seeds of the allied *L. angustifolium*, L., are found among the débris of the lake-dwellings. The neolithic peoples appear to have been the first to introduce spinning, if we may judge from the pottery spindle-whorls found among their remains, and until the discovery of cotton it held its own as a textile fabric among all nations. The species mentioned above, *L. angustifolium*, L., is found with us south of Lancashire, while the beautiful *L. perenne*, L., is much more uncommon, though occasionally found in chalk districts from Durham to Essex. The little white-flowered purging flax, *L. catharticum*, L., is a Warwickshire plant, and quite at home on old walls and dry banks.

In the plays its inflammable nature is twice mentioned—of course in the form of tow—viz., in *2 Henry VI.*, V. ii. 55, and in *Two Noble Kinsmen*, V. iii. 113. As lint it is mentioned together with white of egg:

> Go thou : I'll fetch some flax and whites of egg
> To apply to his bleeding face.
>
> *King Lear*, III. vii. 106.

And, lastly, the term "flax-wench" is applied in opprobrium, much as we might use the term "fish-wife," in the *Winter's Tale*, I. ii. 276; while Falstaff is referred to in the *Merry Wives*, V. v. 159, as

A hodge pudding, a bag of flax.

This month we may consider a curious umbelliferous plant belonging to a genus (*Carum*) noticed in June, the *Carum bulbo-castaneum* of Koch. It is a dainty plant with delicate umbels of white flowers and bright green foliage, and is frequent in damp meadow-land. Its root is peculiar, long and tapering, but terminating in a globose tuber as large as a chestnut and black in colour. Hooker states that this root is used for pigs. It is eaten in the eastern counties by the peasant lads, a custom no doubt alluded to in the *Tempest*, when Caliban says:

I, with my long nails, will dig thee pig-nuts.
Tempest, II. ii. 172.

It is said to be cultivated in some countries for food.

Burs may be either the seed-vessels of the various species of burdock (*Arctium*) or some of the many seeds covered with hooked spines and setæ, such as those of the goosegrass or hound's-tongue. Perhaps the former are the more likely, especially in *King Lear*, IV. iv. 4, where it is one of the plants in the noxious garland already repeatedly referred to.

Hardocks must mean burdocks.* The foliage of these plants (*Arctium lappa*, L.†) is handsome, and their habit massive and pleasing; but, nevertheless, they are troublesome weeds, and the bracts are armed with "long, stiff, spreading, hooked tips,"

---

* The Globe edition reads "burdocks."

† Modern botanists separate the old *A. lappa* into *A. majus*, Bernh.; *A. nemorosum*, Lej.; *A. minus*, Bernh.; and *A. intermedium*, Lange.

which render them troublesome to animals and man.
Shakespeare, as usual, ever observant of natural
peculiarities, has used this tendency in more than
one metaphor.   Thus in *Measure for Measure,* IV. iii.
189 :

> Nay, friar, I am a kind of bur ; I shall stick ;

while Celia cheers Rosalind's mood, saying of the
briars to which she has alluded in picture of her own
troubles :

> They are but burs, cousin, thrown upon thee in holiday
> foolery : if we walk not in the trodden path, our very petti-
> coats will catch them.—*As You Like It,* I. iii. 13.

To which there comes Rosalind's sad reply :

> I could shake them off my coat : these burs are in my
> heart.

And in another play :

> Hang off, thou cat, thou burr !
> *Midsummer-Night's Dream,* III. ii. 260.

But the golden - flowered plant we have already
mentioned as a garden ornament requires to be considered.   It is the bladder senna (*Cassia senna,* L.),
a native of Egypt and Barbary.   The plant was
unknown to Shakespeare, since it was not introduced
into our gardens before 1640, when Parkinson mentions it.   But as a medicine it was well known to
the apothecaries of the day, and they used the
leaves of *Cassia lanceolata* as well as the more common
kind.

> What rhubarb, senna,* or what purgative drug,
> Would scour these English hence ?
> *Macbeth,* V. iii. 55.

If we turn for a while from the flower to the fruit
garden, we shall find the cherry and the gooseberry
to reward our pains.   Twice does the poet directly

---

* The Globe edition reads " cyme."

refer to the former—in *King John*, II. i. 162, where we find:

> Give it a plum, a cherry, and a fig ;

and again in the *Comedy of Errors*, IV. iii. 74, we read of

> A nut, a cherry-stone ;

but more frequently in elegant metaphor, thus :

> So we grew together,
> Like to a double cherry.
> *Midsummer-Night's Dream*, III. ii. 208.

And in the same play :

> Thy lips, those kissing cherries, tempting show ;

and again in *Pericles*, V. i. 8 :

> Twin with the rubied cherry.

Pliny says this fruit was introduced to Britain by the Romans, but Hooker considers all our three species wild, viz., *Prunus cerasus*, L., a small bush with red bark found as far south as the Azores, and the origin of the Morello, Duke and Kentish cherries; *P. avium*, L., the gean, from which has sprung all the garden geans, hearts and bigaroons ; and, lastly, *P. padus*, the bird cherry, a close ally of the common evergreen cherry-laurel, *P. lauro-cerasus*, L., of which more is said under the heading " Bay."

The gooseberry is also a native plant, a member of the order Grossulariaceæ, and a close ally of the black, red, and white currant, none of which are mentioned by Shakespeare. The currants mentioned by him in *The Winter's Tale* are the dried fruit of *Vitio corinthiaca*, L., a species of vine, native of the East, and an early and well-known article of commerce.

The gooseberry, *Ribes* grossularia, L., bears a hairy berry, but there is a variety with the berry smooth, ranked by Linnæus as a species under the name of *Uva-crispa*. It is probably wild in copses in the hilly districts of the North of England, although it is only found as a garden escape elsewhere. It has the usual distribution of European plants throughout the Continent, and stretches into Asia on the one hand, and North Africa on the other. Murray suggests that the name is derived from " goose " and " berry," adding that the grounds on which plants have received names associating them with animals are usually inexplicable. He thinks there is no evidence for a hypothetical gorse or grose berry, although there is a form " gozell " for " grosell," and the country folk still talk of " goosegogs." It was not known to the ancients in a cultivated state, and is said to have been introduced into our gardens by the Netherlanders. It is referred to but once in the plays, in 2 *Henry IV.*, I. ii. 194 :

All the other gifts appertinent to man, as the malice of this age shapes them, are not worth a gooseberry.

From which we may gather that it was not a fruit very highly esteemed in Shakespeare's day.

On hilly heaths we may by chance find this month the fruit of the whortleberry or bilberry, *Vaccinium myrtillus*, L., whose dark-blue glaucous berries are referred to in the words :

To Windsor chimneys shalt thou leap :
Where fires thou find'st unraked and hearths unswept,
There pinch the maids as blue as bilberry.
Merry Wives, V. v. 47.

---

* Ribes, from an Arabic word for rheum, applied to this genus in error (Hooker).

The berries of the plant, Hooker says,* are much used for preserves in Northern countries. Prior tells us the name " whortleberry " is a confusion for "myrtle-berry." The Anglo-Saxon heorot-berie was, he says, the blackberry. The blue-berries, or hurts, of the bilberry gave the name to the azure roundles of the heralds (hurts).† We have two closely allied species, natives—the one of mountainous bogs, from West-morland northwards—viz., *V. uliginosum*, L.; the other the cowberry, *V. vitis-idæus*, L.

In the herb-garden this month camomile, cara-ways and marjoram will be in blossom. The medicinal camomile is but once referred to—1 *Henry IV.*, II. iv. 443 :

Though the camomile, the more it is trodden on, the faster it grows, yet youth, the more it is wasted, the sooner it wears.

The plant *Anthemis nobilis*, L., a native of Spain, Germany, Austria and North Africa, is still used as a tonic and febrifuge, and Gerard says that it was considered good in many stomachic complaints as well as for weariness.

Caraways is a name applied through Middle Latin *carui semina* to the seeds of *Carum carui*, L., an umbelliferous plant naturalized in waste places in our own country, and found wild on the Continent as far east as Western Asia.

It is only once mentioned in the poet, and then as an ingredient in cakes, as the seeds are used to the present day. Ellacombe, however, seems to consider it a variety of apple,‡ though it is hardly likely the guests would be regaled with first one variety, then another :

* " English Flora," 2nd ed., p. 242.
† Woodward, " Brit. and For. Her.," p. 190.
‡ He alters his opinion in a later edition.

5

Nay, you shall see mine orchard; where, in an arbour, we will eat a last year's pippin of my own graffing, with a dish of caraways, and so forth.—2 *Henry IV.*, V. iii. 1.

The sweet-scented marjoram, one of the best of all pot-herbs, the *Origanum marjoram* of L., was introduced to our gardens from its native haunts in Portugal, and has since been deservedly popular for flavouring soups, etc. Perdita mingles this plant with mint and savory amongst her marigolds (*Winter's Tale*, IV. iv. 104); it also occurs in *All's Well*, IV. v. 17, where the clown says:

She was the sweet marjoram of the salad, or, rather, herb of grace,

which brings the retort from Lafeu:

They are not herbs, you knave; they are nose-herbs.

And lastly in the *Sonnets*, xcix.:

Buds of marjoram had stol'n thy hair.

We have allied species among our own native plants. *Origanum vulgare*, L., a bitter, aromatic and balsamic plant, is common in our dry copses and hedge banks from Moray southwards.

It was used as a specific in Gerard's days for colds and diseases of the brain and head, and he especially adds that " it easeth the toothache, being chawed in the mouth " (" Herbal," p. 540). It was also used in ointments.

In the vegetable-garden peas, carrots and mustard will be in flower, and in the fields vetches; to all these Shakespeare makes reference.

The garden pea, *Pisum sativum*, L., is a very ancient vegetable, and its seeds are found among the débris of the Stone Age, from which we may gather that those ancient peoples cultivated it, and, like the

bean, it has continued a favourite ever since.   It is
said to occur in a wild state in Southern Europe.

Shakespeare refers not only to the plant itself, but
to various names for its legumes.   Thus, the young
pods are called squashes, from the French *esquacher*,
as in *Twelfth Night*, I. v. 165 :

Not yet old enough for a man, nor young enough for a
boy, as a squash is before 'tis a peascod.

And again in *Midsummer-Night's Dream* :

Commend me to squash your mother.

Peascod was applied only when the legume
approached maturity, and in one place, 2 *Henry IV.*,
II. iv. 412, it is given as a synonym for summer :

I have known thee these twenty-five years come peascod
time.

In *As You Like It*, II. iv. 51, we read :

I remember the wooing of a peascod instead of her :
from whom I took two cods, and giving her them again, said
with weeping tears, '' Wear these for my sake.''

The reference is to a curious old lovers' custom of
reading good or evil fortune with a pea-pod, which
gave birth to a Devonshire proverb quoted in
Brand :

Winter time for shoeing, peascod time for wooing.

The divination of a peascod was obtained by
selecting one growing on the stem, snatching it away
quickly, and if the good omen of the peas remaining in the husk were preserved, then presenting it
to the lady of one's choice (Brand, '' Pop. Ant.,''
ii. 99).

The carrot, *Daucus carota*, L., is a native plant,

5—2

though long cultivation makes the garden form and
the wild hardly recognisable as close allies. It is,
like many other plants of ours, of wide geographical
range, extending to Northern Africa and North and
Western India. The dense white-flowered umbels
give place to seed petioles curved inwards, these
suggesting the popular name of "bird's nest." As a
garden plant it is said to have been introduced by
Flemish gardeners, and its name was extended to
cover the parsnip, *Pastinaca sativa*, L., which by the
earlier herbalists and gardeners was known as the
yellow carrot. The vegetable is only referred to
once, in *Merry Wives*, IV. i. 55 :

> Remember, William ; focative is caret.
> And that's a good root.

The seeds of both carrot and parsnip have
been found in the Swiss lake-dwellings (Keller,
p. 331).

Mustard is another native plant, or, rather, group of
plants, closely allied to the turnip and cabbage. The
two species used for commerce are the *Brassica nigra*,
Koch, and the *B. alba*, Boiss. The former is truly
wild on sea-cliffs, the latter in cultivated ground, and
both have the usual Europe-Asia distribution.

Shakespeare gives Mustardseed as the name for
one of Titania's fairies (*Midsummer-Night's Dream*,
III. i. 165),

> Peas-blossom ! Cobweb ! Moth ! and Mustard-seed !

and Bottom assigns that fairy the delightful occupation of assisting Cobweb to scratch. The condiment
itself is referred to in the conversation between
Grumio and Katherine, *Taming of the Shrew*, IV. iii. 23 :

> *Gru.* What say you to a piece of beef and mustard ?
> *Kath.* A dish that I do love to feed upon.
> *Gru.* Ay, but the mustard is too hot a little.
> *Kath.* Why then, the beef, and let the mustard rest.

And yet again in a long passage from *As You Like It*, I. ii. 65.

The best mustard of the day, that of Tewksbury, is mentioned in 2 *Henry IV.*, II. iv. 261 :

He a good wit? hang him, baboon! his wit's as thick as Tewksbury mustard.

As an illustration, Ellacombe aptly gives an extract from Coles, who, writing in 1657, says: "In Gloucestershire about Teuxbury they grind mustard and make it into balls, which are brought to London and other remote places as being the best the world affords." Dressing mustard flour was invented in the eighteenth century by Mrs. Clements, of Durham, but appears to have been known to the Anglo-Saxons, and Parkinson says : " The seeds hereof, ground between two stones, fitted for the purpose and called a quern, with some good vinegar added to it to make it liquid and running, is that kind of mustard that is usually made to serve as sauce both for fish and flesh of all sorts."

In the fields the sweet scent of the vetches, which early this month will be cut for fodder, comes to us on the breeze. They are all species of the genus *Vicia*, principally the *Vicia sativa*, L.

These plants are only mentioned once, and that in *The Tempest*, IV. i. 60, as part of the gifts of

Ceres, most bounteous lady, thy rich leas
Of wheat, rye, barley, vetches, oats and peas.

Our cultivated *V. sativa*, L., is not a native plant; indeed, it is unknown out of cultivation. It was probably brought to our island by the Romans. The origin of the popular English name " tares," Prior suggests, is from Low German *töire*, to tether, and as in early works we find it called " tare-fytche ' —*i.e.*,

the vetch that binds or tethers the corn—he may be
correct ; or it may be from the Dutch *terve*, wheat.
Parkinson says, p. 1062, "Th. Bot.": "This ramping
wild vetch, or tare, as the country people call it,
because it is the most pernicious herb that can grow
on the earth, for corn or any other good herb
that it shall grow by, killing and strangling them."
The tare of the Bible (*zizania*) is either darnel, which
is doubtful, or more probably a bastard species
of wheat. Many of our native vetches are handsome, showy plants. The elegant wood-vetch (*V.
sylvestris*) and the beautiful blue *V. cracca* are the
gems, but the delicate foliage and stems of *V. hirsuta*
or the little blue flower of *V. tetrasperma* are not to
be despised.

AUGUST

You sun-burned sicklemen, of August weary,
Come hither from the furrow, and be merry:
Make holiday: your rye-straw hats put on,
And these fresh nymphs encounter every one
In country footing.

Tempest, IV. i. 135.

AUGUST, with its dry days and heat, when the
first fresh green of the early summer has long
passed away, and the leaves seem hot and dusty—and
in very sooth, what with attacks of insects and
variations of climate and atmospheric conditions, no
wonder they show signs of fatigue and their little
breathing mouths become choked—yet even now new
flowers spring up to greet us with their multitudinous
hosts. First of all, in some favoured gardens and
within our greenhouses, that most dainty of all evergreens, the myrtle (*Myrtus communis*), is putting
forth its delicate, wax-like, white flower-buds.
Although no longer considered so delicate and rare
as in Shakespeare's days, few plants are much more
trouble to acclimatize, and it is rarely seen in perfection out-of-doors save on our south-western coasts.
Though said to have been grown more frequently in
the open air in Elizabethan times, yet it was introduced very possibly at an early date, and certainly
by 1629. As the flower of Venus it was in great
request for bridal wreaths, and was looked upon as
the emblem of refined beauty. The poet uses it
chiefly in the *Passionate Pilgrim*, where we read:

[71]

> Venus, with young Adonis sitting by her,
> Under a myrtle shade began to woo him.—xi. 2.

And in *Venus and Adonis*, 865:

> Then sad she hasteth to a myrtle grove.

It is also mentioned in the plays, *Antony and Cleopatra*, III. xii. 8, and *Measure for Measure*, II. ii. 117. The old English name, gale, is still used of the bog myrtle (*Myrica gale*, L.), a plant of our moors and bogs still, employed for tea-making and in cottage medical recipes.

Perhaps few flowers have more popular names than the pansy (*Viola tricolor*, L.). We find in Shakespeare Cupid's flower, love-in-idleness, and pansy, while heart's-ease is inferred; and Prior adds to them: Herb Trinity; three faces under a hood; fancy flamy; kiss me, cull me, or cuddle me to you; tickle-my-fancy; kiss me ere I rise; jump up and kiss me; kiss me at (or over) the garden gate; pink of my John; love-in-idleness.

"Its habit" (he says, p. 171) "of coquettishly hanging its head and half hiding its face, as well as some fancied resemblances in the throat of the *corolla*, have led to many quaint names in our own and foreign languages."

Pansy, or pawnce, comes from French *pensée*, or *menues pensées*, and the German *unnütze sorge ;* Latin *panacea*. Love-in-idleness is quite a common name in Warwickshire to-day. The name heart's-ease is suggested in *Hamlet*, IV. v. 176:

> There is pansies—that's for thoughts.

That of Cupid's flower, said by Ellacombe (p. 207) to be peculiar to Shakespeare, occurs in *Midsummer-Night's Dream*, IV. i. 78:

> Dian's bud o'er Cupid's flower
> Hath such force and blessed power.

But the principal reference is in the same play,
II. i. 165, under the name "love-in-idleness":

> Yet marked I where the bolt of Cupid fell:
> It fell upon a little western flower,—
> Before milk-white, now purple with love's wound,—
> And maidens call it love-in-idleness.
> Fetch me that flower; the herb I showed thee once:
> The juice of it on sleeping eyelids laid
> Will make or man or woman madly dote
> Upon the next live creature that it sees.

Also in the *Taming of the Shrew*, I. i. 155:

> But see, while idly I stood looking on,
> I found the effect of love-in-idleness.

The plant is very closely allied to the sweet violet,
and has the same general arrangement of its petals,
but is placed in the subgenus *Melanium*. It has the
customary geographical distribution of most of our
plants—Europe, North Africa, Asia, to North-West
India. In our own land it is a cornfield weed, with
purple-whitish or golden petals. The type has
purple upper petals; it is the origin of the splendid
colours of our garden varieties.

In dealing with flowers this month, the mallow is
not to be despised; rough though it be and the companion of coarse weeds, its satin-like flowers of deep
pink and dark-green reniform leaves set off many a
bit of barren waste. Our commonest and largest
species is *Malva sylvestris*, L., the fruit of which,
known as "cheeses" to village children, are often
picked and eaten by them. Handsomer still is the
delicate pink musk mallow (*M. moschata*, L.), whose
bright green leaves, much divided, make a specially
elegant setting to the flower. Our other species,
the dwarf mallow (*M. rotundifolia*, L.), has small
flowers of white streaked with lilac. The mallows
are generally distributed, but their allies, the tree

and marsh mallows, are only found in Southern Europe. It must not be forgotten that to this order belongs the handsome hollyhock of our gardens and the cotton (*Gossypium*) of commerce. Only once does the poet mention our plant, and that in *The Tempest*, II. i. 143 :

> *Gon.* Had I plantation of this isle,—
> *Ant.* He'd sow't with nettle-seed.
> *Seb.*   Or docks, or mallows.

Since docks and nettle occur in these lines, we will deal with them next. The former are also referred to in *Henry V.*, V. ii. 51 :

> And nothing teems
> But hateful docks, rough thistles, kecksies, burs.

Prior tells us that the name " dock " comes from the early English " docca," which in Ælfric's glossary is given as the equivalent of Latin *dilla*. It is not unlikely, he thinks, to be the plant meant in Latin by *dorcus*, from its healing powers, such as that of soothing nettle-stings, as the dills were used to heal internal pains, and the word " rumex " is translated " edroc " in an early glossary. Few of our native plants are more stately than the docks ; their handsome artistic leaves and lofty flower-stalks, rich in varied tints of green, crimson, and brown, commend them strongly to the lover of the beautiful. But they are terrible weeds to the farmer. To the botanist, again, they are of great interest ; the peculiar method of flowering and seeding give him both trouble and pleasure. And, honestly, are not these two things, trouble and pleasure, synonyms ? We care little for what we easily get, while that which takes trouble in the getting is highly valued. We have twelve native species and two naturalized, and these vary in height from the 6-foot flower-spike of *Rumex hydrolapathum,* Huds., to the 3-inch stem of *Rumex acetosella,* L.

Monk's rhubarb (*Rumex alpinus,* L.), a naturalized species, has a root used in medicine and its leaves for a pot-herb. It must not be confused with the true rhubarb (*Rheum*). *Rumex acetosa,* L., a common British plant, is cultivated for salads, and abounds in binoxalate of potash. Its name "sorrell," Prior says (p. 1209), is derived from the French *surelle* and German *sur,* from the acidity of its leaves, due to the oxalic acid it contains.

The nettle needs little description. We all know from experience that it has the power to inflict an extremely irritating sting. Each hair is hollow, and has at its base a little sac of acrid fluid, set in an elastic envelope of cells ; the point of the hair is sharp, but protected by a little cap. When the nettle is lightly touched, the cap is broken off, the hair pierces the hand, and the incision forces a drop of acrid fluid into the blood. If grasped firmly, the hair is broken lower down, and there is no sharp point to pierce the skin. There are thirteen references in the poet, most of which, without doubt, refer to the common nettle of our waste lands (*Urtica dioica,* L.). Some we have already quoted in connection with other flowers. Others we now give :

> We call a nettle but a nettle, and
> The faults of fools but folly.
> > *Coriolanus,* II. i. 207.

And, again :

> Goads, thorns, nettles, tails of wasps.
> > *Winter's Tale,* I. ii. 329.

> Look for thy reward
> Among the nettles at the elder-tree.
> > *Titus Andronicus,* II. iii. 271.

Our other species are *U. ureus*, L., a small weed of cultivated ground, and the curious alien said by Camden to have been brought to us by the Romans to chafe their bodies with in this Northern cold. This is the *U. pilulifera*, L., and, like the Roman snail, is said to be only found on the sites of Roman encampments—a statement to be received, like that of Camden, *cum grano salis*. Prior tells us (p. 161) that its name is derived from *netel*, German *nessel*, from the root form *ne*, to spin or sew, and that it meant that with which one sews. That thread was spun from it in Scotland we have the evidence quoted by Prior in illustration—" Scotch cloth is only house-wifery of the nettle "; and Ellacombe quotes a letter of the poet Campbell: " I have slept in nettle sheets, and dined off a nettle tablecloth, and I have heard my mother say that she thought nettle cloth more durable than any other linen." It has also been used for paper and in rope manufacture, and has always been in request as a vegetable. Indeed, the young shoots are considered to be equal to spinach ; and in 1596 Coghan wrote : " Cunning cookes at the spring of the year, when nettles first bud forth, can make good pottage with them." They are much used still to pack garden fruit, and this is but the survival of an old custom, for nettles are supposed to preserve the " bloom " on the fruit. To nettles the insect world owes much. From the tortoiseshell butterfly (*Vanessa urticæ*) to the nettle gall-fly (*Chironomus urticæ*), many dozens of species find in it a home either in a larval or pupate condition, and it is a prey to more than fifty species of fungi, which attack it living or dead. It must not be forgotten that the male and female flowers are on separate plants, and that the order is allied to that to which the hop and hemp belong.

The candied root of a plant called eringoes is once

mentioned, and that in the *Merry Wives of Windsor,*
V. v. 20 :

Let the sky rain potatoes . . . hail kissing-comfits, and
snow eringoes.

The method of preparing the roots is thus given
in Gerard's " Herbal," p. 1000, Ed. 1597 :
"Refine sugar fit for the purpose, and take a
pound of it, the white of one egge, and a pint of
cleere water, boile them togither and scum it, then
let it boile untill it become to a good strong syrupe,
and when it is boiled, as it cooleth adde thereto a
sawcer full of rose water, a spoonfull of cinnamon
water, and a graine of muske, which have beene
infused togither the night before, and now strained ;
into which syrupe, being more than half colde, put in
your rootes to soke and infuse untill the next day :
your rootes being ordered in maner heer after
following."
The root is taken from the sea-holly (*Eryngium
maritimum,* L.), a plant common on our coasts, but
a very handsome one, notwithstanding.   It has
curious glaucous blue spiny foliage, and grows to
the height of 1 to 2 feet.   The flowers are bluish-
white, and each head is surrounded by a spinescent
involucre.   One or two other species are locally
naturalized, and of late years the plants have become
garden favourites.
We now come to the sweet-scented purple thyme,
spoken of in the lines so often quoted in *Midsummer-
Night's Dream,* II. i. 209,

I know a bank where the wild-thyme blows

—a place always conjectured to be either near the
mill at Hampton Lucy or on the summit of Borden
Hill, spots which fit in well with the poet's description, and even to-day harmonize with the spirit of

his creation. Sweet as the plant is, lading the air with its aromatic scent, yet has it no native name—at least, none that we can with certainty assign to it. That we call it by, was the Greek name for some sweet-scented plant or shrub used in sacrifice. We have two native species, *serpyllum*, Tr., and *chamædrys*, Tr. The latter is scarce, the former common, and ranging from Greenland to the Himalayas. It is a well-known garden herb.

By the river-bank this month reeds and sedges will be found in luxuriance, and this seems a fitting place in which to record their lore. Along the banks of Avon no less than along " swift Severn's flood" (1 *Henry IV.*, I. iii. 103) the reeds grow thickly and wave their long, grassy leaves and silky plumes in every passing breeze. Few plants are more graceful. By the poet every grassy plant by the riverside was grouped either as a reed or sedge.

Reeds, properly speaking, are graminaceous plants, (the *Phragmites communis*, Trin., of botanists), with a very wide geographical distribution in Europe, Asia, Africa, America, and Australia, but there are none of them in the extreme North. They are mentioned in *Antony and Cleopatra*, II. vii. 13, *Cymbeline*, IV. ii. 267, in both instances in allusion to their want of stability, and in *Lucrece*, l. 1437 :

To Simois' reedy banks the red blood ran.

Their use in thatching is referred to in *The Tempest*, V. i. 16 :

Like winter's drops
From eaves of reeds.

For its employment as a musical instrument, the Pan or shepherd's pipes, we get :

And speak . . . with a reed voice.
Merchant of Venice, III. iv. 66.

Other references are metaphorical.

Sedges are, more correctly speaking, members of the Cyperaceæ, an order very generally distinguished by its triangular stems. Of the principal genus, *Carex*, some sixty or more species are native, some in dry, the majority in moist situations, and ranging in size from a few inches to 5 feet (*Carex riparia*, Curtis).

The gentle Severn's sedgy bank (1 *Henry IV.*, I. iii. 98)

calls up to the poet's mind some very pretty allusions. Thus, we have (*Taming of the Shrew*, Induct. ii. 53):

And Cytherea all in sedges hid,
Which seem to move and wanton with her breath,
Even as the waving sedges play with wind.

And, again (*Tempest*, IV. i. 128):

You nymphs, called Naiads, of the winding brooks,
With your sedged crowns and ever harmless looks.

And in *Two Gentlemen of Verona*, II. vii. 25 :

The current that with gentle murmur glides,. . .
He makes sweet music with the enamell'd stones,
Giving a gentle kiss to every sedge.

In connection with these reeds and sedges we may well take the more highly organized rushes, members of the order Juncaceæ. Of these we have two groups : the true rushes and the woodrushes.

The former, of which twenty-three species are found along our rivers or in our marshes, are noticed by Shakespeare no less than eighteen times. Some may, as Ellacombe suggests, refer to the bulrush and sweet rush, members of other orders. As mere trifles

used, but useless for their assigned purpose, we get
the phrases:

> Our gates,
> Which yet seem shut, we have but pinned with rushes;
> They'll open of themselves.—*Coriolanus*, I. iv. 16.

> A rush will be a beam
> To hang thee on. —*King John*, IV. iii. 129.

> But a rush against Othello's breast
> And he retires.—*Othello*, V. ii. 270.

Rings were made from the rush for rustic be-
trothals, a custom much abused, so much so that
as early as 1217 Richard, Bishop of Salisbury, issued
a decree against the use of *annulum de junco*
(Ellacombe, p. 279). Rings of the same character
are made to the present day in parts of Norfolk.
Shakespeare refers to them:

> As fit as Teb's rush for Tom's forefinger.
> *All's Well that Ends Well*, II. ii. 24.

> Rings she made
> Of rushes that grew by, and to 'em spoke
> The prettiest posies.
> *Two Noble Kinsmen*, IV. i. 109.

But their principal use lay in strewing the halls
of the wealthy and churches. Brand tells us that
rushes intermingled with flowers—primroses, maidens'
blushes and violets—were strewn at weddings, and
that in summer-time " many in the country do use
them to strowe their parlors and churches, as well for
coolness as for their pleasant smell." Churches were
certainly so strewn on the feast of their respective
patron saints, and the ceremonial rush-bearing on
the occasion is thus described by Brand:

" They cut hard rushes from the marsh, which
they make up into long bundles, and then dress them
in fine linen, silk ribbons, flowers, etc. Afterwards
the young women of the village, who perform the

ceremony that year, take up the burdens erect, and begin the procession (precedence being always given to the churchwardens' burden), which is attended with music, drums, etc. Setting down their burdens, in the church they strip them of their ornaments, leaving the heads or crowns of them decked with flowers, cut paper, etc. Then the company return and cheerfully partake of a cold collation, and spend the remaining part of the day and night in dancing round a maypole adorned with flowers" (vol. ii. p. 14).

There are several allusions to rush-strewing in the plays, viz. :

Let wantons light of heart
Tickle the senseless rushes with their heels.

Romeo and Juliet, I. iv. 35.

She bids you on the wanton rushes lay you down.

1 *Henry IV.*, III. i. 214.

Our Tarquin thus
Did softly press the rushes.

Cymbeline, II. ii. 12.

By the light he spies
Lucretia's glove . . .
He takes it from the rushes where it lies.

Lucrece, l. 316.

One other use is mentioned, that of rush-wicks for candles called "rushlights," now fast dying out, but which were extensively made in most farm-houses, and called "dips." The green bark of the rush was dexterously peeled by means of a special instrument, and the dry pith dipped in melted grease until the candle obtained its required thickness and shape. The candles so made were burnt in stands of sheet iron perforated with holes, which had the weird effect of growing bigger as the candle burned down. In Wales many varieties of rushlight-stands are still used.

6

> Be it moon or sun, or what you please,
> And if you please to call it a rush-candle.
>> *Taming of the Shrew*, IV. v. 13.

One cannot proceed without alluding to the beautiful flowering rush, *Botomus umbellatus*, L. (Nat. Ord., *Alismaceæ*), which shows its fine pink umbel above the waters of the Avon in close proximity to Stratford, and is also found in the river Stour.

In the fruit-garden this month we have apricots and figs. The first-named is a plum (*Prunus armeniaca*, L.). Its name lends itself to a study in language. A native of Armenia, it passed to the West, and its name travelled with it, passing back to the East with constant variations. We have in Shakespeare "apricock," older "abricot" and "abrecot," from the Latin *præcocia* ("early," as an early peach), and Spanish *albaricocque*, Italian *albericoca*, and even Arabic, *al burqûq*. As Prior says: "One would have supposed that the Arabs living near the region of which the fruit is a native might have either had a name of their own for it, or at least have borrowed one from Armenia; but they have apparently adopted a slight variation of the Latin." It is said to have been introduced into English gardens *temp.* Henry VIII., and was known before Turner wrote his "Names of Herbes" in 1548, though it is doubtful if Shakespeare is not mistaken in placing it in the garden of Richard II., when the gardener is told to

> Go, bind up yon dangling apricocks.
>> *Richard II.*, III. iv. 29.

And, lastly, we have Titania's command to the fairies to be

> Kind and courteous to this gentleman;
> Hop in his walks and gambol in his eyes;
> Feed him with apricocks and dewberries.
>> *Midsummer-Night's Dream*, III. i. 167.

Another fruit worth considering is the fig, mentioned in the continuation of the last lines,

> With purple grapes, green figs and mulberries,

and in eleven other places. The most interesting
are the following :

> Give it a plum, a cherry, and a fig.—*King John*, II. i. 162.

> Here is a rural fellow
> That will not be denied your highness's presence;
> He brings you figs.—*Antony and Cleopatra*, V. ii. 233.

> I'll pledge you all, and a fig for Peter.
> 2 *Henry VI.*, II. iii. 66.

Many other of the quotations are a reference to
an insulting and indecent gesture called " making
the fig," which we cannot enter upon.

The fig* itself is a tree with handsome palmately-
lobed leaves of curious texture and a very peculiar
flower usually called the fruit. It is what botanists call
a hypanthodium ; *i.e.*, the end of the flower-stalk is
hollowed out, and the flowers grow within it. Its
introduction has been attributed to the Romans ; it
certainly was grown at Lambeth by Cardinal Pole.

The curious word " coloquintida " is used in *Othello*
in the line (I. iii. 354) :

> The food that to him now is as luscious as locusts
> Shall be to him shortly as bitter as coloquintida.

The word of which colocynth is a synonym was
applied in Shakespeare's day to a drug well known
to the apothecaries, and prepared from the dried
fruit of *Cucumis colocynthis,* a native of Turkey,
which Gerard may have grown in his London
garden, though it is not quite certain. Our only
native member of the order to which gourds,
cucumbers, melons, pumpkins, and vegetable
marrows belong is the poisonous black bryony

* *Ficus carica*, L.

6—2

(*Bryonia dioica*, L.), whose long trailing stems, with their dainty cucumber-like leaves and greenish-white flowers, smother the plants by which they have climbed into sunlight, and in autumn festoon them in garlands of berries, red, green, and orange. This plant in Shakespeare's birthplace garden is labelled " Mandrake." Prior says the roots of it were cut to the shape of men and women, and dried in a hot sand-bath, and thus sold by fraudulent dealers. It is certain the English plant is not the " mandrake" of the poet. The pumpion is also mentioned once. Since it belongs to the same natural order, we may deal with it here. It is in *The Merry Wives of Windsor*, III. iii. 42, and Falstaff is the person referred to :

Go to, then : we'll use this unwholesome humidity, this gross watery pumpion.

It is probably not the pumpkin of our modern gardens, which is useful both for food and in preserve, but one of the large useless gourds grown even then as ornamental plants. Of this group Gerard says : " The gourd groweth into any forme or fashion you would have it . . . being suffered to clime upon an arbour where the fruit may hang ; it hath beene seen to be nine foot long." He says they are used to " cure copper faces, red and shining fierce noses with pimples, pumples, rubies, and such-like precious faces." It is true that he speaks of the cucumber, but his words may be extended. Gerard figures the cucumber pompion, apparently our vegetable-marrow, and a variety which is now our custard marrow, and of which he says : " It maketh a man apt and ready to fall into the disease called colericke passion, and of some the felonie."

Among the umbel-bearing plants this month comes the aromatic fennel, with its curious smooth,

glaucous green stems, extremely divided leaves, and
yellowish flower. In the East of England it grows
in luxuriance in chalk-pits, and is much used chopped
fine with mackerel and other fish ;* hence the poet's
allusion :

> A' plays at quoits well, and eats conger and fennel.
> > 2 *Henry IV.*, II. iv. 266.

It is sometimes used as an emblem of flattery,
as in *Hamlet*, IV. v. 180 :

> There's fennel for you and columbines ;

and by Ben Jonson in " The Case altered," II. ii.† :

> *Chris.* No, my good lord.
> *Count.* Your good lord ! Oh, how this smells of fennel !

The plant is the *Fœniculum vulgare*, Mill., and is
found on the Continent south of Belgium.

Burnet is a herb still grown in our gardens, and,
as salad burnet, abundant in our meadows. It is a
pretty little rosaceous plant with serrated, pinnate
leaves, no corolla, and large pendent stamens. It
is known to science as *Poterium Sanguisorba*, L.,
Another species, *P. officinale*, Hook. fil., the great
burnet, is also found in our islands. The name,
formerly, says Prior (p. 35), applied to a brown cloth,
is diminutive, and in French *brunette*, Italian *brunetto*,
so called from its brown flowers. It is only once
referred to, and that with the cowslip and clover, in—

> The even mead, that erst brought sweetly forth
> The freckled cowslip, burnet, and green clover.
> > *Henry V.*, V. ii. 48.

Other plants, like burnet, of a sweet smell, and
equally admired by Bacon, are the mints—twice
mentioned :

* Periwinkles are cooked with it in Norfolk.
† Quoted by Ellacombe, p. 91.

Here's flowers for you;
Hot lavender, mints, savory, marjoram.
Winter's Tale, IV. iv. 103;

and in *Love's Labour's Lost*, V. ii. 662, " that mint."

The mints (*Mentha*) constitute a difficult group in a difficult order (the Labiates), but many very striking and handsome species occur among our fourteen natives. There are the true peppermint (*Mentha piperita*, L., var. *officinalis*) and the two water mints, the *pubescens* of Willd., and the *hirsuta* of Hudson, formerly included under the name *aquatica*, L. A variety of the last is the bergamot of the rustics. Pennyroyal, still used in medicine, is also a mint (*M. Pulegium*, L.). These were probably all known to Shakespeare, and many others. Red garden mint, crosse or curled mint, speare and cat mint, great cat mint, horse or water mint, sweet water mint, and calamint, were all cultivated by Gerard (" Herbal," p. 552).

The last plant to consider this month is the curious samphire, a close relative, though one would never believe it, of the fennel. It grows on maritime rocks, where its fleshy stems and leaves are gathered to pickle.* It has small flowers with no calyx and minute petals borne in little umbels. This plant (*Crithmum maritimum*, L.) is dedicated to St. Peter, from which, obviously enough, its name is derived. The trade was once of considerable importance, but the pickle has gone out of fashion in the last thirty years. The danger of samphire-gathering is told us in our only quotation:

Half-way down
Hangs one that gathers samphire, dreadful trade!
Methinks he seems no bigger than his head.
King Lear, IV. vi. 14.

---

* The glass-worts were used when true samphire was unattainable.

SEPTEMBER

Earth's increase, foison plenty,
Barns and garners never empty :
Vines, with clustering bunches growing,
Plants with goodly burthen bowing ;
Spring come to you at the farthest
In the very end of harvest !
Scarcity and want shall shun you ;
Ceres' blessing so is on you.

Tempest, IV. i. 110.

THAT glorious month when the "fair tilled glebe"
is golden with waving grain and the hillsides
purple with ling or heath, or glinting every gleam of
gold and red and brown from the perishing bracken ;
the month of Ceres and her reapers, of harvest-homes
and rejoicing for the gathering in of the world's store ;
the month when earth below and sky above reflect
and vary in one another Nature's thousand colourings, and paint them on a background of opal and ruby.

The autumn flowers are here in full vigour at last.
In our gardens the great golden sunflowers and lilac
Michaelmas daisies* are replacing the phloxes, and our
late summer favourites in the lanes, the scabious, rag-
wort, and harebell, tell us the year's work is all but
over, and, as we have said, on moorland and mountain-
side the ling is purpling—a fit lair for the "whirring
partridge."

There was a time when the genus *Erica* was sought

* Called in Warwickshire parlance "Farewell Mid-
summers."

[87]

after and admired in our gardens, the time when the
Cape provided a vast variety of handsome greenhouse
species ; but now, alas ! heaths are unpopular. The
family, almost wanting in the New World, is most
profusely found in South Africa, but is neither an
insignificant feature in mass nor in the individual plant
in our Northern latitudes. In our own islands we
have five species, three of which, the Cornish,
Mackay's, and Mediterranean heaths, are very rare ;
while the others, the cross and fine leaved, are fairly
common. But the reading of the only passage in
which any plant of this group is named leads us to
suppose an allied plant, *Calluna Erica*, D.C., is meant.
The words are generally given :

> Now would I give a thousand furlongs of sea for an acre
> of barren ground, ling, heath, brown furze, anything.
> *Tempest*, I. i. 70.

But some for " ling " put " long " ; in either case
Calluna is meant. It is a small plant, of 1 to 2 feet
in height, with wiry stems and elegant pink bells
growing spikelike on its short pedicels, and ranges
over Arctic Europe, Western Siberia, Greenland, the
Azores, Newfoundland, and very rarely in the United
States.

In Gerard's London garden several heaths found
a home, and among them, in his " Herbal," he
describes and figures the common heath, with a white
variety, the greater heath, the crossed and steeple
heath, and others which he calls *Erica baccifera lati-
folia* and *tenuifolia* (" Herbal," p. 1146).

The name " heath " is from the Anglo-Saxon
" hæth," a word connected with the Early English
" hætu," heat, fitly applied to that plant, which a
few years back was sought after in the East of
England as fuel, and a trade carried on in ling,
brought round to the villages in carts. Ling was,

however, replaced, owing to its increasing scarcity, by the prickly gorse.

A plant of the moor and wayside, of the river-bank and meadow, is the prickly thistle, which in its many forms is a striking, handsome plant, artistic in the fittest sense. Even in old Tusser's days they were considered a sign of strong land, though of bad husbandry. Of the pretty feathered pappus, Coles (quoted by Ellacombe) says : " If the down flyeth off coltsfoot, dandelyon or thistles when there is no winde, it is a signe of rain."

Twice the thistle is alluded to, once in *Henry V.*, V. ii. 51 :

> And nothing teems
> But hateful docks, rough thistles, kecksies, burs ;

and, again, Bottom commands Cobweb to

> Kill me a red-hipped humble-bee on the top of a thistle.
> *Midsummer-Night's Dream*, IV. i. 10.

The British thistles (Early English " thistel," from *thydan*, to stab), close allies of the burdocks, are contained in four genera : *Carduus*, the musk thistle ; *Cnicus*, spear thistles, which includes the plume and melancholy thistles ; *Onopordon*, the cotton thistle ; and, the handsomest of all, *Mariana lactea*, Hill, the milk thistle, a plant with large dark-green, glossy leaves elegantly reticulated with white veins, and assigned to our Lady as one of her special flowers— hence St. Mary's thistle. Its stems were formerly eaten.

Speaking of this thistle reminds us of another Shakespearian plant, the holy thistle, *Carduus Benedictus*, L., a native of Southern Europe, and a sovereign specific with the herbalists, especially for the plague. Thomas Brasbridge (1578) wrote a treatise on its virtues, entitled : " The Poore Man's Jewell ; that is to say, a Treatise on the Pestilence : unto which is annexed a Declaration of the Virtues of the Hearbes Carduus Benedictus and Angelus."

The distilled leaves, it is said, "helpeth the hart." He concludes: "I counsell all them that have gardens to nourish it, that they may have it always to their own use, and the use of their neighbours that lack it." The lines in which it is mentioned are those playful ones between Margaret and Beatrice where the couple pun upon the word, *Much Ado about Nothing*, III. iv. 73 :

Marg. Get you some of this distilled Carduus Benedictus, and lay it to your heart : it is the only thing for a qualm.

Hero. There thou prickest her with a thistle.

Beat. Benedictus! why Benedictus? you have some moral in this Benedictus.

Marg. Moral! no, by my troth, I have no moral meaning ; I meant, plain holy-thistle.

But even wild thistles had medical properties assigned to them ; witness the following cure for hydrophobia (Alexis of Piedmont, "Mysteries," i. 28, in d.) :

"Take the blossomes of flowers of wylde thystles dryed in the shadow, and beaten into powder, give him drynke of the same powder, in whyte wyne halfe a walnuttshell full, and in thrise takynge it, he shall bee healed : a thynge found true by experience."

As the badge of Scotland the thistle deserves a more than parting notice. Woodward ("Brit. and For. Her.," p. 334) tells us it was first used in 1474, on the silver groats of King James II., while the arras in the background of an altar diptych at Holyrood, with portraits of James III. and his Queen, Margaret of Denmark, is powdered with it. The painting dates from 1485. The thistle badge is first seen on Scotch gold coins in 1525. The Order of the Thistle was created in 1540 by James V., although there is

an absurd legend stating it to have been founded by
King Achaius in 809.   The real origin of the adop-
tion of the badge is unknown, although the story of
the Danish invader at the Battle of Largs has been
repeated *ad nauseam*.

In the fruit-garden the trees are daintily set with
peaches, and purple or golden with plums, and in the
hedge banks blackberries are turning from their
scarlet hue.

The peach (*Persica vulgaris*, Mill.) is a native of
China, but found its way into English gardens long
before the days of the poet ; in fact, it has a place
under the name Perseoctreow in Ælfric's vocabulary,
since which time it has passed through the forms
"peske," "peshe," and "peche."   The apricot was
considered, as we have seen, an early peach.   Shakespeare alludes twice to peach colour, but never to
the tree itself or its fruit (2 *Henry IV.*, II. ii. 17, and
Measure for Measure, IV. iii. 12).   It is a handsome
tree when grown among other shrubs for the sake of
its flowers, whether single or double.

The plum is a hardier, more generally useful and
widely-grown fruit, mentioned also by the poet as
damsons and as prunes.

The plum-tree itself is spoken of in *Hamlet*, II.
ii. 198 :

> Their eyes purging thick amber and plum-tree gum.

And in 2 *Henry VI.*, II. i. 96, in a comic scene
between Simpcox and his wife and the Duke of
Gloucester :

> *Simp.*   A fall off of a tree.
> *Wife.* A plum-tree, master. . . .
> *Glouc.* Mass, thou lovedst plums well, that wouldst venture
> so.
> *Simp.* Alas, good master, my wife desired some damsons,
> And made me climb with danger of my life.

The unripe green fruit is mentioned in *Venus and Adonis*, 527 ; ripe plums in *Merry Wives of Windsor*, V. iv.;* while stewed prunes are named in the same play, I. i. 295, 1 *Henry IV.*, III. iii. 128 ; *Measure for Measure*, II. i. 93 ; the uncooked fruit in *Winter's Tale*, IV. iii. 51 ; mouldy prunes in 2 *Henry IV.*, II. iv. 158.

The damason, or damson, a word derived from "Damascus" (Fr. *damascene*), is no doubt an Eastern variety of the common plum (*Prunus domestica*, L.), now regarded as a species distinct from our wild blackthorn, or sloe and bullace (*P. spinosa*, L., and *P. insititia*, Huds.). As Ellacombe remarks (pp. 230, 231), it is very strange that Shakespeare should not mention the blackthorn, with its showy masses of white flowers against its dark stems, its name applied to the cold spell of the end of March ("the blackthorn winter") or to the proverbs which its fruit gives a point to—"As black as a sloe" or "Not worth a sloe"; though, in spite of the proverb, the fruit had its value, and still has in the manufacture of the liqueur fast coming into favour, "sloe gin."

Blackberries are the delicious fruit (technically an etærio of drupes) of various brambles (*Rubi*), a class of very difficult plants, much given to minute variation, and which none but a specialist may hope to thoroughly master. At the present time, according to the Rev. W. Moyle Rogers, we have ninety-nine perfectly distinct kinds natives of our islands, and many of these have several named varieties.† It must not be forgotten that the common raspberry is a bramble (*Rubus idæus*, L.), and a native of our woodlands.

Before quoting Shakespeare's words, a few short lines of Lilly's (from his "Campaspe," 1584, II. ii.)

* Omitted in the Globe edition.
† "Lond. Cat. Brit. Pl.," 1895, 9th ed.

may be worth recording, since they give a pretty notice of the changing colour of the fruit : " Beauty is like the blackberry, which seemeth red, when it is not ripe, resembling precious stones that are polished with honey, which the smoother they look the sooner they break."

In 1 *Henry IV.*, II. iv. 265, we have the remark,

If reasons were as plentiful as blackberries ;

and, again (*ibid.*, 450):

Shall the blessed sun of heaven prove a micher and eat blackberries ?

and in *Troilus and Cressida*, V. iv. 13, the dog-fox, Ulysses, " is not proved worth a blackberry." They are vehicles for the suspension of a lover's elegies in *As You Like It*, III. ii. 379 ; and, lastly, in *Venus and Adonis*, l. 629, we read :

The thorny brambles and embracing bushes,
As fearful of him, part, through whom he rushes.

A foreign fruit, locusts (*Othello*, I. iii. 354), may be considered here. The bean so called is the legume of the carob-tree (*Ceratonia siliqua*), a native of South Europe and Western Asia, much cultivated. The beans are full of pulp of a sweet taste, and cattle and swine are exceedingly fond of them. In Dodoens-Lyte's " Herball " he says (of England): " They grow not in this countrie . . . yet for all that, they be sometimes in the gardens of some diligent Herboristes, but they be so small shrubbes that they can bring forth neither flowers nor fruite."

The bean was at an early date used as a weight, and from it our name " carat " is said to be derived.*

* It may be remembered that the early form of Troy weight ran : 4 grains 1 carat, 24 carats 1 ounce, 12 ounces 1 Troy pound. See Cripps, " Old English Plate," p. 6. Ed. 1881.

From the assumption that St. John the Baptist ate these beans, the tree obtained its name of St. John's beans and St. John's bread.

The herb-garden provides two subjects for our pen this month, the lavender and wormwood. The former is referred to but once, in a passage from *The Winter's Tale*, IV. iv. 103, already quoted:

> Here's flowers for you;
> Hot lavender, mints, savory, marjoram;

but it is not unknown to other Elizabethan playwriters. Thus, we have: "Then she'll put thee into her chest and lay thee into lavender" (Greene's "Friar Bacon," 1594).

The plant itself (*Lavendula officinalis,* L.) is a native of Southern Europe, and was known, though not too frequently, to Elizabethan gardeners.

To-day it is very popular. Its sweet-scented flowers, dried and twisted with ribbons, are made into "lavender pokers," and used to scent linen and houses. From the essential oil the well-known scent is prepared, and it is extensively grown with this object about Mitcham in Surrey and at Carshalton. The flower belongs to the order Labiatæ. Its name is derived, Prior says (p. 133), from the German *lavendel,* Middle Latin *lavendula,* to wash; hence our word "laundress," because it was used to scent freshly-washed clothes. A sprig of lavender was carried to church by peasant girls in clean white print dresses, fastened in the knotted handkerchief which held their service-books until living memory. How differently they looked in those early nineteenth-century Sundays to the hideous colours and cheap, ill-fitting finery with which they deck themselves in the twentieth.

Along our banks and waste places we shall be sure to find the grayish, deep-cut foliage and curious

composite flowers of the wormwood (" wyrme
wyrt "), *Artemisia*, of which we have four species
native, viz., *A. campestris*, L. ; *A. vulgaris*, L., the
mugwort ; *A. Absinthium*, L., the true wormwood,
from which absinthe is distilled ; and *A. maritima*,
L., a plant of our sea-shores. In our herb-gardens
we find the shrub called variously lad's-love, old-man,
and southernwood (*A. Abrotanum*, L.), a native of
Southern Europe. Alexis tells us the wormwood,
which originally took its name from a powder made
from it, which was very generally in use as a preservative of books and manuscripts, was used to keep
moth and vermin from clothes, mingled with cedar
and valerian (Alexis, ii. 14 in d.). It was also considered a sovereign specific in sea-sickness. In Shakespeare it is referred to metaphorically or actually
in three places: *Love's Labour's Lost*, V. ii. 85 ; *Romeo
and Juliet*, I. iii. 26 ; *Hamlet*, III. ii. 191 ; and *Lucrece*,
l. 893 ; but none are worth quoting here, unless it
be the last, where, in a list of comparisons, we
read :

> Thy sugar'd tongue to bitter wormwood taste.

" Artemisia " is a name derived from Artemis, *i.e.*
Diana, who is said to have found the herb and given
it to Chiron the centaur ; and so we get " Dian's
bud " of the *Midsummer-Night's Dream*, IV. i. 78 :

> Dian's bud o'er Cupid's flower
> Hath such force and blessed power.

The cornfields are, however, as we have hinted,
the feature of the month. The principal corn
grown in England in Shakespeare's day was such
as we moderns grow : barley, oats, rye and wheat.
Of each something must be said. The barley has
been cultivated by man since the Eastern neolithic
farmers invaded Europe. Several varieties of it

have been found among the débris of Swiss lake-
dwellings and elsewhere. Dr. Oswald Heer ("Lake-
Dwellings," p. 529) tells us of two six-rowed barleys, a
small and large; from the smaller he thinks the
common four-rowed barley has descended, cultivation
tending to lengthen the axes of the ears, and from this
came at length the two-rowed species. The small-
grained six-rowed barley (*Hordeum hexastichum sanc-
tum*) he considers the most ancient cultivated form;
the other (*H. hexastichum densum*) was cultivated by
the Stone Age people merely for experiment. The
H. vulgare of to-day is the four-rowed descendant.
Barley was grown at an early date in Egypt. From
the barley, the beere plant, as its name implies, was
early brewed "barley-broth," which was assumed
to be the food of English soldiers in the jeering
passage, *Henry V.*, III. v. 18:

> Can sodden water,
> A drench for sur-rein'd jades, their barley-broth,
> Decoct their cold blood to such valiant heat?

And Gerard says: "Our London Beere-Brewers
would scorne to learne to make beere of either
French or Dutch."

Barley is named in one other place, viz., the
Tempest, IV. i. 60, in connection with other cereals.
The oat is named in the same passage, and as the
food for horses in *Midsummer-Night's Dream*, IV. i.
35, *Taming of the Shrew*, III. ii. 207, and other places.
In *Love's Labour's Lost*, V. ii. 912, we have:

> When shepherds pipe on oaten straws;

again, we read how Oberon

> in the shape of Corin sat all day,
> Playing on pipes of corn, and versing love.
> *Midsummer-Night's Dream*, II. i. 66.

Shepherds had imitated with the oat straws the

reeds of their great god Pan from the time of Ovid, and probably many centuries before (see "Met.," i. 677, and Virgil's "Ecl.," i. 1). The grain does not appear to have been cultivated by our forefathers until the Bronze Age ("Lake-Dwellings," p. 579), but was then used both as a food for horses, and for oaten cakes and oatmeal, and it has retained its popularity till the present time. The true oat is the *Avena sativa*, L. We have several native species of the order, as we have of barley and wheat.

The rye (*Secale cereale*, L.) is comparatively little grown to-day, and then only as food for cattle. The old-world rye bread has quite died out of use among us, though on the Continent it is still used. It is the black bread (Schwarzbrod) of the German peasants. Gerard says: " It is harder to digest than wheat, yet to Rusticke bodies that can well digest it, it yields good nourishment." Not only is it quoted in the general list of grain given above, but in *As You Like It*, V. iii. 23:

> Between the acres of the rye,
> These pretty country folks would lie

—that is, on the grass strips between the ploughed acres and half-acres of the common fields. And again we get in the *Tempest*, IV. i. 136,

> Make holiday—your rye-straw hats put on,

which sufficiently explains itself.

The rye is not such an ancient cereal as barley, and scarcely appears until the Age of Bronze.

The principal grain has ever been wheat—*i.e.*, white, in contradistinction to black oats and rye. We get the forms "hwæte" and " hvaiteis." In the Stone Age it was largely grown, as, indeed, it had been for many centuries in Egypt, and we get several forms of the typical *Triticum vulgare*, Vill.—one a

7

small form, from which all our cultivated varieties
have been derived, called *T. antiquorum*, M.   There
has also been found a beardless form (*T. compactum
muticum*), as well as the Egyptian wheat,* spelt
"emmer" and "einkorn" (*T. monococcum*, L.).   The
poet mentions wheat in many places, once as forming the crown of peace, *Hamlet*, V. ii. 41 :

> As peace should still her wheaten garland wear.

"White wheat" is spoken of in *King Lear*, III. iv.
120, red in 2 *Henry IV.*, V. i. 15.

The generic term, "corn," occurs some twenty-three
or more times, but it needs no comment here.   The
end of our month reminds us of another ending—that
of harvest, with its harvest home, mell supper,
kern supper, call it what you will, another old
English custom now, alas! dying fast, and yet, doubtless, as old as the ending of the first harvest.   As
good a description as may be had is that quoted in
Brand (vol. ii., p. 18,) from Stevenson's, " Twelve
Moneths " (1661, p. 37) :

" The furmenty-pot† welcomes home the harvest
cart, and the garland of flowers crowns the captain
of the reapers ; the battle of the field is now stoutly
fought.   The pipe and the tabor are now busily set
a-work ; and the lad and the lass will have no lead
on their heels.   O ! 'tis a merry time wherein honest
neighbours make good cheer, and God is glorified in
His blessings on the earth."

---

* The absurd legend of the mummy wheat has been too
often killed to need any further attacks on its veracity.
† A dish still much used in Yorkshire.

OCTOBER

That time of year . . .
When yellow leaves, or none, or few, do hang
Upon those boughs which shake against the cold,
Bare ruin'd choirs, where late the sweet birds sang.
In me thou seest the twilight of such day
As after sunset fadeth in the west;
Which by-and-by black night doth take away,
Death's second self, that seals up all in rest.

Sonnets lxxiii.

IN this month the artist Nature completes her
work of rendering the foliage of tree and flower
resplendent in its death; lavish indeed is her hand
with every shade of yellow, brown, and red, until
the masses of elm-trees stand up upon their background of blue, as though wrought in molten gold,
while away in the far distance the hills shade to
purple and the deepest blues under the mellowing
autumnal vapours.

Two or three flowers come forth to tell us the frost
and sun are not yet here; the pink hue of the
saffron, the gold of the marigold, and the honey-laden
ivy, all blossom this month, as, too, does the clover,
the honey-stalks of the poet, which, indeed, has been
blossoming for many months past. A strange plant
is the saffron (*Crocus sativus*, L.), largely cultivated in
England in Shakespeare's time, but when introduced
first is difficult to say. So important, however, was its
cultivation that it has given the name to an Essex
town, Saffron Walden, and to Saffron Hill in London.

Gerard tells us: "The moderate use of it is good for the head and maketh sences more quicke and lively, shaketh off heavy and drowsy sleep and maketh a man mery."

In the "Maison Rustique" we read that it was used for "weaknes of the stomacke and fainting of the hart: it keepeth from being drunke, and healeth the bitings of serpents and spiders" (p. 229).

It was much used as a dye, especially for the rich golden yellow of illuminations. Gerard in his "Herball" says: "The chives steeped in water serveth to illumine, or as we say limme pictures and imagerie, as also to colour sundry meats and confections;" but, according to Hooker, the saffron drug is principally yielded by another plant, the meadow saffron (*Colchicum autumnale*, L.), an undoubted native plant found both in the Stour Valley and in that of the Avon in several places near Stratford-on-Avon.

Ellacombe apparently pleads in favour of the *Crocus nudiflorus* and *Crocus sativus*, L., which are certainly not native plants. Shakespeare refers to the plant only as a colour; in one place as a beautiful thing—the colour of the wings of Iris,

> Who with thy saffron wings upon my flowers
> Diffusest honey-drops, refreshing showers.
> *Tempest*, IV. i. 78;

while its use in cooking is noticed by him in the line

> I must have saffron to colour the warden pies.
> *Winter's Tale*, IV. iii. 48.

The other two references are:

> Did this companion with the saffron face
> Revel and feast it at my house to-day?
> *Comedy of Errors*, IV. iv. 64.

Your son was misled by a snipt-taffeta fellow there, whose
villainous saffron would have made all the unbaked and
doughy youth of a nation his colour.
All's Well that Ends Well, IV. v. 1.

The name is said by Prior (p. 194) to come from
the Spanish *azafran,* from the Arabic *al zahafaran,*
but it is named as " safurroun " and " sayfryn " in the
fourteenth century. It seems possible that it may
be one of the plants brought here by Roman
civilization.

The marigold is so bright that its flower might
well be dyed with the plant we have just discussed.
It is called by botanists *Calendula officinalis,* L. ; the
former name it obtained from its being in bloom on
the kalends of every month, the latter from its use
in medicine, which, as old Fuller said, " We all
know the many and sovereign virtues in your leaves,
the Herb Generall in all pottage " (" Antheologie,"
1655, p. 52). Among the ailments for which it was
specific are mentioned headache, jaundice, red eyes,
toothache, and ague (Stevens, p. 224). Its flowers
are still used among the peasantry dried, as they are
still supposed to affect what Gerard gave as their
chief virtue—" to strengthen and comfort the heart."
Prior says (p. 145) it is called in " The Grete Herball " " Mary Gowles," and originated in the Saxon
" mersc-mear-gealla," marsh-horse-gowl—that is, the
marsh-marigold *(Caltha)*—from which it has been
transferred to the *Calendula,* which is called in Sloane
MS. 5 the " Seynte Marie rode."* Be all this as
it may, the manner in which it opens with the sun
and follows that orb through its glorious course is
well known ; as Shakespeare sings :

The marigold, that goes to bed wi' the sun
And with him rises weeping.
Winter's Tale, IV. iv. 105;

* Another pretty name is *Spousa solis*, bride of the sun.

and :

> Great princes' favourites their fair leaves spread
> But as the marigold at the sun's eye.
>
> *Sonnets* xxv.

The old herbalists knew its habits well. Thus
Dodoens-Lyte (book ii., chap. xiii., p. 163) :

"It hath pleasant, bright, and shining yellow
flowers, the which do close at the setting downe of
the sunne, and do spread and open againe at the
sunne rising."

There can be little, if any, doubt that our flower is
the heliotropium or solsequium of our forefathers, but
can hardly be that meant by Ovid ("Met.," iv.
244-270), into which the unhappy nymph Clytie
was transformed for giving information of the love
intrigue of her rival Leucothoë with the Sun-God,
which mad jealousy impelled her to do, and hence
she was transformed, so that a flower very like a
violet conceals her face. Though she is held fast
by a root, she turns towards the sun, and though
changed she still retains her passion.

The other quotation from the poet specially worth
noting is that in which the flower is called " Mary
buds "—

> And winking Mary buds begin
> To ope their golden eyes.
>
> *Cymbeline*, II. iii. 25.

As a special favourite for decking graves it is
mentioned thus :

> The purple violets, and marigolds,
> Shall as a carpet hang upon thy grave,
> While summer-days do last.
>
> *Pericles*, IV. i. 16.

This month, clustering on tree and rúined wall,
ever tightening its hold upon that which supports it,

the thick, glossy masses of the ivy break out into blossom, and prove a most delicate banquet for the myriads of insects about to hibernate, and which flit about its flowers day and night to extract the rich honey from its nectaries.

The plant itself is our only native member of the Araliaceæ, and, although a plant of infinite variation, but two really distinct species are known. It is the *Hedera helix*, L. Prior (p. 124) tells us its name was originally " ivyne " from the Saxon " ifig," but became confused with the yew, so that its name was brought about by the error of a copyist. Pliny called it *abiga*, the copyist *ajuga*, which was further misquoted as *iva*, a form from which we get " ivy."

Shakespeare, as is his wont, knew well the nature of the plant. He says (*Midsummer-Night's Dream*, IV. i. 48) that—

> The female ivy so
> Enrings the barky fingers of the elm.

In this connection the present writer remembers well one lovely autumn day the avenue of elms leading to the disused church of Thundridge in Hertfordshire, where the trunks were wreathed in glossy green, and the leaves in liquid gold against the deep blue sky, a sight never to be forgotten.

The poet calls it " usurping ivy " (*Comedy of Errors*, II. ii. 180), and woe to the ruined building whose shattered walls this monster enwreathes, to decorate and destroy, painting death with the hue of life. Then, in speaking of his lost sheep, in the *Winter's Tale* the shepherd says (III. iii. 66) :

> If any where I have them, 'tis by the seaside, browsing of ivy.

The ivy was used by the herbalists as a cure for the

pestilence, or, rather, as a preventative. Alexis has the following recipe:

"Take the seede or bearies of yvy, that groweth on trees or walles, and not of that whyche is founde lowe by the grounde, and you muste gather the sayde bearies very rype and towarde the northe; yf it bee possible, yf not, take theym as you maye gette them, although they bee not verye rype: drye them in shadowe, and kepe them in a boxe of woode, as a precious thynge. And yf anye bee infected with the pestilence, take of the sayde herbes, and beate them to poulder in a cleane morter and gyve the pacient of the sayd poulder, in halfe a glassefull of white wyne" (Alexis, i. 42).

There seems to have been some variation in different localities as to the use of ivy in decoration; as the special plant of Bacchus, it would naturally be unfit in places of worship, and yet there is no doubt it was so used. Coles says (p. 64): "In some places setting up of holly, ivy, rosemary, bayes, yewes, etc., in churches at Christmas is still in use"; and Stow tells us that every man's house, "as also their parish churches," were so decked; nor are entries wanting in old churchwardens' accounts, such as those of St. Martin Outwich, where in 1524-25 we get: "Item, for Holy and Ivye at Christmas." But as the special symbol of Bacchus it was very fitly appropriated to the front of taverns, where a tod or bush of ivy was suspended, and hence the proverb, "Good wine needs no bush"; and, again, "Be merry and wise"—that is, "An owl in an ivy-bush."

The clover as clover is mentioned by the poet in *Henry V.*, V. ii. 48, in connection with cowslip and burnet, and as "honey-stalks" in *Titus Andronicus*, IV. iv. 89:

> I will enchant the old Andronicus
> With words more sweet, and yet more dangerous,
> Than baits to fish, or honey-stalks to sheep.

The name "clover" is the Anglo-Saxon " clæfer "—
i.e., the claver of herbals, from *clava*, a club, and the
origin of our "clubs" in a pack of cards (French
trèfle). The name is loosely applied to a number of
plants of the pea order, which we can hardly find space
to describe, but they include the true clovers, such as
the splendid crimson clover (*Trifolium incarnatus*),
the Dutch clover (*T. repens*, L.), which is generally
considered the true shamrock of St. Patrick, the
national badge of Ireland, and also as the source of
all heraldic trefoils, whether used in France or Germany—where the curious nenuphar, a stalkless tre-
foil, is found—and has been considered the *bouterolle*
of a sword, a heart, or the horns of a beetle, as the
fancy or ignorance of the writer dictated. Besides
the true clovers, the name is also given to melilot as
"hart's-clover," to medic as "heart-clover," and some
others.

The principal vegetable this month is a plant of
the nightshade order (*Solanum tuberosum*, L.). The
English name, according to Prior (p. 181), belongs
to the sweet potato, a plant of the order Convol-
vulaceæ, called by the Spaniards *batatas*.

The two passages in Shakespeare are among the
earliest mention of the tuber after its introduction. The plant is said to have been brought to
Ireland in 1584 by Sir Walter Raleigh. Gerard
grew them as curiosities in 1597, and ends by saying
they are eaten "either rosted in the embers, or
boiled and eaten with vinegar and pepper, or dressed
in any other way by the hand of some cunning in
cookerie " ("Herbal," p. 782).

It ought to be remembered that the plant is
extremely poisonous uncooked, and the green berries
borne in the autumn have been fatal more than once.
It is a plant of so poisonous an order that it is
reported Linnæus refused to eat it.

The passages from the poet are :

How the devil Luxury, with his fat rump and potato-finger, tickles these together !

Troilus and Cressida, V. ii. 55 ;

and in the *Merry Wives*, V. v. 20 :

Let the sky rain potatoes.

To the order belong many of our well-known garden plants—tobacco, petunia, winter cherry, and tomato ; and among our wild ones none are more interesting than the thorn-apple, henbane, and bella-donna.

Another vegetable grown on a large scale in our fields as food for cattle is the turnip and its allies. Only once is it mentioned, and that in the *Merry Wives*, III. iv. 90 :

I had rather be set quick i' the earth
And bowl'd to death with turnips.

As Ellacombe says (p. 316) : " If we did not get the vegetable from the Romans, we got its name." Prior gives it as equivalent to the Latin *terræ napus,* and certainly in England its old name was nep, or næp, but its scientific name is *Brassica Rapa,* L. The plant is considered native, but has a variety *sativa,* the cultivated plant, which is only naturalized. The rape (*B. Napus*) and the swede (*B. Rutabaga,* D.C.) are also escapes of cultivation when met with apparently wild. The authors of " Maison Rustique" tells us that turnips are used as a cure for gout, and are also mingled with the juice of earthworms to harden steel.

Fruits are the principal feature of the month. There is much to be done in the orchard and store-room, and although we have elected to consider the apple under the month in which its flowers appear, yet it may not be thought amiss to refer to it again, if only to include an old Shakespearian recipe for a pomander :

"*To make a Pomander.*—Take pyppyns or other lyke melowe apples, and laye them upon a tyle for to bake in an oven, then take out the core and the kernels, and make theym cleane wythin, brayenge and breakynge the reste, and strayne it throughe a fyne canvesse or straynour. Thys done, take as much fat or grease of a kydde as you have apples and strayne it lykewyse, boylinge it all together in a newe vessell well leaded, untyll the rose water bee consumed : then adde to it muske, cloves, nutmegges and such lyke substances of a reasonable quantitye according to your discretion : provided alwayes that they be well brayed and broken in pyeces as is above sayed, and boyle them in the like manner aforesayed, then straine them and kepe them" (Alexis, 57).

Very closely related to the apple is the pear (*Pyrus communis*, L.), in its wild state another of our native fruit-trees, but a tree confined in range to the Continent of Europe. Twice the poet refers to a dried pear ; first :

> As crestfallen as a dried pear.
> *Merry Wives*, IV. v. 101 ;

and again :

> Marry, 'tis a withered pear.
> *All's Well that Ends Well*, I. i. 177.

Once in *Romeo and Juliet* reference is made to "a poperin pear" (II. i. 38), and once to warden pies— that is, pies made from Warden pears (*Winter's Tale*, IV. iii. 48).

Ellacombe suggests (p. 211) that by Warden pears Shakespeare refers to any large keeping kinds, originally ‚brought to perfection by the Cistercian

Monks of Warden Abbey, co. Beds., who bear those pears as their armorial ensign. The Poperin is mentioned by Parkinson as a summer and winter variety, good firm dry pears, spotted and brownish on the outside. It was perhaps brought from Flanders by old Leland, who was Rector of Popering.

Another ally of the apple and pear is the quince (*Pyrus Cydonia*, L.), the fruit especially assigned to Venus by the youthful Paris, and henceforth sacred to that goddess and love. The quince was undoubtedly used to a large extent as a love token or symbol among the ancients, and an old English custom of eating a quince pear at a wedding feast is told by Brand. The passage is quoted by Ellacombe (p. 249), and, since it serves to illustrate the reference in *Romeo and Juliet*, may be here given :

" I come to marriages, wherein, as our ancestors did fondly, and with a kind of doating, maintaine many rites and ceremonies, some whereof were either shadowes or abodements of a pleasant life to come, as the eating of a quince peare to be preparative of sweet and delightful dayes between the married persons."

The name is said to be a corruption of " coynes," itself derived from Cydonia, a city of Crete, where the quince grows naturally. The fruit is now used for marmalade and cooked with apples, but it has lost the popularity it once had. The only place it is mentioned in the poet is in the line

> They call for dates and quinces in the pastry.
> *Romeo and Juliet*, IV. iv. 2.

Yet another fruit-tree this month, and again a close ally of the quince and pear—the medlar (*Pyrus germanica*, L.), a tree long since naturalized amongst us, and exceedingly handsome when in flower. It is called, Prior tells us, *meslier* in Nor-

mandy, from which we get our English "medlar."
It was, however, more used for medicine than for
food in the time of Shakespeare; and in speaking
as he does contemptuously, playing on the word and
alternating it with the epithet "rotten," we seem
to be feeling the pulse of contemporary popularity.

The best example, perhaps, is that in *As You
Like It*, III. ii. 122 :

Touch. Truly, the tree yields bad fruit.
Ros. I'll graff it with you, and then I shall graff it with
a medlar : then it will be the earliest fruit i' the country;
for you'll be rotten ere you be half ripe, and that's the right
virtue of the medlar.

Another tree, a handsome and stately one, fruits
this month—namely, the walnut (*Juglans regia*, L.),
a tree of majestic proportions and dense shade, a
native of the East—Persia and elsewhere—called by
the Greeks of old "Persicon," the Persian, and
"Basilikon," the royal, tree, the Roman people giving
it the high honour of Jove's own nut. In the old
English vocabularies it was "knuta," the nut, and
later on "bannenote-tree," and then "walnote-tre."
Lyle calls it "walshe nut tree," from *wilix*, a
foreigner, so that it is only the foreign nut, after all.
It was a common tree in Shakespeare's day, especially
on a chalky soil. It is now prized chiefly for its
beautiful wood, much in request for gunstocks. In
the East an oil is extracted from it; it is said to have
been this oil that was used by Van Eyck and Cor-
regio in conjunction with amber varnish as a vehicle
for paint, it drying more slowly than any other
known oil (quoted by Ellacombe from "Arts of
the Middle Ages"). As an antidote for poison it
was also thought highly of. A recipe attributed
to Mithridates, King of Pontus, contained "Two
Nuttes and two Figges and twenty Rewe leaves stamped

together with a little salt and eaten fasting. This doth defend a man from poison and from Pestilence all day" (Bullein, "Government of Health," 1558). It is no longer that we prize the tree as an antidote, but from its fruit excellent pickle is made, and in winter the nuts form a useful addition to dessert.

Twice only does the poet refer to the walnut—first as a mere trifle, "a walnut shell" (*Taming of the Shrew*, IV. iii. 170), and, again :

> As jealous as Ford, that searched a hollow walnut.
> *Merry Wives of Windsor*, IV. ii. 170.

The grape (the fruit of *Vitis vinifera*, L.) grows in profusion in our English gardens, and has done so since the days of Roman supremacy, though it rarely ripens. To obtain satisfactory fruit we must seek it in our greenhouses. And yet at one time it must have been very widely cultivated, and in the open, too, for wine. Domesday Book mentions some thirty-eight vineyards, and one in Essex yielded 20 hogsheads of wine in a year. Roman vineyard sites are found in many places. There is one at Weston-sub-Edge in Gloucestershire still so called, in which numbers of coins, etc., have been found, and of which the terraces remain.

In Shakespeare's time they were grown, as along the Rhine to-day, trained to poles. Gerard says in his "Herbal," : "The vine is held up with poles and frames of wood, and by that means it spreadeth all about and climbeth aloft ; it joyneth itself unto briers, or whatsoever standeth next to it." There are many place-names in England derived from the vine and marking the site of former vineyards. Among the most famous are those at Hatfield and Warwick, the former a terraced garden glowing with peacocks in a semi-wild state, the latter a royal garden, once of some celebrity, and of which the Earls of Warwick were hereditary keepers, but now built over by stabling. Ellacombe mentions the lynches of the Cotswolds, and seems to misunderstand their nature. Many may be vineyard terraces, but a lynch, as a rule, is merely a remnant of the cultivation of common field. When the land to be ploughed lay on the side of a hill, the plough travelled only one way, cutting the furrow and returning without working. In this way the land was always turned outwards and downhill, making a succession of terraced ridges.

The vine is referred to some twenty-seven times by the poet. From these we cannot do more than pick a few passages of interest.

Its dedication to the jovial Bacchus is told us in *Antony and Cleopatra*, II. vii. 120 :

> Come, thou monarch of the vine,
> Plumpy Bacchus with pink eyne !
> In thy fats our cares be drown'd,
> With thy grapes our hairs be crown'd.

As a local example in sculpture, we may see on the Warwick vase the delicately-carved grape tendrils surrounding the basin of that magnificent specimen of ancient art, together with the groups of thyrsi and heads of Bacchanals.

We get it mentioned as a tavern sign in *Measure for Measure*, II. i. 133 :

> 'Twas in the Bunch of Grapes ;

and, finally, a description of the vineyard itself in the same play, IV. i. 28 :

> He hath a garden circummured with brick,
> Whose western side is with a vineyard back'd ;
> And to that vineyard is a planched gate,
> That makes his opening with this bigger key :
> This other doth command a little door
> Which from the vineyard to the garden leads,

We may here fitly notice the darnel, a name now given to the wild rye-grass (*Lolium perenne*, L.) and its allies, but in Shakespeare's time applied generically to many cornfield weeds.   Thus,

> Darnel, and all the idle weeds that grow
> In our sustaining corn.
>
> *King Lear*, IV. iv. 5 ;

and again in *King Henry V.*, V. ii. 44 :

> Her fallow leas
> The darnel, hemlock, and rank fumitory
> Doth root upon.

NOVEMBER

Therefore the winds, piping to us in vain,
As in revenge, have suck'd up from the sea
Contagious fogs: which falling in the land
Have every pelting river made so proud
That they have overborne their continents.
Midsummer-Night's Dream, II. i. 88.

THE last golden leaf has fallen or is about to fall,
and the tall branches of the trees stand up
dark and bare against the leaden sky, and later on
rifts of snowflakes heap themselves on the masses
of red-brown leaves which lie huddled together in
sheltered nooks, into which the sportive currents
of air have driven them. But in our woods and
along our meadows flowers of another class take
the place of those we have lost. They are little
known, as a rule; their delicate colouring, now as
fiery as the setting sun, now as soft as silvery moon-
light, pass unnoticed; the elegance and infinite
variety of their shapes have, if we would but pause,
much of delight, whether we be botanists, artists,
nature-lovers, or only *blasé* men and women of the
world, trying to kill time till the next empty social
function be due. I speak of toadstools first, since
precedence is theirs for beauty, but the humbler
mosses, vivid in their varied greens; the gold and
gray of the lichen; the texture of the liverworts;
the waving fern-fronds—all serve to impress upon
us that cryptogamic botany deserves all the admira-
tion we can give it, and in spite of its difficulties is a

8

most fascinating study. Surely the pleasure of recording a new plant for our county or country, or, rarer
still, one unknown to science, is a far surer and more
enduring memorial than a perishing gravestone on a
forgotten grave. The second great natural kingdom
of plants—the cryptogamic plants, which have no
true flowers, and are reproduced by naked spores—
are divided into ferns, club-mosses and their allies,
liverworts, mosses, lichens, algæ, and fungi, and
vary from most minute diatoms to gigantic tree-
ferns. Shakespeare, as we have said before, was
not a botanist, yet most of these classes were recog-
nised by him. To begin with the highest, the ferns,
we read :

> *Gads.* We have the receipt of fern-seed, we walk invisible.
> *Cham.* Nay, by my faith, I think you are more beholden to
> the night than to fern-seed for your walking invisible.
> 1 *Henry IV.*, II. i. 95.

The power of invisibility conferred by "fern-seed"
sprang from the common belief that plants revealed
by their size or some striking feature the diseases
they were created to cure ; and in this case, since no
one could detect the seed or methods of reproduction,
an idea gained ground that it conferred invisibility.
It is not probable that any special species was meant,
but it has been assumed that it was the royal fern
(*Osmunda regalis*, L.), which received its generic name
from the Scandinavian god Thor. The order *Os-
mundeæ* have the spores collected on a fertile frond,
which varies in shape from the barren one. It is a
magnificent plant in its native haunts—marshy
woods, etc.—reaching from 2 to 10 feet. A miserable, weak plant, starved from drought, grows in the
Birthplace Garden at Stratford, where it is labelled
" Fernseed." It is not at all likely that this fern
was known to Shakespeare.

Many other of our British ferns are interesting. We have the hart's-tongue and male-fern, the latter much used in medicine by the herbalists, and still in the pharmacopœia ; but more peculiar than any others are the adder's-tongue and moon-wort. The former took its name from the Dutch *adderstong*, and was at an early period called *Nedderis gras* and *Nedderis tonge*, from its curious fertile spikelet of spores, standing up in the one ovate leaf. The moon-wort is so called from its leaves being pinnately divided into half-moon-like segments. These plants are called by botanists *Ophioglossum vulgare*, L., and *Botrychium Lunaria*, L. But of all our English ferns none is more beautiful in its haunts than the brake or bracken (*Pteris aquilina*, L.), a plant of wide distribution, as, indeed, is the genus to which it belongs. It brings with it the thoughts of the moor and hillside, purple with heather, golden with furze, and mottled with every shade of red and brown by the dying bracken, a word which is evidently the plural form of brakes, applied to the fern by a transfer to the plant of its place of growth. The plant is said to have Solomon's seal, the double triangle, in its rootstock, if cut transversely.

The liverworts (*Hepaticæ marchantiaceæ*, etc.) are a small order of membranous leaves, plants with curious peltate receptacles or cup-shaped vessels. They love damp situations, but are not mentioned by the poet.

Mosses (*Musci*) are, however, so mentioned. We get—

> Bring thee all this ;
> Yea, and furr'd moss besides, when flowers are none.
> *Cymbeline*, IV. ii. 226,

where it is probable that he refers to one or more of the elegant feather mosses (Hypnaceæ) which deck every shady bank with a feathery undergrowth, and

8—2

are found not only upon the banks, but even in
the water of brooks.   Some species of moss attach
to trees and flourish in the interstices of old bark.   It
may be to these, plants of the genera of *Hypnum,
Tortula, Grimnia,* etc., that the poet refers in the
lines :

> The trees, though summer, yet forlorn and lean,
> O'ercome with moss and baleful mistletoe.
>> *Titus Andronicus*, II. iii. 94.

To man they are a specially useful group.   Moss
is used in packing flowers and vegetables, and one
genus, *Polytrichum,* a slightly astringent group, was
at one time used in medicine.   We have about 570
native species and about 190 liverworts.

In other places in which the poet mentions moss
he is thinking of another group of plants, no wit less
beautiful—plants of a humble crustaceous nature,
but which stain our ancient buildings and rugged
trees with a thousand beautiful tints.   The bright
golden Lecanora, the snow-white Lecidea, each play
their part in the adornment of Nature, and help to
make the landscape more varied and pleasant to the
eye of man.   In Shakespeare we get :

> These moss'd trees,
> That have outlived the eagle.
>> *Timon of Athens*, IV. iii. 223 ;

and, again :

> Under an oak, whose boughs were moss'd with age
> And high top bald with dry antiquity.
>> *As You Like It*, IV. iii. 105.

The lichens weathering with gray the "moss'd
trees" are chiefly of the genus Ramalina, and such
lichens as *Evernia prunastri* and its allies.   There are
also the olive and gray foliaceous lichens of the
genus *Parmelia,* many of which are used in dyeing.

On the other hand, those growing on "steeples and moss-grown towers" (1 *Henry IV.*, III. i. *33*) are almost entirely crustaceous, and chiefly of the genera *Lecidea*, *Lecanora*, *Variolaria*, etc.

These lowly plants are more useful to man than even their green allies, the mosses. For, apart from dyes, they are useful as food. We need but mention Iceland moss (*Cetraria Islandica*, L.) which, with *C. Nivalis*, *Sticta pulmonacea*, and *Alectoria usneoides*, are used, not only as food, but as a tonic. The most interesting from a popular point of view are the pretty little "chalice moss" and the reindeer moss.

The algæ, whether the glorious pink-green or olive-coloured species of the sea, or the many denizens of our stagnant water, plants which to the casual observer seem mere masses of odoriferous green or yellow slime, are not mentioned by the poet; but under the microscope the arrangement of their cell contents are as beautiful and instructive as any other portion of the vegetable kingdom. Fungi, under the term "mushroom" and "toadstool," are, however, noticed. We get first a pleasant reference in the *Tempest* to the fairy rings of our meadows, the dark circles of grass, due for the greater part to the annual concentric growth of an edible fungus. The *Marasmius oreades* of botanists, the Champignon of the French. The dark hue is due to the manuring properties of last year's decayed growths:

> You demi-puppets that
> By moonshine do the green sour ringlets make,
> Whereof the ewe not bites, and you whose pastime
> Is to make midnight mushrooms.
> *Tempest*, V. i. 36.

Or, again, how pretty are the lines:

> I do wander everywhere,
> Swifter than the moon's sphere;

And I serve the fairy queen,
To dew her orbs upon the green.
Midsummer-Night's Dream, II. i. 6.

The fairy rings are again referred to in the *Merry Wives of Windsor*, V. v. 69:

And nightly, meadow-fairies, look you sing,
Like to the Garter's compass, in a ring:
The expressure that it bears, green let it be,
More fertile-fresh than all the field to see.

It is not well for any but an expert to eat toad-stools, although there are at least 300 edible species among us. Folk-lore gives various safeguards to insure safety. If they bruise with a gold ring they are poisonous, and if they do not readily peel, or if they turn green when touched; but none of these can at all be relied on; nothing but individual knowledge of the species will suffice. Gerard speaks strongly: " Poisonous Mushrooms groweth where old rusty iron lieth, or rotten clouts or neere to serpent's dens or rootes of trees that bring forth venomous fruit. Few of them are good to be eaten, and most of them do suffocate and strangle the eater, therefore I give my advice unto those that love such strange and new-fangled meates to beware of licking honey amongst thornes lest the sweetnesse of the one do not counteracte the sharpnesse and pricking of the other." But this was all very wise and well on the part of old Gerard. The beefsteak fungus (*Fistulina hepatica*, L.) is not only wholesome, but very palatable, even though it grow on tree-trunks, and from it much of the ketchup of our shops is made. The young of the large puffball fried with eggs and bread-crumbs is a most delicate dainty. The curious spiney hydnum is quite as tasty as an oyster, and not nearly so dangerous, and, above all, the bright yellow wood-loving *Lactarius deliciosus*, breaking all the canons of good taste, and turning vivid green to the touch, is fully what its name implies. With a little useful knowledge and a willingness to adopt new ideas the fare of the poorest in our country villages might be considerably bettered, but we have insular dislike to innovation to contend with, and a contempt for all that may be had cheaply, which render it a new labour of Hercules to improve the household menage of the English rustic.

Fairies, according to the usual description of those beings, were said to live underground, to emerge from molehills. They had material bodies with the power of making themselves invisible, with the power of passing through all enclosures. They were frequently mischievous, but occasionally helped to labour. What were they if not the small dark aborigines of our island, hiding by day, active at night, now milking their enemies' cows, now stealing. Their chief diversion was dancing, and that in circles on the meadow-lands, from which no maiden would gather dew to bathe her face, or even place a foot within its enchanted round.

DECEMBER.

How like a winter hath my absence been
From thee, the pleasure of the fleeting year!
What freezings have I felt, what dark days seen!
What old December's bareness everywhere!
And yet this time removed was summer's time,
The teeming autumn, big with rich increase,
Bearing the wanton burden of the prime,
Like widow'd wombs after their lord's decease:
Yet this abundant issue seem'd to me
But hope of orphans and unfather'd fruit;
For summer and his pleasures wait on thee,
And, thou away, the very birds are mute;
    Or if they sing, 'tis with so dull a cheer
    That leaves look pale, dreading the winter's near.
                        Sonnet xcvii.

DECEMBER chill and frosty, no matter though
the sky be blue and the short arc'd sun be
shining. It is a time for the death of things, a
harbinger of winter near, the advent hymn of Nature
prophetic of a new awakening into life, when the
dainty decking of her nakedness has passed, when
the white snow mantle is dissolved away and the
crystal jewellery falls from the branches of tree and
shrub.

Within doors it is also a time of preparation, a
time for laying in Christmas store and making
Christmas fare, a time for kneading the Christmas
pudding, in which all must have their share "for
luck," and of compounding mince-meat; and since
flowers we have none, save, perhaps, a few chrysan-

themums in our garden, and the trees have lost both leaf and fruit, save only the sturdy undying ever-greens, it may be as well to hear what the poet has to tell us of such species as he mentions. The catalogue is not a long one, and will not take long in the telling.

In *Love's Labour's Lost*, V. ii. 651, we come to trenchant critiques of the players, and in one the omnipotent Mars is compared to—

> *Long.* A gilt nutmeg.
> *Biron.* A lemon.
> *Long.* Stuck with cloves.

The whole connection is suggestive of the small dried Seville oranges stuck with cloves given as a Christmas present, as, indeed, gilded nutmegs were given and considered also needful accessories of every china bowl of pot-pourri.

The spice as sold to-day is, as then, the unopened flower-buds of a tree (*Caryophyllus aromaticus*, L.), a native of the Moluccas, first introduced into our English greenhouses in 1800.

When these cloves were first an article of com-merce, the Dutch took every means, fair and unfair, to keep the trade in their own hands, and afford an example of double dealing and treachery unmatched elsewhere in the annals of trade. As a flavouring cloves have lost none of their popularity to the present day. With them the nutmeg is also men-tioned, and it also occurs as a colour in *Henry V.*, III. vii. 20, where the Dauphine's horse is described thus by Orleans :

He's of the colour of the nutmeg.

And again, in the *Winter's Tale*, IV. iii. 39, where

in the "Sheep-shearing Feast," we find, the Clown
requires

three pound of sugar, five pound of currants, rice,—what
will this sister of mine do with rice ? But my father hath
made her mistress of the feast, and she lays it on. She hath
made me four-and-twenty nosegays for the shearers, three-
man-song-men all, and very good ones ; but they are most of
them means and bases ; but one puritan amongst them, and
he sings psalms to hornpipes. I must have saffron to colour
the warden pies ; mace ; dates ?—none, that's out of my
note ; nutmegs, seven ; a race or two of ginger, but that I
may beg.

The whole is worth quoting, since it calls up to our
mind what was once a very popular rustic festival,
now, like many others, extinct.

Old Tusser, in his "Five Hundred Points of Good
Husbandry," thus alludes to it :

Wife, make us a dinner, spare flesh neither corne,
Make wafers and cakes, for our sheepe must be shorne ;
At sheepe shearing, neighbours none other things cran,
But good cheese and welcome like neighbours to han.

But to return to the nutmeg. It is the fruit, or
part of it, of the tree called by botanists *Myrista
officinalis*, a native of the Moluccas, principally in
those known as the Islands of Banda. Gerard
describes it, but could not have done so except from
hearsay, as it is not supposed to have been introduced into these islands until 1795. Mace is the
name given to the curious perforated coat (*arillus*)
which grows up round the nut, and is really developed
from the hilum after fertilization. We get an
example in other forms in the so-called "berries" of
the yew and the silky hairs of the willow. Mace is
only once referred to in the lines we have given. It
was known and used as early as the fourteenth
century. Among the names generally used for spices
in Shakespeare's time we may take "pepper," by us

confined to a special plant (*Piper nigrum,* L.), a
native of the tropics. Its name is a native one,
pippali, latinized into piper.   It was apparently well
known and used among the Romans, but not so much
among the Greeks.   By the former it was probably
introduced into our islands, and hence we may
account for its mention in Saxon literature.   It may
be added that in medieval times a pound of pepper
was one of the commonest rents at which land was
held in socage.   In this description of nominal pay-
ments, we find not only a pound of pepper, or even
a peppercorn, but such things as a sparrow-hawk, a
pair of gloves, a pair of gilt spurs, or a pound of
cummin, or a red rose payable on St. John the
Baptist's Day.

Shakespeare uses the word pepper in several
senses; as a general name for spice, we have the
words "pepper gingerbread" (1 *Henry IV.,* III.
i. 260).

The single flower-bud occurs

> An I have not forgotten what the inside of a church is
> made of, I am a peppercorn, a brewer's horse.
> > 1 *Henry IV.*, III. iii. 8.

In a metaphorical sense it is used twice again in
the same play, II. iv. 212, and V. iii. 36, as well
as in *Romeo and Juliet,* III. i. 102 :

> I am peppered I warrant for this world.

And, lastly, in *Twelfth Night,* III. iv. 157 :

> Here's the challenge, read it: I warrant there's vinegar
> and pepper in't.

The vessel, call it what you will, in which the
ground spice was kept is mentioned as a pepper-box
in the *Merry Wives of Windsor,* III. v. 147.

In concluding these brief notes on some of the

spices mentioned in the plays, let us give one short quotation from Beaumont and Fletcher's *Knight of the Burning Pestle*, I. iii., which serves to illustrate their use as ingredients in the hot spiced ale our forefathers loved :

> Nutmegs and ginger, cinnamon and cloves,
> And they gave me this jolly red nose.

But we have not yet touched on ginger, although we have mentioned it in the quotation from the *Winter's Tale*, IV. iii. 50. It occurs in nine other places. Its heat is referred to in *Twelfth Night*, II. iii. 125, when Sir Toby queries :

> Dost thou think because thou art virtuous there shall be no more cakes and ale ?

And Clown replies :

> Yes, by Saint Anne, and ginger shall be hot i' the mouth too.

And in the *Merchant of Venice*, III. i. 9, we get :

> I would she were as lying a gossip in that as ever knapped ginger.

Razes of ginger are not only mentioned in the *Winter's Tale*, but in 1 *Henry IV.*, II. i. 25 :

> I have a gammon of bacon and two razes of ginger to be delivered as far as Charing Cross.

Gingerbreads occur in *Love's Labour's Lost*, V. i. 74 :

> An I had but one penny in the world, thou shouldst have it to buy gingerbread.

And in 1 *Henry IV.*, III. i. 258 :

> Swear me, Kate, like a lady as thou art, a good mouth-

filling oath, and leave " in sooth " and such process of pepper to velvet guards and Sunday-citizens.

The commodity was well known at a very ancient date, and derived, together with its name, Zingiberi, from Arabia.   It is produced from the roots of *Zingiber officinale,* L.

JANUARY

When icicles hang by the wall
 And Dick the shepherd blows his nail
And Tom bears logs into the hall
 And milk comes frozen home in pail,
When blood is nipp'd and ways be foul,
Then nightly sings the staring owl,
   Tu-whit ;
Tu-who, a merry note,
While greasy Joan doth keel the pot.
When all aloud the wind doth blow,
 And coughing drowns the parson's saw,
And birds sit brooding in the snow,
 And Marian's nose looks red and raw,
When roasted crabs hiss in the bowl,
Then nightly sings the staring owl,
   Tu-whit ;
 Tu-who, a merry note,
While greasy Joan doth keel the pot
     Love's Labour's Lost, V. ii. 922.

THE month of rejoicing, the month of Christmas, old style, of Twelfth Night sports and pastimes, of open hospitality to rich and poor alike, of genial hand-shaking and joyous welcome — in Shakespeare's time more so even than our own. For is it not true of these latter years that cheap postage and railways have served to break down the ties of family affection, and severed the bonds of friendship, and an age essentially self-seeking and pleasure-seeking cares little for the simple gathering about the family board, the reunion of scattered units ; but, nevertheless, some semblance of old-world forms are

[126]

kept, and it is our pleasing duty this month to trace some of these by aid of Shakespeare's genius.

It may be biting cold, it may be merely damp and uncomfortable, but what matter the atmospheric conditions, the whirling, twirling, eddying snow-flakes, or the sobbing of the wind moaning round the chimney-stacks, till it seems the very sighing of lost souls, so that within both palace and cot the warm, bright firelight throws its glinting beams, lighting up with mellow beauty the rough flooring, and homely furniture of the one, or the ancestral portraits, gazing from their gilded frames, of the other. Over both garlands of holly and ivy, box and bay, laurel and mistletoe, may be found. Fitting resting-places for the sylvan spirits driven from their native woodlands by lack of cover from the nipping frosts. Or, if we would seek a Christian symbol in this so-called Christian land, surely the shining leaves and glossy berries can teach us eternal hope.

The royal place among the evergreens is truly assigned to the holly, with its leaves smooth or prickly, variegated or plain, its berries yellow or red; in all its forms it stands easily first.

From the earliest times—indeed from ancient temple worship—decking of house and sanctuary with evergreens has come, and as the temples of old were twined with the several flowers, shrubs, and garlands sacred to their god, so are our homes and churches to-day. The plants dedicated to some of the chief deities are thus assigned by Shakespeare's contemporary, Greene—

> Apollo's heliotropion then shall stoop,
> And Venus' hyacinth shall vail her top,
> Juno shall shut her gilliflowers up,
> And Pallas' bay shall bush her brightest green;
> Ceres' carnation in consort with those
> Shall stoop and wonder at Diana's rose.
>
> *Friar Bacon.*

Stow, in his "Survey of London," says that "against the feast of Christmas, every man's house, as also their parish churches, were decked with holme, ivy, bayers, and whatsoever the season of the year afforded to be green."

And so, too, in Herbert's "Country Parson," 1675, p. 56, the author tells us: "Our parson takes order that the church be swept and kept clean, without dust or cobwebs, and at great festivals strawed and stuck with boughs, and perfumed with incense."

It must be remembered in this connection that the decoration of our parish churches in medieval and later times was not carried on with the reckless extravagance of the modern decorator, whose one ambition seems to be to destroy as much of the fabric of the church as possible, or to cramp Nature's grace and beauty into inartistic, graceless flower-stands. The earlier and better way was that of strewing cut sprays of evergreen as a warm and living carpet, and placing bushes of holly in available corners. These early customs gradually drifted down into the little holly sprays our great-grandfathers decked the corners of their "pews" with, sticking them upright, as the cook still does the spray in the Christmas pudding.

Shakespeare mentions the holly but once, and then in an outburst of rollicking, jubilant song, sung in the holly glades of the beloved Arden, where to this day it freely grows. This breezy song of Amiens seems to bid defiance to all the bitterness of mankind, the hollowness of society, its shams and mockeries, and prefers the unfettered life "under the greenwood tree," with a "Heigho!" to the never downcast holly (*As You Like It*, II. vii. 180).

Gerard does not seem to consider the holly much of an ornament, though English folk-song had sung its praises many a long year under names it still bears in part—Holme and Hulver (Hulwun tre).

The common holly, the only plant known to Shakespeare, is the *Ilex aquifolium* of Linnæus our only British species of the order *Ilicaceæ*, and is found wild throughout Europe, from Southern Norway to Turkey, and also in West Asia. Not the least of its beauties are the little cymes of waxy, white flowers which appear from May till August in the setting of green.

Side by side with holly that most curious parasitic plant, the mistletoe (*Viscum album*, L.), has ever been placed, the position of high honour, held apparently from the very earliest times; but Shakespeare says nothing of all this. He entirely ignores the stolen salutation beneath its protective shadow. Neither does he tell us ought of its occult powers, in banishing evil spirits, nothing of its heathen use, as tradition has handed down of white-robed Druids with golden sickles, cutting the mystic plant from the sacred oak. He looks upon it as a "baleful" thing killing its host.

The plant itself belongs to a genus containing almost one hundred species, chiefly natives of the tropics. Our plant is parasitical on many trees, but rarest on the oak; it is a native of Europe and Northern Asia, and bears flowers in threes, small and green, the reverse of conspicuous in March or May; and in this island is not found north of Yorkshire.

There was always a mystery attached to this plant, as in the ancient world it was not supposed to grow from its seed.

The mode of its propagation severely exercised the minds of the Elizabethan writers, who were ultimately divided into two camps—those who said it was due to the agency of birds, as indeed it is now well-known to be, and those who declared that this notion was absurd and impossible, among whom Bacon and Gerard ranked themselves.

One other evergreen merits a place here, not only on account of its ancient reputation, when it shared as the predominant partner with ivy the honour of forming the poet's crown, but on account of its graceful form and delicate fragrance, as well as its Christmastide usage — I mean the bay (*Laurus nobilis*, L.).

It cannot be too much insisted upon that Shakespeare nowhere mentions the shrub grown so commonly in our gardens and shrubberies to-day, that which we call the laurel, a name derived from the Latin *laurellus*, and applied, Prior tells us, to many evergreen shrubs, though originally solely to the classical laurel or bay. The common laurel of our gardens is *Cerasus laurocerasus*, D.C. ; the laurustinus (*Viburnum Tinus*, L.). In this connection can we help uttering a protest against such learned and august bodies as the trustees of Shakespeare's birthplace, and others offering garlands of this foreign plum, which was not introduced until 1629, on such ceremonial occasions as the memorial service in Shakespeare's church, or as a tribute to the memory of Goethe at his memorial festival ?

The curious allusion in *Richard II.*, II. iv. 7 when Salisbury says :

> 'Tis thought the King is dead ; we will not stay,
> The bay-trees in our country are all withered,

is difficult to understand, since there is no folk-saying of the kind known at the present day—at least, so far as the writer has seen.

There is little difficulty with the second allusion : bays were and are used to crown the boar's head at Winchester College, and were among the the ever-

greens most in request for decking houses at
Christmas :

Marry, come up, my dish of chastity, with rosemary and
bays.
Pericles, IV. vi. 159.

In *Henry VIII.*, iv. 2 we get the mention of
garlands of bay upon the head, and branches of bay
in the hand. The objections of Ellacombe that the
bay had been too lately introduced (1561) to be
known to Shakespeare does not appear to me to
exclude it from the passages, even if it were not
actually known here in a living state, which is doubtful. It was well enough known by its classical fame
and in contemporary medicine, as witness Alexis :
" Take the rype Berries of a Baye Tree, and pylle
of the blacke skynne that is uppon them beate them
in powder wyth a lyttel salte . . . for plague to be
taken " (Alexis, 37).
It was also used frequently by the other Elizabethan dramatists. Two examples of their use must,
however, suffice us here : " Crown me with laurel, as
they all have done " (Greene's " Friar Bacon ").

Cut is the branch that might have grown full straight,
And burnéd is Apollo's laurel bough.
MARLOWE : *Doctor Faustus.*

We cannot do better than end our account of this
sweet-scented, popular plant than by giving a
quotation from Parkinson's " Garden of Flowers,"
p. 426 :
" The bay leaves are necessary both for civil use
and for physic, yea, both for the sick and the sound,
both for the living and the dead. It serveth to
adorn the house of God as well as man, to crown
or encircle, as with a garland, the heads of the
living, and to sticke and decke forth the bodies of
9—2

the dead, so that, from the cradle to the grave, we have still use of it."

Twined with the foregoing we find the ivy most in favour, but this we have already dealt with; but it seems a pity not to quote one little piece of sarcasm from Brand, p. 520.

> At Christmas men do always ivy get,
> And at each corner of the house it set:
> But why do they then use that Bacchus-weed?
> Because they mean then Bacchus-like to feed.

Another companion of this garland of evergreens is the yew (*Taxus baccata*, L.), whose curious and beautiful juicy arillus we have already referred to. The tree is a native, not only of England, but with a geographical range extending throughout the north temperate regions. Twice the tree is referred to without any directly uncanny feeling, though with an echo of something dread and supernatural (*Romeo and Juliet*, V. iii. 3). Its use for bows is mentioned in *Richard II.*, III. ii. 116, when the epithet "doubly fatal" is applied to it, first, perhaps, since it is poisonous to man, and, second, since it brings him death through the bow. This brings up the controversy respecting the planting of yews in our churchyards. It has been variously assumed that they were so planted to protect the building from the wind, to supply the villagers with bows, and as a symbol of the Resurrection, on account of their gloomy appearance and noxious qualities, more fittingly morbid than any other tree to this garden of death. Brand quotes Hecate's answer to the air-spirit in this connection:

> With new fall'n dew
> From churchyard yew.

And the poet mentions it also as an ingredient in the magic potion :

> Gall of goat and slips of yew.
> *Macbeth*, IV. i. 27.

There is no doubt, too, that slips of yew were used with flowers in funeral ceremonies, as the poet himself witnesses :

> My shroud of white stuck all with yew.
> *Twelfth Night*, II. iv. 56.

No one seems to have suggested that the yew-trees were utilized for church decoration. To make the carpet of yew-sprigs, which custom ordered, much would be required, and the trees would be close at hand ; they were, however, no doubt used for all or most of the other purposes : bows were occasionally made from them, and their gloomy appearance may have lent solemnity to the yard, but their symbolical character and utility in sheltering the edifice seem more questionable. Be it as it may, there is little doubt they came down to us from Roman mythology as plants sacred to the gods of the lower regions, for which purpose they were used both by Gauls and Celts.

The cypress, a yet more mournful shrub, is alluded to twice as a shady grove :

> Their sweetest shade a grove of cypress-trees.
> *2 Henry VI.*, III. ii. 322.

And :

> I am attended at the cypress grove.
> *Coriolanus*, I. x. 30.

And again as a wood much valued as a preservative medium :

> I have stuff'd . . .
> In cypress chests my arras counterpoints.
> *Taming of the Shrew*, II. i. 351.

The tree is *Cupressus sempervirens*, L., a native of the
Levant; it has usually been connected, like the
yew, with funerals and churchyards, and Sir John
Mandeville says: "The Cristene men, that dwellen
beyond the See, in Grece, seyn that the tre of thee
Cros, that we callen cypresse, was of that tree that
Adam ete the appule of" (quoted by Ellacombe,
p. 69).

We have wandered from the gay to the grave,
from the holly to the cypress, and lost sight for a
while of our Christmas cheer. It may be as well to
return this time from the decking evergreens to the
table laden with its fruits—to the golden oranges,
lemons, and pomegranates, of all of which the poet
has something to say.

The orange—*naranji*, Arabic; early Latinized as
anarantium, which became *anrantium*, from its golden
hue, from whence the French made *orangs*—(*Citrus
aurantiacus*, L.) was introduced into Europe from the
East Indies at an early date, and gradually became
known further north: Italy, 1200; Chantilly, 1421;
Fontainebleau, 1532; England, 1578. Lyte says:
"In this countrie the Herboristes do set and plant
orange-trees in their gardens, but they beare no
fruite without they be wel kept and defended from
cold, and yet for all that they beare very seldome."
Gerard describes them in his "Herbal," but had not
the tree in cultivation until 1599. The tree has
been considered the golden apple of the Hesperides,
and the famous fruit of the Judgment of Paris, but, as
we have said elsewhere, these were in all probability
quinces. Shakespeare mentions the fruit three times
as a colour, twice in *Midsummer-Night's Dream*,
(I. ii. 95 and III. i. 129), and again in reference to a
saying still in vogue, "yellow for jealous":

The count is neither sad nor sick, nor merry, nor well;

but civil count, civil as an orange, and something of that jealous complexion.

Much Ado About Nothing, II. i. 303.

The other is an allusion to an orange saleswoman under the name of an "orange wife" (*Coriolanus*, II. i. 77).

Many flowers of various kinds were used for wedding wreaths. It is only of recent years that orange blossom, real or artificial, has been considered the flower *par excellence*. Among the Saxon people wreaths were kept in the churches, and sometimes blessed and sprinkled with holy water. Myrtle was used abroad and corn-ears in England (see Brand, vol. ii., p. 124).

The beautiful old-fashioned garden shrub, the mock orange (*Philadelphus coronarius*, L.), was, no doubt, used in this connection also.

But not only was the orange grown to eat of or its flowers used in the wedding ceremony : it was also used for medicine and as a scent. Thus :

"Take fresh flowres of Rosemarye pounde twoo, amber a scrupule, three pounde of the flowres of oranges, lemons and citrons, all confuselyve together whyche the Frenche menne call eau de naphe, leave all together in somme vesselle welle steepte tenne dayes. Thenne the water beynge dystylled in Baheo Marie lette it bee kepte in a vyolle of glasse very close and stopped " (Alexis, 146 in d.).

Of the former we get a curious cure :

" *For Biliousness and Cattsheare.*—Take a cytron or orange, and parte hym in the myddes, take a lyttle towe in a dyshe, and . . . presse or wryng it in your hand, and put to it a lyttell commune salt well beaten to powder, and laye it so hotte upon the sore, puttyng uppon the sayde towe halfe the citron or orange, and so bynde all this with some bande, chaungynge it evenynge and mornynge, and incontinente the corrupte matter wylle dissolve " (Alexis, i. 34, in d.).

Once only is the lemon (*Citrus acida*, L.) referred to, and that in *Love's Labour's Lost*, V. ii. 653. It is closely allied to the orange, but a native of the continent of Asia. The word is derived from its Armenian name, *laimun ;* French, *limon*. It was introduced into Europe in much the same way and about the same time as the orange.

The pomegranate is mentioned three times by the poet, first in the humorous lines :

Go to, sir, you were beaten in Italy for picking a kernel out of a pomegranate.
All's Well that Ends Well, II. iii. 275.

And twice in reference to the shrub, once in 1 *Henry IV.*, II. iv. 41, and again in *Romeo and Juliet*, III. v. 4 :

It was the nightingale, and not the lark,
That pierced the fearful hollow of thine ear ;
Nightly she sings on yon pomegranate-tree.

No tree exceeds the pomegranate (*Punica Granatum*, L.) in beauty ; none has a richer history or has been more admired and loved. Far back in the earliest palaces of Assyria and Babylonia we find it used as a mysterious and sacred decoration on the robes of deities and demi-gods. From thence it was carried into the Jewish worship and religion, both of tabernacle and temple. Nor was it any the less beloved and honoured in Egypt. It has a place, moreover, in English heraldry as the royal badge of Katherine of Arragon, who derived it from the *armes parlantes* of Grenada, Argent, a pomegranate vert (now gules), seeded and slipped proper. Turner, in

the "Grete Herball," says : "Pomegranat trees
growe plentuously in Italy and in Spayne, and there
are certayne in my Lorde's gardene at Lyon, but
their fruite cometh never with perfection." So that
Shakespeare may well have seen and known the tree,
though not in fruit.

FEBRUARY

A February face,
So full of frost, of storm and cloudiness?
Much Ado About Nothing, V. iv. 41.

"AS the day lengthens the cold strengthens" is the country proverb, and it is often true. The great ice fair on the Thames lasted well into this month ; but, nevertheless, the first signs of re-awakening life commence. The "lambs' tails" of our childhood and the golden gorse are in flower, and even the rosemary in very sheltered nooks, and to these we can add one or two other plants the poet names, which do not seem to have any more fitting resting-place—a round dozen Shakespeare's references to the hazel mount to—under the name of filbert, nut. The first name, filbert, is derived from a barbarous rendering of *feuille* leaf and beard, to denote its distinguishing peculiarity, the permanent leafy calyx ; others say it is derived from King Philibert, but why they do not explain. Nut (Saxon, *knut*, connected with "knot") implies a mere hard, round lump ; and hazel (Saxon, *hæsl* or *hæsel*, from *hase*, a husk, or *hæs*, a behest), a hazel-stick being in general use in management of slaves and cattle. Only twice is the word "hazel" used—viz., in the pretty comparison of the fiery Kate, who,

Like the hazel-twig
Is straight and slender and as brown in hue
As hazel-nuts and sweeter than the kernels.
Taming of the Shrew, II. i. 255.

[138]

And the word "filbert" occurs but once (*Tempest*, II. ii. 175):

> I'll bring thee clustering filberts.

The other reference is to the nut, where, in *Romeo and Juliet*, I. iv. 67, an empty hazel-nut is Queen Mab's chariot—

> Made by the joiner squirrel or old grub,
> Time out o' mind the fairies' coachmakers.

A nut unadorned by any phrase is named in the *Comedy of Errors*, IV. iii. 72, as one of the requirements of devils:

> Some devils ask but the parings of one's nails,
> A rush, a hair, a drop of blood, a pin,
> A nut, a cherry-stone.

And again:

> I have a venturesome fairy that shall seek
> The squirrel's hoard and fetch thee new nuts.
> *Midsummer-Night's Dream*, IV. i. 39.

And yet again in *Romeo and Juliet*, III. i. 20:

Wilt thou quarrel with a man for cracking nuts, having no other reason but because thou hast hazel eyes.

As a fusty, sour, and worm-eaten nut, we find several references, chiefly—

Hector shall have a great catch if he knock out either of your brains: a' were as good crack a fusty nut with no kernel.

> *Troilus and Cressida*, II. i. 110.

> Sweetest nut hath sourest rind,
> Such a nut is Rosalind.
> *As You Like It*, III. ii. 115.

Among the Old World customs connected with this tree must be mentioned, going a nutting on

Holy Rood Day, September 14. Brand quotes
(i. 353) "Status Scholæ Etonensis," 1560, which
orders the boys of Eton, on a certain day in September, to go out to gather nuts, having first written
verses on the fruitfulness of autumn and the cold of
advancing winter; and also from "Poor Robin,"
1709:

> The devil, as the common people say,
> Doth go a nutting on Holyrood day;
> And sure some leachery in some doth lurk
> Going a nutting do the devil's work.

There was also the All Hallows E'en ("Nutcrack
Night"), when around the fire fortunes were told by
the cracking of nuts. The custom is referred to in
Goldsmith's "Vicar of Wakefield": "They kept up
the Christmas carol, sent true-love knots on Valen-
tine morning, ate pancakes on Shrovetide, showed
their wit on the first of April, and religiously cracked
nuts on Michaelmas Eve" (chap. iv.). Brand quotes
Hutchinson's "Northumberland," (vol. ii., p. 18):
"The 1st of November seems to retain the celebra-
tion of a festival to Pomona, when it is supposed the
summer stores are opened on the approach of winter.
Divinations and consulting of omens attended all
these ceremonies in the practice of the heathen.
Hence, in the rural sacrifice of nuts propitious omens
are sought touching matrimony: If the nuts be still
and burn together, it prognosticates a happy marriage
or a hopeful love; if, on the contrary, they bounce
and fly asunder, the sign is unpropitious." To the
present day the ceremony is used, but chestnuts are
the medium; as they are placed on the grate bars
the following distich is repeated:

> If you love me, pop and fly,
> If not, lie there silently.

Nor must the use of the forked hazel rod in divination be omitted. The writer knows from experience that it has been used, and succeeded; on the other hand, it has almost as often failed.

The stick, about 9 inches long, is simply forked, and held in the palm of the hand; it is supposed to become agitated when there is water beneath. In a note on " The Divining Rod," as used by Mr. John Mullins, of Chippenham, in search for water at Grantham, in 1891 (*Antiquary*, vol. xxiii., p. 190), we get the following:

" On Exmoor, faith in the occult powers of a V-shaped twig of hazel used to be quite common up to a recent date. An old woman who was in the habit of 'hurting'—that is, of picking bilberries— carried with her a twig, that she might insure lighting on the earliest and ripest. When we used to follow the Devon and Somerset staghounds thirty years ago, the boldest and best rider always carried a small forked twig of hazel in his breeches pocket, as a sure preventative against galling. The late Sir Thomas Acland's head gamekeeper was similarly equipped for luck in black-game shooting."

The hazel (*Coryllus avellana*, L.) is found throughout Europe, North Africa, Siberia, and Dahuria. The nuts yield oil; the wood is elastic. The fertilized female flowers produce nut-bearing peduncles after fertilization.

A far more showy plant, and one that flowers so long as to give rise to the motto, " When the gorse is out of flower, kissing is out of favour," is the furze, whin, or gorse (*Ulex Europæus*, L.). The first of its three names is difficult to account for. Prior gives it as " fir," from its use as firing; others suggest that it is from the likeness of its spines to those of a fir-tree. Gorse is also an obscure word, perhaps from the Welsh *goresta*, waste, or Middle Latin *gorra*; while " whins" is from the Danish *hviin*, the

whistling of the wind, in allusion to its native
windy heaths.

Shakespeare alludes to the first two of these
names in the *Tempest*, IV. i. 180 :

Tooth'd briars, sharp furzes, pricking goss, and thorns.

There is another reference to furze in the same
play (I. i. 71) :

Long heath, brown furze.

It does not seem to me sufficiently clear that there
was any real distinction in Shakespeare's day between goss and furze. Ellacombe quotes the en-
closure of Greenwich Park, where vrises and gorste
are distinguished, but it is only an English method
of expressing the usual formula for manorial waste
common to all early deeds. The heath and waste
(*bruera et campus*). There are two other English
species of the genus—*U. gallii*, Planch. and *U. nanus*,
Forster, but both are comparatively uncommon.

One quotation—

And thy broom groves,
Whose shadow the dismissed bachelor loves,
Being lass-lorn ;

Tempest, IV. i. 66.

—has led to a good deal of misunderstanding.

It has been suggested to be the common broom,
growing in clumps sufficiently high to shelter the
unfortunate bachelor, which it rarely, if ever, does,
and would scarce be a suitable place to wander in if
it did. Another far-fetched idea has been that
birchen groves are meant, and that the name of the
useful " birch broom " has been applied to the grove
of living trees from which the twigs are cut; but
there is no doubt in the writer's mind that the plant,
loving the shady retirement of a dusky copse wood,

the curious butcher's broom is that referred to. It
is, moreover, plentiful in a natural state close to
Shakespeare's town. The " groves " would then be
the shady copses generally bare of other undergrowth,
" broom'd " by the clustering masses of this shade-
loving plant, in all ways most suitable to the inatten-
tive wanderings of the distraught lover.

As said above, it is a most curious plant; the
apparent rigid leaves are really flattened flower-
stalks—technically, cladodes—while the leaves are
mere minute scales, from the axils of which these
cladodes rise. The flowers are borne on their mid-
rib, and are yellowish with red veins, while the fruit
is a berry. It is a native of Europe and Western
Asia ; it grows freely in shady woods and coppices.
Parkinson tells us of this plant, " Butchers made
brooms to sweep their stalls," but it is called in
Italian prick-mouse (*pongitopo*). And Dr. Prior
quotes Lonicerus, "Kraüterb." p 204: "Die Weiber
hencken ihn auch bey das Fleisch, dann er vertreibt
und hält mit seiner scheusslichen Gestalt die Fleder-
maüss darvon ab "—that is, that it was used much
as gauze-covers are used to-day to lay over meat to
protect it from the ravages of bats and mice.

In the herb-garden rosemary sometimes flowers
this month, a labiate of great fragrance, and to
which many medicinal virtues were assigned. It is
the *Rosmarinus officinalis*, L., and is summed up in
the highest praise by old Parkinson :

" Rosemary is almost of as great use as bays, as
well for civill as physical purposes : for civill uses, as
all doe know, at weddings, funerals, etc., to bestow
among friends " (" Garden of Flowers," 1629, p. 598).

It was furthermore used at weddings and perhaps at
funerals also, and, together with bays, was occasionally gilded. The rosemary appeared to have been
sometimes dipped in scented water, as in the query,

" Were the rosemary branches dipped ?" (Beaumont and Fletcher's " Scornful Lady ").

> Well, well, since wedding will come after wooing,
> Give me some rosemary, and letts be going.
> > FLETCHER : *Woman's Pride.*

Ellacombe (p. 273) quotes a pleasing fragment in its favour from Sir Thomas Moore :

" As for Rosmarine, I lett it run alle over my garden walls, not onlie because my bees love it, but because 'tis the herb sacred to remembrance, and therefore to friendship ; whence a sprig of it hath a dumb language that maketh it the chosen emblem at our funeral wakes, and in our buriall grounds."

The plant is a native of the South of Europe, and derives its name from *ros maris* (spray of the sea), since it flourishes on the foreshore.

Its evergreen habits are referred to in the *Winter's Tale,* IV. iv. 74 :

> Rosemary and rue ; these keep
> Seeming and savour all the winter long ;
> Grace and remembrance be to you both.

And again in *Hamlet,* IV. v. 175 :

> There's rosemary, that's for remembrance.

Its use in funeral rites occurs in *Romeo and Juliet,* IV. v. 79 :

> Stick your rosemary
> On this fair corse.

The flower is a curiously pale bluish-white, and is not lacking in a beauty of its own, while the lasting scent which remains long after it has been gathered endeared it to the heart of the people. It is still considered a sovereign specific against cramp.

There are three foreign plants, the products of which are mentioned by the bard. One is the tree of trees, the olive (*Olea Europæa*, L.), which is a native of the South of Europe, flowering in July, and introduced to us in 1570. Its fruit is well known, and as much appreciated to-day as in the sixteenth century. A good deal of this is no doubt due to its biblical lore, where it is ever set forth as the symbol of fatness, plenty, and honour — from the time the dove first brought back the olive leaf to expectant Noah (Gen. viii. 11) until the time when the Gentile Church was likened to a wild olive-tree grafted into the cultivated stem of the Jewish (Rom. xi. 17)— but a good deal is also due to the classical honour paid to it as the sacred emblem of Minerva, the gift, she believed, and rightly so, the most blessed offering to mankind, the symbol of Peace. Can we forget the great scene of contest carved by the matchless skill of Phidias high on the pediment of that most perfect of temples the Parthenon, the snorting war-horse of Neptune, the dignity of Athene Glaucopus and her gift? All but two of the poet's references are to the olive in this aspect. The exceptions are *As You Like It*, III. v. 74:

> If you will know my house,
> 'Tis at the tuft of olives here hard by.

And again, IV. iii. 77:

> Where in the purlieus of this forest stands
> A sheep-cote fenced about with olive-trees.

Ebony, the wood of *Diospyros ebenum* and various trees of the genera *Ebenaster, Mabola*, etc., was known to the poet only from hearsay; at least, he could not have seen the living tree, although the wood itself was imported from the East long before his time. It was well enough known to ancient peoples, and prized for cabinet work, and the bed of sleep in his dark abode is said by Ovid to have been com-

10

posed of it ("Met.," xi. 610). There are five references to the wood in the poet's lines, but one of
which is literal :

The clearstores towards the south north are lustrous as ebony.
Twelfth Night, IV. ii. 41.

Otherwise we get, " ebon-coloured ink " (*Love's
Labour's Lost*, I. i. 246, and the amusing—

> *King.* By heaven, thy love is black as ebony.
> *Biron.* Is ebony like her? O wood divine!
>   A wife of such wood were felicity.
> *Ibid.*, IV. iii. 247.

MARCH

When daffodils begin to peer,
  With heigh ! the doxy over the dale,
Why, then comes in the sweet o' the year ;
  For the red blood reigns in the winter's pale.

The white sheet bleaching on the hedge,
  With heigh ! the sweet birds, O, how they sing !
Doth set my pugging tooth on edge ;
  For a quart of ale is a dish for a king.

Winter's Tale, IV. iii. 1.

HOW the boisterous equinox bends almost to the breaking, the naked branches of the trees! How it howls about the chimney-stacks and whistles through the keyhole and tosses the catkins of hazel and the reddening purples of the willows fringing the brooks ! But for all that

> March winds,
> April showers,
> Bring forth May flowers ;

so runs the jingling adage of the rustic. In leafy Warwickshire the reddish-green balls of flowers crowd on the branches of the typical tree of the county, the elm, just as they did in Shakespeare's day. The elm is a handsome tree in early summer, raising its verdure some 120 feet from the ground, but by-and-by, when the sun and rain have marred its first beauty, how dingy it appears. Its brightness vanishes, and nought but a dull, lifeless, neutral green takes its place. We have two species, one native, *Ulmus*

10—2

montanus, L., the wych elm ; the other naturalized, *U. surculosa*, Syme, and this may have been brought to us by the Romans.

Two of Shakespeare's references are exceedingly pretty :

> Thou art an elm, my husband, I a vine,
> Whose weakness married to thy stronger state
> Makes me with thy strength communicate.
> > *Comedy of Errors*, II. ii. 176.

And in a similar train of thought we get:

> The female ivy so
> Enrings the barky fingers of the elm.
> > *Midsummer-Night's Dream*, IV. i. 48.

The word " wych " elm is equivalent to hutch elm, because it was used to make coffers to keep provisions in, called hucches, wyches, or whycchs. Thus Dr. Prior quotes :

> His hallrofe was full of bacon flytches,
> The chambre charged was with wyches,
> Full of eggs, butter, and cheese.

The other component word, elm, often pronounced " hell-um " by the villagers, is a word nearly identical in all the Germanic and Scandinavian dialects, but is really a foreign word, the Latin *ulmus*, adopted and varied by them. The use of it points to a South European origin, and would help to bear out the suggestion that we may thank Rome for this tree, as we have for the vine and chestnut.

The most delicate and graceful of our native poplars, the aspen, also flowers this month. It rears its crown of constantly vibrating leaves some 40 to 80 feet, and has the usual European distribution of most of our native trees, reaching into Asia and Northern Africa. Its curious trembling form, from which its specific name (*Populus tremula*, L.) is

derived, is still said to be in accordance with long
tradition, due to the fact that from it the wood of
the holy rood was made which bore our Saviour's
body on Calvary. Ellacombe quotes a verse which
gives what he describes as " a rude libel " (p. 50),
from " The Schoolhouse of Women " (511-545), which
thus concludes:

> The aspin lefe hanging where it be,
> With little wind or none it shaketh ;
> A woman's tung in like wise taketh
> Little ease and little rest ;
> For if it should the hart would brest.

And old Gerard has much the same idea in his
concluding remarks on the tree :

" In English Aspe and Aspen tree, and may also be
called Tremble, after the French name, considering
it is a matter whereof women's tongues were made
(as the poets and some others report) which seldom
cease wagging."

Dr. Prior says it was called in Chaucer's time apse,
from " æpse," from the hissing sound of the leaves
(p. 12).

The willow, in favourable seasons, towards the end
of this month puts out a multitude of golden catkins
on the male tree, and as many green or silvery on the
female. The willows belong to a difficult order of
plants, and some 160 species, are known, of which we
ourselves, under the latest arrangement—that of
Dr. White and the Rev. E. P. Linton—are considered
to have endless named varieties. The most important are the trees, such as (*Salix fragilis*) the crack
willow or withy, which reaches 80 feet, and the white
willow (*S. alba*, L.). The goat willow or sallow
(*S. Capræa*, L.) is well-known, and the basket osier
(*S. viminalis*, L.) also. From the earliest times the
use of the pliable twigs of these plants, has been
known, and in Britain this class of work was carried to

great perfection, and was used for houses, boats, and, in the form of baskets, was even imported to Rome, and looked upon there as an article of rarity and beauty.   These basket-work dwellings are referred to by the poet in *Twelfth Night*, I. v. 287 :

> Make me a willow cabin at your gate.

But the willow was looked upon by the sixteenth-century poets as the plant of jilted love, and a spirit of sadness prevailed in connection with it, both in ancient and more modern times.   Thus we get—

> In such a night
> Stood Dido with a willow in her hand
> Upon the wild sea banks.
> *Merchant of Venice*, V. i. 9 ;

and—

> Tell him, in hope he'll prove a widower shortly,
> I'll wear the willow garland for his sake.
> 3 *Henry VI.*, III. iii. 227.

Osiers are also spoken of thus :

> The rank of osiers by the murmuring stream.
> *As You Like It*, IV. iii. 80.

> When Cytherea, all in love forlorn,
> A longing tarriance for Adonis made
> Under an osier growing by a brook.
> *Passionate Kinsman*, vi.

The most beautiful early flowering tree is undoubtedly the almond, one of our showiest garden ornaments this month.   It was early known in Britain and called the " Eastime-nutte-beam."   The tree is the *Amygdalus communis*, L., of botanists, and is said to have come from Barbary.   It was cultivated in 1570, in England, and probably many centuries earlier.   It is only once mentioned by the poet, and

that in *Troilus and Cressida*, V. ii. 193, in the form of
a proverb :

> The parrot will not do more for an almond.

But Shakespeare's contemporaries mention it freely,
thus : " The blooms of the almond-tree grow in a
night and vanish in a morn " (Greene's " Friar
Bacon ").

And again :

> Bright Bathsabe shall wash in David's bower
> In water mix'd with purest almond flower.
>> PEELE : *Love of King David*, 1599.

Almonds were used in Elizabethan times in the
manufacture of marchpanes—the prototypes either
of macaroons or the Italian marzipan :

> Save me a piece of marchpane.
>> *Romeo and Juliet*, I. v. 9.

If we turn for a while from trees to shrubs, and
search the hedgebanks, we cannot help thinking of
Tennyson's beautiful lines :

> The meadows your walks have left so sweet
>> That whenever a March wind sighs
> It sets the jewel-print of your feet
>> In violets blue as your eyes.

It matters little ; the violet, with its delicious
colour and scent, its coy half-revealed, half-hidden
habit, appeals not only to the poet, but to the most
untutored clod that ever was born on Midland clay,
and William Shakespeare was no exception.   In
eighteen separate passages this flower is quoted, and
always with a tender poet's love.

Several of these passages are too beautiful to miss.
First for the violet's catholicity :

> I think the king is but a man, as I am ; the violet smells to
> him as it doth to me.
>> *Henry V.*, IV. i. 105.

The delicate scent is, however, the most constant theme ; thus we get :

> The forward violet thus did I chide :
> Sweet thief, whence didst thou steal thy sweet that smells,
> If not from my love's breath ?
>
> <div align="right"><i>Sonnet</i> xcix.</div>

> To gild refined gold, to paint the lily,
> To throw a perfume on the violet,
> To smooth the ice, or add another hue
> Unto the rainbow, or with taper-light
> To seek the beauteous eye of heaven to garnish,
> Is wasteful and ridiculous excess.
>
> <div align="right"><i>King John</i>, IV. ii. 11.</div>

For the combination of colour and odour we cannot better

> Violets dim,
> But sweeter than the lids of Juno's eyes
> Or Cytherea's breath.
>
> <div align="right"><i>Winter's Tale</i>, IV. iv. 120.</div>

The delicate veining of the petals is thus spoken of :

> These blue-vein'd violets whereon we lean
> Never can blab, nor know not what we mean.
>
> <div align="right"><i>Venus and Adonis</i>, 125.</div>

Perhaps of all Warwickshire flowers none are so plentiful as violets; our own little churchyard of Whitchurch is sheeted with them. They grow in every hedgebank, until the whole air is filled with their fragrance, and even the wood-violets and their allies are equally common. The wastes near Stratford are sometimes purple as far as eye can see with the flowers of *V. canina*, L. Our English violets are twelve in number, including some, such as *V. rupestris* and *V. stagnina*, of great rarity ; one the pansy, has been already dealt with. The best known are the marsh, sweet, hairy, and wood violets, and their varieties, while in the north we get *Viola lutea*, Huds. The cultivated species are chiefly from Southern Europe.

It is not generally known that the violet has a
secondary* apetalous flower in the autumn, which
produces most of the seed.   This is not confined to
the sweet violet, but to all Hooker's section *Nominium.*
The plant is still used in medicine, and acquired of late
a notoriety as a suggested cancer cure, and in Shakespeare's time was eaten raw with onions and lettuces
("History of Gardening," Amherst, p. 59), and also
mingled in broth and used to garnish dishes, while
crystallized violets are not unknown in the present
day.

Daisies, too, may be found this month, although
they are not in profusion until later on in the year,
when they whiten the whole expanse of meadow-
land, as it were, with frosted silver, awaiting the
brand of the gilder in buttercup-time.   Shakespeare
mentions it five times in all, but the two best
passages we have already quoted more than once.†
We have left *Lucrece,* 394—

> Whose perfect white
> Show'd like an April daisy on the grass ;

and *Hamlet,* IV. v. 183, Ophelia's offering to her
brother :

> You must wear your rue with a difference.   There's a
> daisy.

The daisy (*Bellis perennis,* L.) belongs to a small
genus of three or four species distributed in the
temperate regions of the old and new world.   Our
own plant is confined to Europe.   It belongs to the
gigantic order *Compositæ.*

Yet another March flower in forward seasons is the
daffodil (*Narcissus pseudo-Narcissus,* L.), the Lent-lily
of the countryside, our principal representatives of

---

* Dimorphic.
† *Love's Labour's Lost,* V. ii. ; *Hamlet,* IV. vii.

a class of flowers of singular beauty, which have become great garden favourites in the last quarter of a century. Its name, daffodil, varied into daffadown-dilly, daffodilly, came from a confusion of asphodel, affodilly, with another plant, sapharoun-lily—at least, so Prior says.

The legend of Narcissus and his shadowy love is told in Ovid ("Met.," Book IV., vi.-vii.), where we learn that Juno, to punish Echo, who has detained her with stories while Jupiter's mistresses escape, allows her to fall in love with Narcissus, and to be slighted by him in return. One of the many nymphs who, like Echo, had been thus despised, prayed to Rhamnusia (*i.e.*, Nemesis), the goddess of Retribution, thus : "Though he should love, let him not enjoy what he loves." This seeming to Rham-nusia reasonable, the prayer was granted, and Narcissus fell in love with his shadow, reflected in a spring, when he pined away. Ovid ends: "And now they were preparing the funeral pile, and the shaken torches, and the bier. The body was nowhere to be found. Instead of his body they found a yellow flower, with white leaves encompassing the middle."

It appears the flower was known to the ancients, and its praises sung by the poets of Greece and Italy.

Shakespeare alludes to it in the pretty song in the *Winter's Tale*, IV. iii. 1, given as our heading :

> When daffodils begin to peer,
>   With heigh! the doxy over the dale,
> Why, then comes in the sweet o' the year ;
>   For the red blood reigns in the winter's pale.

And, again, in the same, IV. iv. 118 :

>   Daffodils,
> That come before the swallow dares, and take
> The winds of March with beauty.

As early as Turner's time (1548) the narcissus was with us as a garden plant. He says :

"Narcissus is of diverse sortes. There is one wyth a whyte floure, which groweth plenteously in my lorde's gardine in Syon, and it is called of diverse whyte claus tibi."

Gerard had twenty-four species in his London garden, and speaks of their popularity. Flower lovers had "them all and every of them in the London gardens in great abundance."

Even in the flower-garden, and that, with our modern wealth of foliage plants, few plants are more stately in flower and leaf than the *Rhubarbs* (*Rheum*). One species is popular, and deservedly so, as a spring vegetable, but this popularity appears to be of comparatively recent growth. Ellacombe tells us (p. 256) that its culinary properties are not mentioned in 1807, but by 1822 it was largely grown for the London market. There seems some little doubt as to what species the drug Turkey rhubarb was obtained from ; the botanists, apparently, thought it came from the plant they called *Rheum officinale*, which is to this day grown for the sake of the drug near Banbury. As a people, we are nothing if not conservative ; but why, in spite of this, should we refuse a place among our flowers to such plants as rhubarb, such trees as apple and quince, and even such foliage plants as parsley ? Where natural beauty is sought for rather than the trim neatness of a suburban villa garden, nothing can be out of place that fits in with its surroundings, and is not an artificial mockery. With rhubarb either isolated as a single plant or grown on an eminence of the rock-garden against a background of shrubs, nothing is more majestic, and when the flower is over the glorious reddish-gold fruit is more beautiful still.

What a wealth of weird lore gathers round the

mandrake (*Mandragora officinalis*, L.), a member, together with henbane, belladonna, nightshade, and many other noxious plants, of the order *Solanaceæ*.

The plant is a native of Syria, and has purple flowers with orange-coloured berries. The root is long, fleshy, and forked, and from this root, with a little careful manipulation, came the grotesquely weird mandrake of the medievalist, which was said to be torn from the ground with screams, thus alluded to by the poet:

> Would curses kill as doth the mandrake's groan.
> 2 *Henry VI.*, III. ii. 310.

> And shrieks like mandrakes' torn out of the earth,
> That living mortals, hearing them, run mad.
> *Romeo and Juliet*, IV. iii. 47.

With regard to this plant Gerard says:

"There hath been many ridiculous tales brought up of this plant, whether of old wives or some runagate surgeons or physicke-mongers, I know not. . . . They adde that it is never or very seldome to be found growing naturally but under a gallowes, where the matter that has fallen from a dead body hath given it the shape of a man and the matter of a woman, the substance of a female plant, and many other such doltish dreams. They fable further and affirme that he who would take up a plant thereof must tie a dog thereunto to pull it up, which will give a great shreeke at the digging up, otherwise if a man should do it he would surely die in a short space after."

That these fables are neither English nor medieval may at once be seen by a note ot Dr. Daubeny, quoted by Ellacombe, p. 163, where the Goddess of Discovery is represented as giving the root to Dioscorides; the dog she had used to pull up the plant is shown in the agonies of death. On its use in medicine, Lyle says, p. 437:

"The wine wherein the roote of mandrage hath been stieped or boyled, swageth all paine; wherefore men to geve it, very wel, to such as they intende to cut, sawe, or burne in any part of their bodies, because they shall feel no payne."

From the roots images were made called "puppettes and mammettes," and these fetched high prices among the superstitious. Shakespeare indirectly refers to these in *2 Henry VI.*, I. ii. 16, and III. ii. 338. Its use as an opiate is also not forgotten. Thus we get:

> *Cleo.* Give me to drink mandragora.
> *Char.* Why, madam?
> *Cleo.* That I might sleep out this great gap of time.
> *Antony and Cleopatra*, I. v. 4.

And, again, in *Othello*, III. iii. 330:

> Not poppy nor mandragora,
> Not all the drowsy syrups of the world,
> Shall ever medicine thee to that sweet sleep
> Which thou owedst yesterday.

As an uncomplimentary epithet we have it in *2 Henry IV.*, I. ii. 16, when Falstaff calls his page—

> Thou whoreson mandrake.

And, again, III. ii. 338, when Justice Shallow is described in terms hardly fit for repetition:

> For all the world like a forked radish with a head fantastically carved upon it with a knife.

This mention of radish reminds us of that very pleasant early vegetable of the same name (*Raphanus sativus*, L.). Beyond the quotation just given, the plant is but once referred to, namely—in *1 Henry IV.*, II. iv. 205, where we find:

> If I fought not with fifty of them, I am a bunch of radish.

It was used by the Romans much as we use melons

and other fruit to this day, as a stimulus before dinner, and it was, no doubt, introduced to these islands by them, and they seem to have thought it the root above all other roots. In Elizabethan times marvellous properties were attributed to it as a prevention to the bite of serpents and other noxious reptiles; it was thus prepared:

"Take a radishe roote and make hym hollowe wythin unto the bottome, then take thre unces of oyle of roses and an unce of turpentin or more, according to the greatnes of the radish, and then cover the said radishe and leave it in the hote ashes or embers, until it be half consumed, then take it out, and anointe your handes with it ("Alexis," II., p. 18).

SHAKESPEARE'S GARDEN
NEW PLACE, STRATFORD-ON-AVON

APPENDIX

A TABLE OF QUOTATIONS FROM THE PLAYS AND POEMS

THE TEMPEST

Gon. I'll warrant him for drowning; though the ship were no stronger than a nutshell.

I. i. 48.

Gon. Now would I give a thousand furlongs of sea for an acre of barren ground, long heath, brown furze, any thing. The wills above be done! but I would fain die a dry death.

I. i. 70.

> That now he was
> The ivy which had hid my princely trunk,
> And suck'd my verdure out on't.

I. ii. 85.

> She did confine thee,
> By help of her more potent ministers
> And in her most unmitigable rage,
> Into a cloven pine.
>
>   *   *   *   *
> With hair up-staring,—then like reeds not hair.

I. i. 213.

> Sea-water shalt thou drink; thy food shall be
> The fresh-brook muscles, wither'd roots, and husks
> Wherein the acorn cradled.   Follow.

I. ii. 462.

> When I arrived and heard thee, that made gape
> The pine, and let thee out.

I. ii. 275.

[159]

Pro. If thou more murmur'st, I will rend an oak
And peg thee in his knotty entrails till
Thou hast howl'd away twelve winters.

I. ii. 294.

Gon. How lush and lusty the grass looks! how green!
Ant. The ground indeed is tawny.
Seb. With an eye of green in't.

II. i. 52.

Seb. I think he will carry this island home in his pocket,
and give it his son for an apple.
Ant. And, sowing the kernels of it in the sea, bring forth
more islands.

II. i. 90.

Gon. Had I plantation of this isle, my lord—
Ant. He'ld sow't with nettle-seed.
Seb.   Or docks, or mallows.
Gon. And were the king on't, what would I do?
Seb. 'Scape being drunk, for want of wine.
Gon. I' the commonwealth I would by contraries
Execute all things; for no kind of traffic
Would I admit; no name of magistrate;
Letters should not be known; riches, poverty,
And use of service, none; contract, succession,
Bourn, bound of land, tilth, vineyard, none;
No use of metal, corn, or wine, or oil;
No occupation.

II. i. 144.

Cal. I pr'ithee, let me bring thee where crabs grow;
And I with my long nails will dig thee pig-nuts;
Show thee a jay's-nest, and instruct thee how
To snare the nimble marmoset; I'll bring thee
To clust'ring filberts, and sometimes I'll get thee
Young scamels from the rock.   Wilt thou go with me?

II. ii. 171

Now I will believe
That there are unicorns; that in Arabia
There is one tree, the phœnix' throne; one phœnix
At this hour reigning there.

III. iii. 21.

Iris. Ceres, most bounteous lady, thy rich leas
Of wheat, rye, barley, vetches, oats, and pease;
Thy turfy mountains, where live nibbling sheep,
And flat meads, thatch'd with stover, them to keep;

Thy banks with pioned and twilled brims,
Which spongy April at thy hest betrims,
To make cold nymphs chaste crowns; and thy broom groves,
Whose shadow the dismissed bachelor loves,
Being lass-lorn; thy pole-clipt vineyard;
And thy sea-marge, sterile, and rocky-hard,
Where thou thyself dost air: the queen o' the sky
Whose watery arch and messenger am I,
Bids thee leave these; and with her sovereign grace,
Here on this grass-plot, in this very place,
To come and sport; her peacocks fly amain:
Approach, rich Ceres, her to entertain.

Enter CERES.

Cer. Hail, many-coloured messenger, that ne'er
Dost disobey the wife of Jupiter;
Who, with thy saffron wings upon my flowers
Diffusest honey-drops, refreshing showers,
And with each end of thy blue bow dost crown
My bosky acres, and my unshrubb'd down,
Rich scarf to my proud earth; why hath thy queen
Summon'd me hither, to this short-grass'd green?
                                        IV. i. 60.

    Cer. Earth's increase, foison plenty,
        Barns and garners never empty:
        Vines, with clustering bunches growing:
        Plants, with goodly burthen bowing:
        Spring come to you, at the farthest
        In the very end of harvest!
        Scarcity and want shall shun you;
        Ceres' blessing so is on you.
                                        IV. i. 110.

Iris. You nymphs, call'd Naiads, of the windring brooks,
With your sedged crowns and ever-harmless looks,
Leave your crisp channels, and on this green land
Answer your summons; Juno does command:
Come, temperate nymphs, and help to celebrate
A contract of true love; be not too late.

Enter certain Nymphs.

You sun-burnt sicklemen, of August weary,
Come hither from the furrow and be merry:
Make holiday; your rye-straw hats put on
And these fresh nymphs encounter every one
In country footing.   IV. i. 130.

11

So I charm'd their ears
That, calf-like they my lowing follow'd through
Tooth'd briers, sharp furzes, pricking goss, and thorns.

IV. i. 178.

Just as you left them ; all prisoners, sir,
In the lime-grove which weather-fends your cell;
They cannot budge till your release.

V. i. 9.

And you, whose pastime
Is to make midnight-mushrooms, that rejoice
To hear the solemn curfew; by whose aid,
Weak masters though ye be, I have bedimm'd
The noontide sun, call'd forth the mutinous winds,
And 'twixt the green sea and the azur'd vault
Set roaring war : to the dread rattling thunder
Have I given fire and rifted Jove's stout oak
With his own bolt; the strong-based promontory
Have I made shake ; and by the spurs pluck'd up
The pine and cedar : graves, at my command
Have wak'd their sleepers ; oped, and let 'em forth
By my so potent art.

V. i. 38.

Ari. Where the bee sucks, there suck I,
In a cowslip's bell I lie ;
There I couch when owls do cry.
On the bat's back I do fly
After summer merrily.
Merrily, merrily shall I live now,
Under the blossom that hangs on the bough.

V. i. 88.

THE TWO GENTLEMEN OF VERONA.

And this my father ; A vengeance on't ! there 'tis : now,
sir, this staff is my sister, for, look you, she is as white as a
lily and as small as a wand.

II. iii. 20.

Val. And I will help thee to prefer her too :
She shall be dignified with this high honour—
To bear my lady's train, lest the base earth
Should from her vesture chance to steal a kiss
And, of so great a favour growing proud,
Disdain to root the summer-swelling flower
And make rough winter everlastingly.

II. iv. 158.

Jul. The more thou damm'st it up, the more it burns.
The current that with gentle murmur glides,
Thou know'st, being stopp'd, impatiently doth rage ;
But when his fair course is not hindered,
He makes sweet music with the enamell'd stones,
Giving a gentle kiss to every sedge
He overtaketh in his pilgrimage.

II. vii. 24.

The air hath starved the roses in her cheeks
And pinch'd the lily-tincture of her face,
That now she is become as black as I.

IV. iv. 159.

THE MERRY WIVES OF WINDSOR.

Eva. Pauca verba, Sir John ; goot worts.
Fal. Good worts ! good cabbage. Slender, I broke your
head : what matter have you against me ?

I. i. 123.

Three veneys for a dish of stewed prunes.

I. i. 295.

I will make an end of my dinner ; there's pippins and
cheese to come.

I. ii. 11.

Pist. " Convey," the wise it call. " Steal !" foh ! a fico
for the phrase !

I. iii. 32.

Pist. . . . For gourd and fullam holds,
And high and low beguiles the rich and poor.

I. iii. 95.

What says my Æsculapius ? my Galen ? my heart of
elder ? ha ! is he dead, bully stale ? is he dead ?

II. iii. 29.

> To shallow rivers, to whose falls
> Melodious birds sing madrigals ;
> There will we make our peds of roses,
> And a thousand fragrant posies.

III. i. 17.

Mrs. Ford. Go to, then : we'll use this unwholesome
humidity, this gross watery pumpion ; we'll teach him to
know turtles from jays.

III. iii. 42.

11—2

Come, I cannot cog and say thou art this and that, like a
many of these lisping hawthorn buds, that come like women
in men's apparel, and smell like Bucklersbury in simple
time; I cannot: but I love thee.

III. iii. 76.

Anne. Alas, I had rather be set quick i' the earth
And bowl'd to death with turnips !

III. iv. 89.

He cannot 'scape me; 'tis impossible he should; he
cannot creep into a halfpenny purse, nor into a pepper-box:
but, lest the devil that guides him should aid him, I will
search impossible places.

III. v. 147.

Eva. Remember, William; focative is *caret*.
Quick. And that's a good root.
Eva. 'Oman, forbear.
Mrs. Page. Peace !

IV. i. 55.

" As jealous as Ford, that searched a hollow walnut for
his wife's leman." Satisfy me once more ; once more search
with me.

IV. ii. 170.

Mrs. Page. There is an old tale goes that Herne the
　　　　hunter,
Sometime a keeper here in Windsor forest,
Doth all the winter-time, at still midnight,
Walk round about an oak, with great ragg'd horns ;

*　　　*　　　*　　　*　　　*

Why yet there want not many that do fear
In deep of night to walk by this Herne's oak.

IV. iv. 28.

I warrant they would whip me with their fine wits till I
were as crest-fallen as a dried pear. I never prospered
since.

IV. v. 101.

I'll show you here at large. Hark, good mine host.
To-night at Herne's oak, just 'twixt twelve and one,
Must my sweet Nan present the Fairy Queen.

IV. vi. 18.

How now, Master Brook! Master Brook, the matter will be known to-night, or never. Be you in the park about mid-night, at Herne's oak, and you shall see wonders.

V. i. 10.

Mrs. Page. They are all couched in a pit hard by Herne's oak, with obscured lights; which, at the very instant of Falstaff's and our meeting, they will at once display to the night.

Mrs. Ford. That cannot choose but amaze him.

Mrs. Page. If he be not amazed, he will be mocked; if he be amazed, he will every way be mocked.

Mrs. Ford. We'll betray him finely.

Mrs. Page. Against such lewdsters and their lechery
Those that betray them do no treachery.

Mrs. Ford. The hour draws on. To the oak, to the oak!

V. iii. 14.

Fal. My doe with the black scut! — Let the sky rain potatoes; let it thunder to the tune of "Green Sleeves," hail kissing-comfits and snow eringoes; let there come a tempest of provocation, I will shelter me here.

V. v. 20.

Cricket, to Windsor chimneys shalt thou leap;
Where fires thou find'st unraked and hearths unswept,
There pinch the maids as blue as bilberry.

V. v. 47.

The several chairs of order look you scour
With juice of balm and every precious flower:
Each fair instalment, coat, and several crest,
With loyal blazon, ever more be blest!
And nightly, meadow-fairies, look you sing,
Like to the Garter's compass, in a ring:
The expressure that it bears, green let it be,
More fertile-fresh than all the field to see;
And *Honi soit qui mal y pense* write
In emerald tufts, flowers purple, blue, and white;
Like sapphire, pearl and rich embroidery,
Buckled below fair knighthood's bending knee:
Fairies use flowers for their charactery.
Away; disperse: But till 'tis one o'clock,
Our dance of custom round about the oak
Of Herne the hunter, let us not forget.

V. v. 65.

Ford. What, a hodge-pudding? a bag of flax?

V. v. 159.

MEASURE FOR MEASURE.

> Now, as fond fathers,
> Having bound up the threatening twigs of birch,
> Only to stick it in their children's sight
> For terror, not to use, in time the rod
> Becomes more mock'd than fear'd.

I. iii. 23.

And longing, saving your honour's reverence for stewed prunes ; sir.

*   *   *   *   *

Longing, as I said, for prunes; and having but two in the dish, as I said, Master Froth here, this very man, having eaten the rest, as I said, and, as I say, paying for them very honestly ;—for, as you know, Master Froth, I could not give you threepence again.

Froth. No, indeed.

Clo. Very well; you being then, if you be remembered, cracking the stones of the foresaid prunes.

II. i. 92.

Clo. Why, very well; I hope here be truths. He, sir, sitting, as I say, in a lower chair, sir ; 'twas in the Bunch of Grapes, where indeed you have a delight to sit, have you not ?

II. i. 131.

> Nothing but thunder !   Merciful Heaven,
> Thou rather with thy sharp and sulphurous bolt
> Split'st the unwedgeable and gnarled oak
> Than the soft myrtle.

II. ii. 114.

> But it is I
> That, lying by the violet in the sun,
> Do as the carrion does, not as the flower,
> Corrupt with virtuous season.

II. ii. 164.

He's not past it yet, and I say to thee, he would mouth with a beggar, though she smelt brown bread and garlic: say that I said so.   Farewell.

III. 2. 193.

> *Isab.* He hath a garden circummured with brick,
> Whose western side is with a vineyard back'd ;
> And to that vineyard is a planched gate,

That makes his opening with this bigger key:
This other doth command a little door
Which from the vineyard to the garden leads.

IV. i. 28.

Come, let us go:
Our corn's to reap, for yet our tithe's to sow.

IV. i. 75.

Here be many of her old customers. First, here's young Master Rash; he's in for a commodity of brown paper and old ginger, nine score and seventeen pounds; of which he made five marks, ready money: marry, then ginger was not much in request, for the old women were all dead. Then is there here one Master Caper, at the suit of Master Threepile the mercer, for some four suits of peach-coloured satin, which now peaches him a beggar.

IV. iii. 4.

Clo. He is coming, sir, he is coming; I hear his straw rustle.

IV. iii. 37.

Lucio. Yes, marry, did I: but I was fain to forswear it; they would else have married me to the rotten medlar.

IV. iii. 182.

Nay, friar, I am a kind of burr; I shall stick.

IV. iii. 189.

THE COMEDY OF ERRORS.

Thou art an elm, my husband, I a vine,
Whose weakness, married to thy stronger state,
Makes me with thy strength to communicate:
If aught possess thee from me, it is dross,
Usurping ivy, briar, or idle moss;
Who, all for want of pruning, with intrusion
Infect thy sap, and live on thy confusion.

II. ii. 176.

Dro. S. 'Tis true; she rides me and I long for grass.
'Tis so, I am an ass.

II. ii. 202.

Dro. S. Some devils ask but the parings of one's nail,
A rush, a hair, a drop of blood, a pin,
A nut, a cherry-stone.

IV. iii. 72.

Did this companion with the saffron face
Revel and feast it at my house to-day,
Whilst upon me the guilty doors were shut
And I denied to enter in my house?

IV. iv. 64.

MUCH ADO ABOUT NOTHING.

D. John. I had rather be a canker in a hedge, than a rose
in his grace.

I. iii. 28.

Bene. Even to the next willow, about your own business,
count. What fashion will you wear the garland of?

II. i. 194.

Bene. Alas, poor hurt fowl! Now will he creep into
sedges.

II. i. 209.

Bene. O, she misused me past the endurance of a block!
An oak, but with one green leaf on it, would have answered
her!

II. i. 246.

Civil as an orange, and something of that jealous complexion.

II. i. 302.

And bid her steal into the pleached bower,
Where honeysuckles, ripen'd by the sun,
Forbid the sun to enter, like favourites.

III. i. 7.

So angle we for Beatrice; who even now
Is couched in the woodbine coverture.

III i. 29.

Marg. Get you some of this distilled Carduus Benedictus,
and lay it to your heart: it is the only thing for a qualm.
Hero. There thou prickest her with a thistle.
Beat. Benedictus! Why Benedictus? You have some
moral in this Benedictus.
Marg. Moral! No, by my troth, I have no moral meaning: I meant, plain holy thistle.

III. iv. 73.

Give not this rotten orange to your friend.

IV. i. 33.

LOVE'S LABOUR'S LOST

Long. He weeds the corn and still lets grow the weeding.
I. i. 96.

At Christmas I no more desire a rose
Than wish a snow in May's new-fangled shows.
I. i. 106.

The ebon-coloured ink, which here thou viewest.
I i. 245.

Cost. No egma, no riddle, no l'envoy, no salve in the mail,
sir: O, sir, plantain, a plain plantain ! no l'envoy, no l'envoy ;
no salve, sir, but a plain plantain !
III. i. 73.

Cost. Pray you, sir, how much carnation riband may a
man buy for a remuneration ?
III. i. 146.

Hol. The deer was, as you know, sanguis, in blood; ripe as
a pomewater, who now hangeth like a jewel in the ear of cœlo,
the sky, the welkin, the heaven ; and anon falleth like a crab
on the face of terra,—the soil, the land, the earth.
IV. ii. 3.

Though to myself foresworn, to thee I'll faithful prove ;
Those thoughts to me were oaks, to thee like osiers
bowed.
IV. ii. 111.

So sweet a kiss the golden sun gives not
To those fresh morning drops upon the rose,
As thy eye beams, when their fresh rays have smote
The dew of night that on my cheeks down flows.
IV. iii. 25.

Dum. As upright as the cedar.
IV. iii. 89.

But alack, my hand is sworn
Ne'er to pluck thee from thy thorn.
IV. iii. 111.

King. By heaven, thy love is black as ebony.
Biron. Is ebony like her ? O wood divine !
A wife of such wood were felicity.
IV. iii. 247.

Biron. Allons ! allons ! Sow'd cockle reap'd no corn ;
And justice always whirls in equal measure.
IV. iii. 383.

Cost. An I had but one penny in the world, thou shouldst
have it to buy gingerbread.

V. i. 74.

Boyet. Under the cool shade of a sycamore,
I thought to close mine eyes some half an hour.

V. ii. 89.

King. Say to her, we have measured many miles
To tread a measure with her on this grass.

V. ii. 184.

Boyet. Therefore change favours; and, when they repair
Blow like sweet roses in this summer air.
Princess. How blow? How blow? Speak to be under-
stood.
Boyet. Fair ladies masked, are roses in their bud;
Dismask'd, their damask sweet commixture shown,
Are angels vailing clouds, or roses blown.

V. ii. 292.

Biron. This fellow pecks up wit as pigeons peas,
And utters it again when God doth please.

V. ii. 315.

Now by my maiden honour, yet as pure
As the unsullied lily, I protest.

V. ii. 351.

Hol. Begin, sir; you are my elder.
Biron. Well follow'd: Judas was hanged on an elder.
Hol. I will not be put out of countenance.
Biron. Because thou hast no face.

V. ii. 608.

Dum. A gilt nutmeg.
Biron. A lemon.
Long. Stuck with cloves.
Dum. No, cloven.
Arm. Peace!—

V. ii. 651.

Dum. That mint.
Long. That columbine.

V. ii. 661.

To weed this wormwood from your fruitful brain.

V. ii. 857.

When daisies pied and violets blue
And lady-smocks all silver-white
And cuckoo-buds of yellow hue
Do paint the meadows with delight.

V. ii. 904.

When shepherds pipe on oaten straws.

V. ii. 913.

When all aloud the wind doth blow
And coughing drowns the parson's saw
And birds sit brooding in the snow
And Marian's nose looks red and raw,
When roasted crabs hiss in the bowl,
Then nightly sings the staring owl,
Tu-whit;
Tu-who, a merry note,
While greasy Joan doth keel the pot.

V. ii. 931.

A MIDSUMMER-NIGHT'S DREAM.

But earthlier happy is the rose distill'd,
Than that which withering on the virgin thorn
Grows, lives and dies in single blessedness.

I. i. 76.

Lys. How now, my love! Why is your cheek so pale?
How chance the roses there to fade so fast?

I. i. 128.

And your tongue's sweet air
More tuneable than lark to shepherd's ear,
When wheat is green, when hawthorn buds appear.

I. i. 183.

Lys. Helen, to you our minds we will unfold:
To-morrow night, when Phœbe doth behold
Her silver visage in the wat'ry glass,
Decking with liquid pearl the bladed grass,
A time that lovers' flights doth still conceal,
Through Athens' gates have we devis'd to steal.
Her. And in the wood, where often you and I
Upon faint primrose-beds were wont to lie,
Emptying our bosoms of their counsel sweet,
There my Lysander and myself shall meet.

I. i. 208.

Bot. I will discharge it either in your straw-colour beard,
your orange-tawny beard.

I. ii. 93.

Quin. At the duke's oak we meet.

I. ii. 113.

The cowslips tall her pensioners be:
In their gold coats spots you see;
Those be rubies, fairy favours,
In those freckles live their savours:
I must go seek some dew-drops here,
And hang a pearl in every cowslip's ear.
Farewell, thou lob of spirits; I'll be gone:
Our queen and all her elves come here anon.

II. i. 10.

And jealous Oberon would have the child
Knight of his train, to trace the forests wild;
But she perforce withholds the loved boy,
Crowns him with flowers and makes him all her joy:
And now they never meet in grove or green,
By fountain clear, or spangled star-light sheen,
But they do square, that all their elves for fear
Creep into acorn cups and hide them there.

II. i. 24.

When I a fat and bean-fed horse beguile,
Neighing in likeness of a filly foal:
And sometime lurk I in a gossip's bowl,
In very likeness of a roasted crab.

II. i. 45.

Tita. Then, I must be thy lady: but I know
When thou has stol'n away from fairy land,
And in the shape of Corin sat all day,
Playing on pipes of corn and versing love
To amorous Phillida.   Why art thou here?

II. i. 64.

And never, since the middle summer's spring,
Met we on hill, in dale, forest or mead,
By paved fountain or by rushy brook.

II. i. 82.

The ploughman lost his sweat; and the green corn
Hath rotted ere his youth attain'd a beard.

II. i. 94.

Hoary-headed frosts
Fall in the fresh lap of the crimson rose,
And on old Hiems' thin and icy crown
An odorous chaplet of sweet summer buds
Is, as in mockery, set.

II. i. 107.

It fell upon a little western flower,
Before milk-white, now purple with love's wound,
And maidens call it, love-in-idleness.
Fetch me that flower; the herb I showed thee once:
The juice of it on sleeping eyelids laid
Will make or man or woman madly dote
Upon the next live creature that it sees.
Fetch me this herb; and be thou here again.

II. i. 166.

I know a bank where the wild thyme blows,
Where ox-lips and the nodding violet grows,
Quite over-canopied with luscious woodbine,
With sweet musk-roses and with eglantine:
There sleeps Titania some time of the night,
Lull'd in these flowers with dances and delight.

II. i. 249.

Some, to kill cankers in the musk-rose buds.

II. ii. 3.

This green plot shall be our stage, this hawthorn brake our
'tiring-house.

III. i. 3.

Quin. Ay; or else one must come in with a bush of thorns
and a lanthorn.

III. i. 59.

Puck. What hempen home-spuns have we swaggering here,
So near the cradle of the fairy queen?
What, a play toward! I'll be an auditor.

III. i. 79.

Most radiant Pyramus, most lily-white of hue,
Of colour like the red rose on triumphant brier.

III. i. 95.

Puck. I'll follow you, I'll lead you about a round,
Through bog, through bush, through brake, through brier:
Sometime a horse I'll be, sometime a hound,
A hog, a headless bear, sometime a fire.

III. i. 108.

And they shall fetch thee jewels from the deep,
And sing while thou on pressèd flowers dost sleep :
And I will purge thy mortal grossness so,
That thou shalt like an airy spirit go.
Peas-blossom ! Cobweb ! Moth ! and Mustard-seed !

III. i. 161.

Tita. Be kind and courteous to this gentleman ;
Hop in his walks, and gambol in his eyes ;
Feed him with apricocks and dewberries,
With purple grapes, green figs, and mulberries ;
The honey-bags steal from the humble-bees,
And for night tapers crop their waxen thighs
And light them at the fiery glow-worm's eyes,
To have my love to bed and to arise ;
And pluck the wings from painted butterflies,
To fan the moon-beams from his sleeping eyes :
Nod to him, elves, and do him courtesies.

III. i. 167.

He murder cries and help from Athens calls.
Their sense thus weak, lost with their fears thus strong,
Made senseless things begin to do them wrong ;
For briers and thorns at their apparel snatch.

III. ii. 26.

Obe. Flower of this purple dye,
Hit with Cupid's archery,
Sink in apple of his eye.
When his love he doth espy,
Let her shine as gloriously
As the Venus of the sky.
When thou wak'st, if she be by,
Beg of her for remedy.

III. ii. 102.

O, how ripe in show
Thy lips, those kissing cherries, tempting grow.

III. ii. 139.

So we grew together,
Like to a double cherry, seeming parted,
But yet an union in partition ;
Two lovely berries moulded on one stem.

III. ii. 208.

Lys. [*To Hermia.*] Hang off, thou cat, thou burr ! vile
thing, let loose,
Or I will shake thee from me like a serpent !

III. ii. 260.

MULBERRY TREES, WINCOT
SAID TO HAVE BEEN PLANTED BY SHAKESPEARE

Lys.   Get you gone, you dwarf ;
You minimus, of hindering knot-grass made ;
You bead, you acorn !   III. ii. 328.

Then crush this herb into Lysander's eye ;
Whose liquor hath this virtuous property,
To take from thence all error with his might,
And make his eye-balls roll with wonted sight.
When they next wake, all this derision
Shall seem a dream and fruitless vision ;
And back to Athens shall the lovers wend,
With league whose date till death shall never end.
                                        III. ii. 366.

Her. Never so weary, never so in woe,
Bedabbled with the dew, and torn with briers ;
I can no farther crawl, no farther go ;
My legs can keep no pace with my desires.
Here will I rest me till the break of day.
                                        III. ii. 442.

Tita. Come, sit thee down upon this flowery bed,
While I thy amiable cheeks do coy,
And stick musk-roses in thy sleek smooth head,
And kiss thy fair large ears, my gentle joy.
  Bot. Where's Peas-blossom ?
  Peas. Ready.
  Bot. Scratch my head, Peas-blossom.   IV. i. 1.

  Tita. Or say, sweet love, what thou desir'st to eat.
  Bot. Truly, a peck of provender : I could munch your good
dry oats.   Methinks I have a great desire to a bottle of hay :
good hay, sweet hay, hath no fellow.
  Tita. I have a venturous fairy that shall seek
The squirrel's hoard, and fetch thee new nuts.
  Bot. I had rather have a handful or two of dried peas.
But, I pray you, let none of your people stir me : I have an
exposition of sleep come upon me.
  Tita. Sleep thou, and I will wind thee in my arms.
Fairies, be gone, and be all ways away.
                    [*Exeunt Fairies.*]
So doth the woodbine the sweet honeysuckle
Gently entwist : the female ivy so
Enrings the barky fingers of the elm.
O, how I love thee, how I dote on thee !   [*They sleep.*
                    [*Enter* PUCK.]

  Obe. [*Advancing.*] Welcome, good Robin.   Seest thou this
    sweet sight ?

Her dotage now I do begin to pity :
For, meeting her of late behind the wood,
Seeking sweet savours for this hateful fool,
I did upbraid her, and fall out with her ;
For she his hairy temples then had rounded
With coronet of fresh and fragrant flowers ;
And that same dew, which sometime on the buds
Was wont to swell, like round and orient pearls,
Stood now within the pretty flow'rets' eyes,
Like tears, that did their own disgrace bewail.

IV. i. 33.

But first I will release the fairy queen.
    Be as thou wast wont to be ;
    See as thou wast wont to see :
    Dian's bud o'er Cupid's flower
    Hath such force and blessed power.
Now, my Titania ; wake you, my sweet queen.

IV. i. 75.

And, most dear actors, eat no onions nor garlick, for we are to utter sweet breath ; and I do not doubt but to hear them say, it is a sweet comedy. No more words : away ! go, away.

IV. ii. 42.

This man, with lantern, dog, and bush of thorn,
    Presenteth Moonshine ; for, if you will know,
By moonshine did these lovers think no scorn
    To meet at Ninus' tomb, there, there to woo.

V. i. 136.

And Thisby, tarrying in mulberry shade,
    His dagger drew and died.

V. i. 149.

Moon. All that I have to say, is, to tell you that the lantern is the moon ; I, the man in the moon ; this thorn-bush, my thorn-bush ; and this dog, my dog.

V. i. 261.

    This. Asleep, my love ?
        What, dead, my dove ?
    O Pyramus, arise !
        Speak, speak. Quite dumb ?
        Dead, dead ? A tomb
    Must cover thy sweet eyes.
        These lily lips,
        This cherry nose,
    These yellow cowslip cheeks,

Are gone, are gone :
Lovers, make moan :
His eyes were green as leeks.
   *   *   *   *
Adieu, adieu, adieu.

V. i. 331.

I am sent, with broom, before,
To sweep the dust behind the door.

V. i. 396.

Obe. Through the house give glimmering light,
    By the dead and drowsy fire :
Every elf and fairy sprite,
    Hop as light as bird from brier ;
And this ditty, after me,
Sing and dance it trippingly.

V. i. 398.

THE MERCHANT OF VENICE.

I should be still

Plucking the grass, to know where sits the wind.

I. i. 17.

Would scatter all her spices on the stream.

I. i. 33.

His reasons are as two grains of wheat hid in two bushels
of chaff.

I. i. 115.

A goodly apple rotten at the heart.

I. iii. 102.

Pick'd from the chaff and ruin of the times.

II. ix. 48.

Salan. I would she were as lying a gossip in that as ever
knapped ginger or made her neighbours believe she wept
for the death of a third husband.

III. i. 9.

You may as well forbid the mountain pines
To wag their high tops and to make no noise,
When they are fretten with the gusts of heaven.

IV. i. 75.

12

Lor.   In such a night
Stood Dido with a willow in her hand
Upon the wild sea-banks and waft her love
To come again to Carthage.
Jes.   In such a night
Medea gather'd the enchanted herbs
That did renew old Æson.

V. i. 9.

AS YOU LIKE IT

Ros. Where learned you that oath, fool?

Touch. Of a certain knight that swore by his honour they were good pancakes and swore by his honour the mustard was naught : now I'll stand to it, the pancakes were naught and the mustard was good, and yet was not the knight forsworn.

Cel. How prove you that, in the great heap of your knowledge?

Ros. Ay, marry, now unmuzzle your wisdom.

Touch. Stand you both forth now : stroke your chins and swear by your beards that I am a knave.

Cel. By our beards, if we had them, thou art.

Touch. By my knavery, if I had it, then I were ; but if you swear by that that is not, you are not forsworn : no more was this knight, swearing by his honour, for he never had any ; or if he had, he had sworn it away before ever he saw those pancakes or that mustard.

I. ii. 65.

Ros. No, some of it for my child's father. O, how full of briers is this working-day world!

Cel. They are but burrs, cousin, thrown upon thee in holiday foolery.

I. iii. 11.

To-day my lord of Amiens and myself
Did steal behind him as he lay along
Under an oak whose antique root peeps out
Upon the brook that brawls along this wood.

II. i. 29.

And I remember the wooing of a peascod instead of her, from whom I took two cods and, giving her them again, said with weeping tears " Wear these for my sake."

II. iv. 51.

Heigh-ho ! sing, heigh-ho ! unto the green holly :
Most friendship is feigning, most loving mere folly :
    Then, heigh-ho ! the holly !
    This life is most jolly.

                       II. vii. 180.

O Rosalind ! these trees shall be my books
And in their barks my thoughts I'll character.

                       III. ii. 25.

        Sweetest nut hath sourest rind,
        Such a nut is Rosalind.
        He that sweetest rose will find
        Must find love's prick and Rosalind.

                       III. ii. 115.

Ros. Peace, you dull fool ! I found them on a tree.
Touch. Truly, the tree yields bad fruit.
Ros. I'll graff it with you, and then I shall graff it with a
medlar : then it will be the earliest fruit i' the country ; for
you'll be rotten ere you be half ripe, and that's the right
virtue of the medlar.
Touch. You have said ; but whether wisely or no, let the
forest judge.

                       III. ii. 121.

Ros. Look here what I found on a palm-tree. I was never
so be-rhymed since Pythagoras' time, that I was an Irish rat,
which I can hardly remember.

                       III. ii. 185.

I pr'ythee, take the cork out of thy mouth that I may
drink thy tidings.

                       III. ii. 213.

I found him under a tree, like a dropped acorn.

                       III. ii. 248.

Ros. No, I will not cast away my physic but on those that
are sick. There is a man haunts the forest, that abuses our
young plants with carving Rosalind on their barks ; hangs
odes upon hawthorns, and elegies on brambles.

                       III. ii. 375.

Ros. There is none of my uncle's marks upon you : he
taught me how to know a man in love ; in which cage of
rushes I am sure you are not prisoner.

                       III. ii. 387.

Cel. An excellent colour : your chestnut was ever the only
colour.

                       III. iv. 12.

                    Lean but upon a rush,
The cicatrice and capable impressure
Thy palm some moment keeps.

                                        III. v. 22.

Cel. Yes; I think he is not a pick-purse nor a horse-
stealer, but for his verity in love, I do think him as concave
as a covered goblet or a worm-eaten nut.

                                        III. iv. 24.

Besides, I like you not.   If you will know my house,
'Tis at the tuft of olives here hard by.

                                        III. v. 74.

That I shall think it a most plenteous crop
To glean the broken ears after the man
That the main harvest reaps.

                                        III. v. 101.

Oli. Good morrow, fair ones; pray you, if you know,
Where in the purlieus of this forest stands
A sheepcote fenc'd about with olive-trees?
Cel. West of this place, down in the neighbour bottom:
The rank of osiers by the murmuring stream
Left on your right hand, brings you to the place.

                                        IV. iii. 76.

Under an oak, whose boughs were moss'd with age
And high top bald with dry antiquity.

                                        IV. iii. 105.

Touch. Why, thou sayest well. I do now remember a
saying, "The fool doth think he is wise, but the wise man
knows himself to be a fool." The heathen philosopher,
when he had a desire to eat a grape, would open his lips
when he put it into his mouth; meaning thereby that grapes
were made to eat and lips to open.

                                        V. i. 33.

          It was a lover and his lass,
            With a hey, and a ho, and a hey nonino,
          That o'er the green cornfield did pass
            In the spring time, the only pretty ring time,
          When birds do sing, hey ding a ding, ding:
          Sweet lovers love the spring.

          Between the acres of the rye,
            With a hey, and a ho, and a hey nonino,
          These pretty country folks would lie,
            In spring time, etc.

This carol they began that hour,
   With a hey, and a ho, and a hey nonino,
How that a life was but a flower
   In spring time, etc.

And therefore take the present time,
   With a hey, and a ho, and a hey nonino ;
For love is crowned with the prime
   In spring time, etc.

V. iii. 17.

Good wine needs no bush.

Epilogue 3.

THE TAMING OF THE SHREW.

And burn sweet wood to make the lodging sweet.

Induct. i. 49.

What is it your honour will command ?
Let one attend him with a silver basin
Full of rose-water and bestrewed with flowers.

Induct. i. 54.

And if the boy have not a woman's gift
To rain a shower of commanded tears,
An onion will do well for such a shift,
Which in a napkin being close convey'd,
Shall in despite enforce a watery eye.

Induct. i. 124.

  2nd Serv. Dost thou love pictures ? We will fetch thee
       straight
Adonis painted by a running brook,
And Cytherea all in sedges hid,
Which seem to move and wanton with her breath,
Even as the waving sedges play with wind.
  Lord. We'll show thee Io as she was a maid,
And how she was beguiled and surprised,
As lively painted as the deed was done.
  3rd Serv. Or Daphne roaming through a thorny wood,
Scratching her legs that one shall swear she bleeds.

Induct. ii. 51.

  Hor. 'Faith, as you say, there's small choice in rotten
apples.

I. i. 138.

But see, while idly I stood looking on,
I found the effect of love in idleness.

I. i. 155.

And do you tell me of a woman's tongue,
That gives not half so great a blow to hear
As will a chestnut in a farmer's fire?
Tush, tush! fear boys with bugs.

I. ii. 208.

Or shall I send my daughter Kate to you?
   Pet. I pray you do.   I will attend her here,
And woo her with some spirit when she comes.
Say that she rail; why, then I'll tell her plain
She sings as sweetly as a nightingale:
Say that she frown: I'll say she looks as clear
As morning roses newly washed with dew:
Say she be mute and will not speak a word;
Then I'll commend her volubility,
And say she uttereth piercing eloquence.

II. i. 168.

   Pet. Nay, come, Kate, come; you must not look so sour.
   Kath. It is my fashion, when I see a crab.
   Pet. Why, here's no crab; and therefore look not sour.

II. i. 229.

Why does the world report that Kate doth limp?
O slanderous world!   Kate like the hazel-twig
Is straight and slender and as brown in hue
As hazel nuts and sweeter than the kernels.
O! let me see thee walk: thou dost not halt.

II. i. 254.

In ivory coffers I have stuffed my crowns;
In cypress chests my arras counterpoints
Costly apparel, tents, and canopies,
Fine linen, Turkey cushions boss'd with pearl,
Valance of Venice gold in needlework.

II. i. 352.

   Pet.   Grumio, my horse.
   Gru. Ay, sir, they be ready: the oats have eaten the horses.

III. ii. 206.

Where's the cook? Is supper ready, the house trimmed, rushes strewed, cobwebs swept; the serving-men in their new fustian, their white stockings, and every officer his wedding-

garment on ? Be the jacks fair within, the jills fair without,
and carpets laid, and everything in order ?

IV. i. 47.

Bion. [*aside*]. As much as an apple doth an oyster, and all one.

IV. ii. 101.

Gru. I cannot tell ; I fear 'tis choleric.
What say you to a piece of beef and mustard ?
Kath. A dish that I do love to feed upon.
Gru. Ay, but the mustard is too hot a little.
Kath. Why then, the beef, and let the mustard rest.
Gru. Nay then, I will not : you shall have the mustard,
Or else you get no beef of Grumio.
Kath. Then both, or one, or anything thou wilt.
Gru. Why then, the mustard without the beef.
Kath. Go, get thee gone, thou false deluding slave

[*Beats him.*

That feed'st me with the very name of meat.

IV. iii. 22.

Why, 'tis a cockle or a walnut shell,
A knack, a toy, a trick, a baby's cap :
Away with it ! Come, let me have a bigger.

IV. iii. 66.

What's this ? a sleeve ? 'Tis like a demi-cannon :
What, up and down, carved like an apple-tart ?

IV. iii. 88.

Bion. I cannot tarry : I knew a wench married in an afternoon as she went to the garden for parsley to stuff a rabbit ;
and so may you, sir : and so, adieu, sir.

IV. iv. 99.

Kath. Forward, I pray, since we have come so far,
And be it moon, or sun, or what you please ;
An if you please to call it a rush-candle,
Henceforth I vow it shall be so for me.

IV. v. 12.

ALL'S WELL THAT ENDS WELL.

It looks ill, it eats drily ; marry, 'tis a withered pear ; it
was formerly better ; marry, yet 'tis a withered pear.

I. i. 175.

Even so it was with me when I was young :
If ever we are nature's, these are ours ; this thorn
Doth to our rose of youth rightly belong ;
Our blood to us, this to our blood is born.

I. iii. 134.

Laf. O, will you eat no grapes, my royal fox ?
Yes, but you will my noble grapes, an if
My royal fox could reach them.

II. i. 73.

Clo. As fit as ten groats is for the hand of an attorney, as your French crown for your taffeta punk, as Tib's rush for Tom's forefinger.

II. ii. 22.

Laf. There's one grape yet.

II. iii. 105.

Laf. Go to, sir; you were beaten in Italy for picking a kernel out of a pomegranate.

II. iii. 275.

Fare you well, my lord ; and believe this of me, there can be no kernel in this light nut.

II. v. 46.

Dia.   Ay, so you serve us,
Till we serve you ; but when you have our roses
You barely leave our thorns to prick ourselves
And mock us with our bareness.

IV. ii. 16.

Hel.   Yet, I pray you :
But, with the word, the time will bring on summer,
When briers shall have leaves as well as thorns,
And be as sweet as sharp.

IV. iv. 30.

Laf. No, no, no, your son was misled with a snipt-taffeta fellow there, whose villanous saffron would have made all the unbaked and doughy youth of a nation in his colour.

IV. v. 1.

Laf. 'Twas a good lady, 'twas a good lady : we may pick a thousand salads ere we light on such another herb.
Clo. Indeed, sir, she was the sweet-marjoram of the salad, or rather, the herb of grace.
Laf. They are not herbs, you knave ; they are nose-herbs.
Clo. I am no great Nebuchadnezzar, sir : I have not much skill in grass.

IV. v. 14.

Laf. Mine eyes smell onions ; I shall weep anon.

V. iii. 321.

TWELFTH NIGHT.

O, it came o'er my ear like the sweet sound,
That breathes upon a bank of violets.

I. i. 5.

Sir To. Excellent; it hangs like flax on a distaff.

I. iii. 108.

Mal. Not yet old enough for a man, nor young enough for
a boy; as a squash is before 'tis a peascod, or a codling when
'tis almost an apple: 'tis with him in standing water, between
boy and man.

I. v. 165.

I hold the olive in my hand; my words are as full of peace
as matter.

I. v. 225.

Vio. Make me a willow cabin at your gate,
And call upon my soul within the house.

I. v. 287.

Clo. Yes, by Saint Anne, and ginger shall be hot i' the
mouth, too.

II. iii. 126.

For women are as roses, whose fair flower
Being once display'd, doth fall that very hour.

II. iv. 39.

Clo. Come away, come away, death,
    And in sad cypress let me be laid;
Fly away, fly away, breath;
    I am slain by a fair cruel maid.
My shroud of white, stuck all with yew,
        O, prepare it!
My part of death, no one so true
        Did share it.

Not a flower, not a flower sweet,
    On my black coffin let there be strown;
Not a friend, not a friend greet
    My poor corpse, where my bones shall be thrown:
A thousand thousand sighs to save,
        Lay me, O, where
Sad true lover never find my grave,
        To weep there!

II. iv. 52.

Vio. A blank, my lord.   She never told her love,
But let concealment, like a worm i' the bud,
Feed on her damask cheek : she pined in thought,
And with a green and yellow melancholy
She sat like patience on a monument,
Smiling at grief.   Was not this love indeed ?

II. iv. 114.

Sir To. Here comes the little villain.

Enter MARIA.

How now, my nettle of India !
Mar. Get ye all three into the box-tree.

II. v. 15.

Enough is shown : a cypress, not a bosom.

III. i. 132.

Cesario, by the roses of the spring.

III. i. 161.

Sir And. Here's the challenge, read it : I warrant there's
vinegar and pepper in't.

III. iv. 157.

Clo. Why, it hath bay-windows transparent as barricadoes,
and the clearstores toward the south north are as lustrous as
ebony ; and yet complainest thou of obstruction ?

IV. ii. 40.

Ant. How have you made division of yourself ?
An apple, cleft in two, is not more twin
Than these two creatures.   Which is Sebastian ?

V. i. 229.

THE WINTER'S TALE.

How like, methought, I then was to this kernel,
This squash, this gentleman.

I. ii. 159.

My wife's a hobby-horse ; deserves a name
As rank as any flax-wench that puts to
Before her troth-plight.

I. ii. 276.

Which being spotted
Is goads, thorns, nettles, tails of wasps.

I. ii. 328.

1st Lord. Behind the tuft of pines I met them; never
Saw I men scour so on their way: I eyed them
Even to their ships.

II. i. 34.

Whose sting is sharper than the sword's; and will not—
For, as the case now stands, it is a curse
He cannot be compell'd to't—once remove
The root of his opinion, which is rotten
As ever oak or stone was sound.

II. iii. 86.

They have scared away two of my best sheep, which I
fear the wolf will sooner find than the master: if anywhere I
have them 'tis by the sea-side, browsing of ivy.

III. iii. 66.

When daffodils begin to peer,
   With heigh! the doxy over the dale,
Why, then comes in the sweet o' the year;
   For the red blood reigns in the winter's pale.

IV. iii. 1.

Three pound of sugar, five pound of currants, rice—what
will this sister of mine do with rice! But my father hath
made her mistress of the feast, and she lays it on.

IV. iii. 39.

I must have saffron to colour the warden pies; mace;
dates?—none, that's out of my note; nutmegs, seven; a race
or two of ginger, but that I may beg; four pound of prunes,
and as many of raisins o' the sun.

IV. iii. 48.

Give me those flowers there, Dorcas. Reverend sirs,
For you there's rosemary and rue; these keep
Seeming and savour all the winter long:
Grace and remembrance be to you both,
And welcome to our shearing!

IV. iv. 73.

Per.   The fairest flowers o' the season
Are our carnations and streak'd gillyvors,
Which some call nature's bastards: of that kind
Our rustic garden's barren; and I care not
To get slips of them.

IV. iv. 81.

Pol. Then make your garden rich in gillyvors,
And do not call them bastards.

       *   *   *   *

Per.   Here's flowers for you;
Hot lavender, mints, savory, marjoram;
The marigold, that goes to bed wi' the sun
And with him rises weeping: these are flowers
Of middle summer, and, I think they are given
To men of middle age.

                                        IV. iv. 98.

                      O Proserpina,
For the flowers now, that frighted thou let'st fall
From Dis's waggon! daffodils,
That come before the swallow dares, and take
The winds of March with beauty; violets dim,
But sweeter than the lids of Juno's eyes
Or Cytherea's breath; pale primroses,
That die unmarried, ere they can behold
Bright Phœbus in his strength—a malady
Most incident to maids; bold oxlips and
The crown-imperial; lilies of all kinds,
The flower-de-luce being one! O, these I lack,
To make you garlands of, and my sweet friend,
To strew him o'er and o'er!

                                     IV. iv. 116.

Clo.   Come on, strike up!
Dor. Mopsa must be your mistress: marry, garlic,
To mend her kissing with!

                                     IV. iv. 162.

          Lawn as white as driven snow;
          Cyprus black as e'er was crow;
          Gloves as sweet as damask roses.

                                     IV. iv. 220.

Pol. I'll have thy beauty scratch'd with briers, and made
More homely than thy state.

                                     IV. iv. 436.

But O, the thorns we stand upon.

                                     IV. iv. 596.

KING JOHN.

Bast. Madam, an if my brother had my shape,
And I had his, Sir Robert's his, like him ;
And if my legs were two such riding-rods,
My arms such eel-skins stuff'd, my face so thin,
That in mine ear I durst not stick a rose,
Lest men should say, " Look, where three-farthings goes !"
                                                    I. i. 138.

Const. Do, child, go to it grandam, child ;
Give grandam kingdom, and it grandam will
Give it a plum, a cherry, and a fig :
There's a good grandam.
                                                    II. i. 160.

Of Nature's gifts thou mayst with lilies boast
And with the half-blown rose.
                                                    III. i. 53.

Sal. Therefore, to be possess'd with double pomp,
To guard a title that was rich before,
To gild refined gold, to paint the lily,
To throw a perfume on the violet,
To smooth the ice, or add another hue
Unto the rainbow, or with taper-light
To seek the beauteous eye of heaven to garnish,
Is wasteful and ridiculous excess.
                                                    IV. ii. 9.

I am amazed methinks, and lose my way
Among the thorns and dangers of this world.
                                                    IV. iii. 140.

RICHARD II.

Pierced to the soul with slander's venom'd spear,
The which no balm can cure but his heart-blood
Which breathed this poison.
                                                    I. i. 171.

Cap. 'Tis thought the king is dead ; we will not stay.
The bay-trees in our country are all wither'd
And meteors fright the fixed stars of heaven.
                                                    II. iv. 7.

Yield stinging nettles to my enemies.

III. ii. 18.

But when from under this terrestrial ball,
He fires the proud tops of the eastern pines.

III. ii. 41.

Not all the water in the rough rude sea
Can wash the balm off from an anointed king;

III. ii. 54.

Thy very beadsmen learn to bend their bows
Of double-fatal yew against thy state.

III. ii. 116.

Aumerle, thou weep'st, my tender-hearted cousin!
We'll make foul weather with despised tears;
Our sighs and they shall lodge the summer corn,
And make a dearth in this revolting land.

III. iii. 160.

    Gard. Go, bind thou up yon dangling apricocks,
Which, like unruly children, make their sire
Stoop with oppression of their prodigal weight:
Give some supportance to the bending twigs.
Go thou, and like an executioner,
Cut off the heads of too fast growing sprays,
That look too lofty in our commonwealth:
All must be even in our government.
You thus employ'd, I will go root away
The noisome weeds, which without profit suck
The soil's fertility from wholesome flowers.
    1st Serv. Why should we in the compass of a pale
Keep law and form and due proportion,
Showing, as in a model, our firm estate,
When our sea-walled garden, the whole land,
Is full of weeds, her fairest flowers chok'd up,
Her fruit-trees all unpruned, her hedges ruin'd,
Her knots disorder'd and her wholesome herbs
Swarming with caterpillars?
    Gard.   Hold thy peace:
He that hath suffer'd this disorder'd spring
Hath now himself met with the fall of leaf:
The weeds which his broad-spreading leaves did shelter,
That seem'd in eating him to hold him up,
Are pluck'd up root and all by Bolingbroke,
I mean the Earl of Wiltshire, Bushy, Green.

1st Serv. What, are they dead?

Gard. They are; and Bolingbroke
Hath seized the wasteful king. O, what pity is it,
That he hath not so trimm'd and dress'd his land,
As we this garden! We at time of year
Do wound the bark, the skin of our fruit-trees,
Lest, being over-proud in sap and blood,
With too much riches it confound itself:
Had he done so to great and growing men,
They might have lived to bear and he to taste
Their fruits of duty: all superfluous branches
We lop away, that bearing boughs may live:
Had he done so, himself had borne the crown,
Which waste of idle hours hath quite thrown down.

III. iv. 29.

Here did she fall a tear; here in this place
I'll set a bank of rue, sour herb of grace:
Rue, even for ruth, here shortly shall be seen,
In the remembrance of a weeping queen.

III. iv. 104.

With mine own tears I wash away my balm,
With mine own hands I give away my crown,
With mine own tongue deny my sacred state,
With mine own breath release all duty's rites,
All pomp and majesty I do forswear.

IV. i. 207.

The woe's to come; the children yet unborn
Shall feel this day as sharp to them as thorn.

IV. i. 322.

But soft, but see, or rather do not see,
My fair rose wither: yet look up, behold,
That you in pity may dissolve to dew,
And wash him fresh again with true-love tears.

V. i. 7.

Duch. Welcome, my son: who are the violets now
That strew the green lap of the new come spring?

V. ii. 46.

1 HENRY IV.

When on the gentle Severn's sedgy bank,
In single opposition, hand to hand,
He did confound the best part of an hour
In changing hardiment with great Glendower:
Three times they breathed and three times did they drink,
Upon agreement, of swift Severn's flood ;
Who then, affrighted with their bloody looks,
Ran fearfully among the trembling reeds,
And hid his crisp head in the hollow bank,
Blood-stained with these valiant combatants.

I. iii. 98.

To put down Richard, that sweet lovely rose,
And plant this thorn, this canker, Bolingbroke?

I. iii. 175.

2nd Car. Peas and beans are as dank here as a dog, and
that is the next way to give poor jades the bots: this house
is turned upside down since Robin ostler died.
1st Car. Poor fellow, never joyed since the price of oats
rose; it was the death of him.

II. i. 9.

1st Car. What, ostler! come away and be hanged! come
away.
2nd Car. I have a gammon of bacon and two razes of
ginger, to be delivered as far as Charing-cross.

II. i. 24.

Gads. She will, she will ; justice hath liquored her. We
steal as in a castle, cock-sure; we have the receipt of fern-
seed, we walk invisible.
Cham. Nay, by my faith, I think you are more beholding
to the night than to fern-seed for your walking invisible.

II. i. 93.

But I tell you, my lord fool, out of this nettle, danger, we
pluck this flower, safety.

II. iii. 9.

Fran. Anon, anon, sir. Look down into the Pomgarnet.

II. iv. 41.

Fal. What, upon compulsion? 'Zounds, and I were at the
strappado, or all the racks in the world, I would not tell you
on compulsion. Give you a reason on compulsion! if reasons
were as plenty as blackberries, I would give no man a reason
upon compulsion, I.

II. iv. 261.

Fal. All! I know not what ye call all ; but if I fought not
with fifty of them, I am a bunch of radish : if there were not
two or three and fifty upon poor old Jack, then I am no two-
legged creature.

II. iv. 204.

Bard. Yea, and to tickle our noses with spear-grass, to
make them bleed.

II. iv. 340.

For though the camomile, the more it is trodden on, the
faster it grows, yet youth, the more it is wasted, the sooner
it wears.

II. iv. 443.

Shall the blessed sun of heaven prove a micher, and eat
blackberries ? a question not to be asked.

II. iv. 450.

Shakes the old beldam earth and topples down
Steeples and moss-grown towers.

III. i. 32.

Worse than a smoky house : I had rather live
With cheese and garlic in a windmill, far,
Than feed on cates and have him talk to me
In any summer-house in Christendom.

III. i. 161.

Glend. She bids you on the wanton rushes lay you down
And rest your gentle head upon her lap,
And she will sing the song that pleaseth you
And on your eyelids crown the god of sleep,
Charming your blood with pleasing heaviness.

III. i. 214.

Swear me, Kate, like a lady as thou art,
A good mouth-filling oath, and leave "in sooth,"
And such protest of pepper-gingerbread,
To velvet-guards and Sunday-citizens.

III. i. 258.

Fal. Why, my skin hangs about me like an old lady's
loose gown ; I am withered like an old apple-john. Well,
I'll repent, and that suddenly, while I am in some liking ; I
shall be out of heart shortly, and then I shall have no

13

strength to repent. An I have not forgotten what the inside of a church is made of, I am a peppercorn, a brewer's horse : the inside of a church !

III. iii. 3.

Fal. There's no more faith in thee than in a stewed prune.

III. iii. 127.

2 HENRY IV.

Thou whoreson mandrake, thou art fitter to be worn in my cap than to wait at my heels.

I. ii. 16.

The other gifts appertinent to man, as the malice of this age shapes them, are not worth a gooseberry.

I. ii. 194.

Murder, murder ! Ah, thou honey-suckle villain ! wilt thou kill God's officers and the king's ? Ah, thou honey-seed rogue ! thou art a honey-seed, a man-queller, and a woman-queller.

II. i. 55.

Host. Good people, bring a rescue or two. Thou wo't, wo't thou ? thou wo't, wo't ta ? do, do, thou rogue ! do, thou hemp-seed !

II. i. 62.

What a disgrace is it to me to remember thy name ! or to know thy face to-morrow ! or to take note how many pair of silk stockings thou hast, viz. these, and those that were thy peach-coloured ones !

II. ii. 15.

1st Draw. What the devil hast thou brought there ? apple-johns ? thou know'st Sir John cannot endure an apple-john.

2nd Draw. Mass, thou sayest true. The prince once set a dish of apple-johns before him, and told him there were five more Sir Johns, and, putting off his hat, said "I will now take my leave of these six dry, round, old, withered knights." It angered him to the heart : but he hath forgot that.

II. iv. 1.

Host. . . . Your colour, I warrant you, is as red as any rose, in good truth, la ! But, i' faith, you have drunk too much canaries ; and that's a marvellous searching wine, and it perfumes the blood ere one can say " What's this ?"

II. iv. 27.

Host. Do I ? yea, in very truth, do I, an' 'twere an aspen leaf : I cannot abide swaggerers.

II. iv. 116.

He a captain ! Hang him, rogue ! He lives upon mouldy stewed prunes and dried cakes.

II. iv. 157.

His wit's as thick as Tewkebury mustard.

II. iv. 261.

Fal. Because their legs are both of a bigness, and a' plays at quoits well ; and eats conger and fennel.

II. iv. 265.

P. Hen. Look, whether the withered elder hath not his poll clawed like a parrot.

II. iv. 281.

Poins. Answer, thou dead elm, answer.

II. iv. 358.

Host. Well, fare thee well : I have known thee these twenty-nine years, come peascod-time ; but an honester and truer-hearted man,—well, fare thee well.

II. iv. 412.

I do remember him at Clement's Inn like a man made after supper of a cheese-paring : when a' was naked, he was, for all the world, like a forked radish, with a head fantastically carved upon it with a knife.

III. ii. 333.

. . . A' was the very genius of famine ; . . . and . . . called him—mandrake.

III. ii. 338.

We shall be winnowed with so rough a wind
That even our corn shall seem as light as chaff
And good from bad find no partition.

IV. i. 194.

A hoop of gold to bind thy brothers in,
That the united vessel of their blood,
Mingled with venom of suggestion—
As, force perforce, the age will pour it in—
Shall never leak, though it do work as strong
As aconitum or rash gunpowder.

IV. iv. 43.

There is not now a rebel's sword unsheathed,
But Peace puts forth her olive everywhere.

IV. iv. 86.

Let all the tears that should bedew my hearse
Be drops of balm to sanctify thy head:
Only compound me with forgotten dust;
Give that which gave thee life unto the worms.

IV. v. 114.

Davy. Marry, sir, thus; those precepts cannot be served:
and, again, sir, shall we sow the headland with wheat?
Shal. With red wheat, Davy.

V. i. 14.

Shal. Nay, you shall see mine orchard, where, in an
arbour, we will eat a last year's pippin of my own graffing,
with a dish of caraways, and so forth: come, cousin Silence:
and then to bed.

V. iii. 1.

Davy. There is a dish of leather-coats for you.

V. iii. 43.

Harry the Fifth's the man. I speak the truth:
When Pistol lies, do this; and fig me, like
The bragging Spaniard.

V. iii. 122.

1st Groom. More rushes, more rushes.
2nd Groom. The trumpets have sounded twice.

V. v. 1.

HENRY V.

Ely. The strawberry grows underneath the nettle
And wholesome berries thrive and ripen best
Neighboured by fruit of baser quality:
And so the prince obscured his contemplation
Under the veil of wildness; which, no doubt,
Grew like the summer grass, fastest by night,
Unseen, yet crescive in his faculty.

I. i. 60.

Host. A' could never abide carnation; 'twas a colour he
never liked.

II. iii. 35.

Chor. The well-appointed king at Hampton pier
Embark his royalty ; and his brave fleet
With silken streamers the young Phœbus fanning :
Play with your fancies, and in them behold
Upon the hempen tackle ship-boys climbing.

III. Prol. 4.

Mowing like grass
Your fresh fair virgins and your flowering infants.

III. iii. 13.

Con. And if he be not fought withal, my lord,
Let us not live in France ; let us quit all
And give our vineyards to a barbarous people.

III. v. 2

Con. Can sodden water,
A drench for sur-rein'd jades, their barley-broth,
Decoct their cold blood to such valiant heat ?

III. v. 18

Let gallows gape for dog ; let man go free,
And let not hemp his windpipe suffocate :
But Exeter hath given the doom of death
For pax of little price.

III. vi. 45

Pist. The fig of Spain !
Flu. Very good.

III. vi. 62.

Orl. He's of the colour of the nutmeg
Dau. And of the heat of the ginger.

III. vii. 20.

Orl. Foolish curs, that run winking into the mouth of a
Russian bear and have their heads crushed like rotten
apples !

III. vii. 153.

Pist. Tell him, I'll knock his leek about his pate
Upon Saint Davy's day.

IV. i. 54.

K. Hen. . . . I think the king is but a man, as I am : the
violet smells to him as it doth to me.

IV. i. 104.

Will. You pay him then. That's a perilous shot out of
an elder gun, that a poor and a private displeasure can do
against a monarch.

IV. i. 210.

                    And I know
'Tis not the balm, the sceptre and the ball,
The sword, the mace, the crown imperial,
The intertissued robe of gold and pearl,
The farced title running 'fore the king.

                                        IV. i. 277.

Lies foul with chewed grass, still and motionless;
And their executors, the knavish crows,
Fly o'er them, all impatient for their hour.

                                        IV. ii. 50.

Flu. Your majesty says very true : if your majesties is
remembered of it, the Welshmen did good service in a garden
where leeks did grow, wearing leeks in their Monmouth caps ;
which, your majesty know, to this hour is an honourable
badge of the service ; and I do believe your majesty takes no
scorn to wear the leek upon Saint Tavy's day.

                                        IV. vii. 101.

Gow. Nay, that's right; but why wear you your leek to-day?
Saint Davy's day is past.
Flu. There is occasions and causes why and wherefore in
all things : . . . look you, and bid me eat my leek: it was in
a place where I could not breed no contention with him ;
but I will be so bold as to wear it in my cap till I see him
once again, and then I will tell him a little piece of my
desires.
            *   *   *   *   *
Pist. I am qualmish at the smell of leek.
Flu. I peseech you heartily, scurvy, lousy knave, at my
desires, and my requests, and my petitions, to eat, look you,
this leek : because, look you, you do not love it, nor your
affections and your appetites and your digestions doo's not
agree with it, I would desire you to eat it.
            *   *   *   *   *
Flu. . . . If you can mock a leek, you can eat a leek.
Gow. Enough, captain : you have astonished him.
Flu. I say, I will make him eat some part of my leek, or I
will peat his pate four days.—Bite, I pray you ; it is good for
your green wound and your ploody coxcomb.
Pist. Must I bite?
Flu. Yes, certainly, and out of doubt, and out of question
too, and ambiguities.
Pist. By this leek, I will most horribly revenge : I eat, and
eat, I swear——

Flu. Eat, I pray you : will you have some more sauce to your leek ? There is not enough leek to swear by.

Pist. Quiet thy cudgel ; thou dost see I eat.

Flu. Much good do you, scauld knave, heartily. Nay, pray you, throw none away ; the skin is good for your broken cox-comb. When you take occasions to see leeks hereafter, I pray you, mock at 'em ; that is all.

Pist. Good.

Flu. Ay, leeks is good : hold you, there is a groat to heal your pate.

Pist. Me a groat !

Flu. Yes, verily and in truth, you shall take it ; or I have another leek in my pocket, which you shall eat.

V. i.

Her vine, the merry cheerer of the heart,
Unpruned dies ; her hedges even-pleach'd,
Like prisoners wildly overgrown with hair,
Put forth disorder'd twigs ; her fallow leas
The darnel, hemlock and rank fumitory
Doth root upon, while that the coulter rusts
That should deracinate such savagery ;
The even mead, that erst brought sweetly forth
The freckled cowslip, burnet and green clover,
Wanting the scythe, all uncorrected, rank,
Conceives by idleness and nothing teems
But hateful docks, rough thistles, kecksies, burs,
Losing both beauty and utility.
And as our vineyards, fallows, meads, and hedges,
Defective in their natures, grow to wildness,
Even so our houses and ourselves and children
Have lost, or do not learn for want of time,
The sciences that should become our country.

V. ii. 41.

Shall we not ?   What sayest thou, my fair flower-de-luce ?

V. ii. 322.

I HENRY VI.

Awake, awake, English nobility !
Let not sloth dim your honours new-begot :
Cropp'd are the flower-de-luces in your arms ;
Of England's coat one half is cut away.

I. i. 78.

Puc. I am prepared : here is my keen-edged sword,
Deck'd with five flower-de-luces on each side ;
The which at Touraine, in Saint Katharine's churchyard,
Out of a great deal of old iron I chose forth.

I. ii. 98.

Plan. Since you are tongue-tied and so loth to speak,
In dumb significants proclaim your thoughts :
Let him that is a true-born gentleman
And stands upon the honour of his birth,
If he suppose that I have pleaded truth,
From off this briar pluck a white rose with me.
    Som. Let him that is no coward nor no flatterer,
But dare maintain the party of the truth,
Pluck a red rose from off this thorn with me.
    War. I love no colours, and, without all colour
Of base insinuating flattery
I pluck this white rose with Plantagenet.
    Suf. I pluck this red rose with young Somerset
And say withal I think he held the right.
    Ver. Stay, lords and gentlemen, and pluck no more,
Till you conclude that he upon whose side
The fewest roses are cropp'd from the tree
Shall yield the other in the right opinion.
    Som. Good master Vernon, it is well objected :
If I have fewest, I subscribe in silence.
    Plan. And I.
    Ver. Then for the truth and plainness of the case,
I pluck this pale and maiden blossom here,
Giving my verdict on the white rose side.
    Som. Prick not your finger as you pluck it off,
Lest bleeding you do paint the white rose red
And fall on my side so, against your will.
    Ver. If I, my lord, for my opinion bleed,
Opinion shall be surgeon to my hurt
And keep me on the side where still I am.
    Som. Well, well, come on : who else ?
    Law. Unless my study and my books be false,
The argument you held was wrong in you ; [*To* SOMERSET.
In sign whereof I pluck a white rose too.
    Plan. Now, Somerset, where is your argument ?
    Som. Here in my scabbard, meditating that
Shall dye your white rose in a bloody red.
    Plan. Meantime your cheeks do counterfeit our roses ;
For pale they look with fear, as witnessing
The truth on our side

Som.   No, Plantagenet,
Tis not for fear but anger that thy cheeks
Blush for pure shame to counterfeit our roses,
And yet thy tongue will not confess thy error.
   Plan. Hath not thy rose a canker, Somerset?
   Som. Hath not thy rose a thorn, Plantagenet?
   Plan. Ay, sharp and piercing, to maintain his truth;
Whiles thy consuming canker eats his falsehood.
   Som. Well, I'll find friends to wear my bleeding roses,
That shall maintain what I have said is true,
Where false Plantagenet dare not be seen.
   Plan. Now, by this maiden blossom in my hand,
I scorn thee and thy fashion, peevish boy.
                                        II. iv. 25.

   Plan. And, by my soul, this pale and angry rose,
As cognizance of my blood-drinking hate,
Will I for ever and my faction wear,
Until it wither with me to my grave
Or flourish to the height of my degree.
                                        II. iv. 107.

   War. This blot that they object against your house
Shall be wip'd out in the next parliament
Call'd for the truce of Winchester and Gloster;
And if thou be not then created York,
I will not live to be accounted Warwick.
Meantime, in signal of my love to thee,
Against proud Somerset and William Pole,
Will I upon thy party wear this rose:
And here I prophesy: this brawl to-day,
Grown to this faction in the Temple-garden,
Shall send between the red rose and the white
A thousand souls to death and deadly night.
                                        II. iv. 116.

And pithless arms, like to a wither'd vine
That droops his sapless branches to the ground.
                                        II. v. 11.

   Puc. These are the city gates, the gates of Rouen,
Through which our policy must make a breach:
Take heed, be wary how you place your words;
Talk like the vulgar sort of market-men
That come to gather money for their corn.
                                        III. ii. 1.

Puc. Paysans, pauvres gens de France ;
Poor market-folks, that come to sell their corn.

III. ii. 14.

Puc. Good morrow, gallants ! Want ye corn for bread ?
I think the Duke of Burgundy will fast
Before he'll buy again at such a rate :
'Twas full of darnel ; do you like the taste ?

III. ii. 41.

Bur. Scoff on, vile fiend and shameless courtezan !
I trust ere long to choke thee with thine own
And make thee curse the harvest of that corn.

III. ii. 46.

Bas. Crossing the sea from England into France,
This fellow here, with envious carping tongue,
Upbraided me about the rose I wear ;
Saying, the sanguine colour of the leaves
Did represent my master's blushing cheeks,
When stubbornly he did repugn the truth
About a certain question in the law
Argu'd betwixt the Duke of York and him.

IV. i. 89.

I see no reason, if I wear this rose,
[*Putting on a red rose.*
That any one should therefore be suspicious
I more incline to Somerset than York.

IV. i. 152

Shep. Wilt thou not stoop ? Now cursed be the time
Of thy nativity ! I would the milk
Thy mother gave thee when thou suck'dst her breast,
Had been a little ratsbane for thy sake !
Or else, when thou didst keep my lambs a-field,
I wish some rav'nous wolf had eaten thee !

V. iv. 26.

2 HENRY VI.

Then will I raise aloft the milk-white rose,
With whose sweet smell the air shall be perfumed ;
And in my standard bear the arms of York,
To grapple with the house of Lancaster ;
And, force perforce, I'll make him yield the crown,
Whose bookish rule hath pull'd fair England down.

I. i. 254.

Duch. Why droops my lord, like over-ripen'd corn,
Hanging the head at Ceres' plenteous load ?

I. ii. 1.

Car. What, art thou lame ?
Simp.   Ay, God Almighty help me !
Suf. How camest thou so ?
Simp.   A fall off of a tree.
Wife. A plum-tree, master.
Glo.   How long hast thou been blind ?
Simp. O, born so, master.
Glo.   What, and wouldst climb a tree ?
Simp. But that in all my life, when I was a youth.
Wife. Too true ; and bought his climbing very dear.
Glo. 'Mass, thou lov'dst plums well, that wouldst venture so.
Simp. Alas, good master, my wife desired some damsons,
And made me climb, with danger of my life.

II. i. 93.

Suf. Thus droops this lofty pine and hangs his sprays ;
Thus Eleanor's pride dies in her youngest days.

II. iii. 45.

Hor. Let it come, i' faith, and I'll pledge you all ; and a fig
for Peter !

II. iii. 66.

Now 'tis the spring, and weeds are shallow-rooted ;
Suffer them now, and they'll o'ergrow the garden
And choke the herbs for want of husbandry.

III. i. 31.

K. Hen. My lords, at once ; the care you have of us,
To mow down thorns that would annoy our foot,
Is worthy praise : but shall I speak my conscience,
Our kinsman Gloster is as innocent.

III. i. 66.

Q. Mary. I would be blind with weeping, sick with groans,
Look pale as primrose with blood-drinking sighs,
And all to have the noble duke alive.

III. ii. 62.

His well-proportion'd beard made rough and rugged,
Like to the summer's corn by tempest lodg'd.
It cannot be but he was murder'd here ;
The least of all these signs were probable.

III. ii. 175.

Suf. Blunt-witted lord, ignoble in demeanour !
If ever lady wrong'd her lord so much,

Thy mother took into her blameful bed
Some stern untutor'd churl, and noble stock
Was graft with crab-tree slip; whose fruit thou art,
And never of the Nevils' noble race.

III. ii. 210.

Suf. A plague upon them! Wherefore should I curse
    them?
Would curses kill, as doth the mandrake's groan,
I would invent as bitter-searching terms,
As curst, as harsh and horrible to hear,
Deliver'd strongly through my fixed teeth,
With full as many signs of deadly hate,
As lean-faced Envy in her loathsome cave.

III. ii. 309.

Should I not curse them. Poison be their drink!
Gall, worse than gall, the daintiest that they taste!
Their sweetest shade a grove of cypress-trees!
Their chiefest prospect murdering basilisks!
Their softest touch as smart as lizards' stings!
Their music frightful as the serpent's hiss,
And boding screech-owls make the concert full!
All the foul terrors in dark-seated hell.

III. ii. 320.

Suf. You bade me ban, and will you bid me leave?
Now, by the ground that I am banish'd from,
Well could I curse away a winter's night,
Though standing naked on a mountain top,
Where biting cold would never let grass grow,
And think it but a minute spent in sport.

III. ii. 333.

Comb down his hair; look! look! it stands upright,
Like lime-twigs set to catch my winged soul.
Give me some drink; and bid the apothecary
Bring the strong poison that I bought of him.

III. iii. 15.

Cade.   . . . In Cheapside shall my palfrey go to grass.

IV. ii. 74.

Cade. Ye shall have a hempen caudle then and the help
of hatchet.

IV. vii. 95.

Wherefore, on a brick wall have I climbed into this garden, to see if I can eat grass, or pick a sallet another while, which is not amiss to cool a man's stomach this hot weather. And I think this word "sallet" was born to do me good: for many a time, but for a sallet, my brain-pan had been cleft with a brown bill; and many a time, when I have been dry and bravely marching, it hath served me instead of a quart-pot to drink in; and now the word "sallet" must serve me to feed on.

IV. x. 7.

A sceptre shall it have,—have I a soul,—
On which I'll toss the flower-de-luce of France.

V. i. 10.

War. Now, by my father's badge, old Nevil's crest,
The rampant bear chain'd to the ragged staff,
This day I'll wear aloft my burgonet,
As on a mountain-top the cedar shows
That keeps his leaves in spite of any storm,
Even to affright thee with the view thereof.

V. i. 202.

And beauty that the tyrant oft reclaims
Shall to my flaming wrath be oil and flax.

V. ii. 54.

3 HENRY VI.

I cannot rest
Until the white rose that I wear be dy'd
Even in the lukewarm blood of Henry's heart.

I. ii. 32.

And many strokes, though with a little axe,
Hew down and fell the hardest-timber'd oak.
By many hands your father was subdu'd.

II. i. 54.

Ah, what a life were this! how sweet! how lovely!
Gives not the hawthorn-bush a sweeter shade
To shepherds looking on their silly sheep,
Than doth a rich embroider'd canopy
To kings that fear their subjects' treachery?

II. v. 41.

K. Hen. Woe above woe! grief more than common grief!
O that my death would stay these ruthful deeds!
O pity, pity, gentle heaven, pity!
The red rose and the white are on his face,
The fatal colours of our striving houses:
The one his purple blood right well resembles;
The other his pale cheeks, methinks, presenteth:
Wither one rose, and let the other flourish;
If you contend, a thousand lives must wither.

II. v. 94.

K. Hen. From Scotland am I stol'n, even of pure love,
To greet mine own land with my wishful sight.
No, Harry, Harry, 'tis no land of thine;
Thy place is fill'd, thy sceptre wrung from thee,
Thy balm wash'd off wherewith thou wast anointed:
No bending knee will call thee Cæsar now.

III. i. 13.

And I—like one lost in a thorny wood,
That rends the thorns and is rent with the thorns,
Seeking a way and straying from the way.

III. ii. 174.

Tell him, in hope he'll prove a widower shortly,
I'll wear the willow garland for his sake.

III. iii. 227.

Clar. No, Warwick, thou art worthy of the sway,
To whom the heavens in thy nativity
Adjudg'd an olive branch and laurel crown,
As likely to be blest in peace and war;
And therefore I yield thee my free consent.

IV. vi. 32.

My pity hath been balm to heal their wounds,
My mildness hath allay'd their swelling griefs,
My mercy dried their water-flowing tears.

IV. viii. 41.

Thus yields the cedar to the axe's edge,
Whose arms gave shelter to the princely eagle,
Under whose shade the ramping lion slept,
Whose top-branch over-peer'd Jove's spreading tree
And kept low shrubs from winter's powerful wind.

V. ii. 11.

K. Edw. Brave followers, yonder stands the thorny wood,
Which, by the heavens' assistance and your strength,
Must by the roots be hewn up yet ere night.

V. iv. 67.

What ! can so young a thorn begin to prick ?

V. v. 13.

K. Edw. Once more we sit in England's royal throne,
Re-purchas'd with the blood of enemies.
What valiant foemen, like to autumn's corn,
Have we mow'd down in tops of all their pride ?

V. vii. 1.

RICHARD III.

We say that Shore's wife hath a pretty foot,
A cherry lip, a bonny eye, a passing pleasing tongue ;
And that the queen's kindred are made gentlefolks :
How say you, sir ? can you deny all this ?

I. i. 92.

I pour the helpless balm of my poor eyes.

I. ii. 13.

Glo.   But I was born so high,
Our aery buildeth in the cedar's top,
And dallies with the wind and scorns the sun.

I. iii. 263.

Glo. My lord of Ely, when I was last in Holborn,
I saw good strawberries in your garden there :
I do beseech you send for some of them.

*   *   *   *   *

Ely. Where is my lord protector ? I have sent for these
strawberries.

III. iv. 48.

" Their lips were four red roses on a stalk,
Which in their summer beauty kiss'd each other.
A book of prayers on their pillow lay ;
Which once," quoth Forrest, " almost changed my mind ;
But O ! the devil "—there the villain stopp'd ;

When Dighton thus told on : " We smothered
The most replenished sweet work of nature,
That from the prime creation e'er she fram'd."

IV. iii. 12.

The wretched, bloody, and usurping boar,
That spoil'd your summer fields and fruitful vines,
Swills your warm blood like wash, and makes his trough
In your embowell'd bosoms, this foul swine
Lies now even in the centre of this isle,
Near to the town of Leicester, as we learn.

V. ii. 7.

HENRY VIII.

Surv. Not long before your highness sped to France,
The duke being at the Rose, within the parish
Saint Lawrence Poultney, did of me demand
What was the speech among the Londoners
Concerning the French journey.

I. ii. 151.

Almost no grave allow'd me : like the lily,
That once was mistress of the field and flourish'd,
I'll hang my head and perish.

III. i. 151.

*The Vision. Enter, solemnly tripping one after another, six
personages, clad in white robes, wearing on their heads garlands
of bays, and golden vizards on their faces ; branches of bays or
palm in their hands.*

After IV. ii. 82.

Both now and ever bless her !—'tis a girl,
Promises boys hereafter.   Sir, your queen
Desires your visitation, and to be
Acquainted with this stranger : 'tis as like you
As cherry is to cherry.

V. i. 167.

Port. Belong to the gallows, and be hanged, you rogue !
Is this a place to roar in ?   Fetch me a dozen crab-tree
staves, and strong ones : these are but switches to 'em.   I'll
scratch your heads : you must be seeing christenings ?   Do
you look for ale and cakes here, you rude rascals ?

V. iv. 6.

They fell on: I made good my place; at length they came
to the broom-staff with me; I defied 'em still: when suddenly
a file of boys behind 'em, loose shot, delivered such a shower
of pebbles, that I was fain to draw mine honour in, and let
'em win the work: the devil was amongst 'em, I think,
surely.

V. iv. 56.

Port. These are the youths that thunder at a playhouse,
and fight for bitten apples; that no audience, but the
Tribulation of Tower-hill, or the Limbs of Limehouse, their
dear brothers, are able to endure.

V. iv. 63.

She shall be loved and fear'd: her own shall bless her;
Her foes shake like a field of beaten corn,
And hang their heads with sorrow: good grows with her:
In her days every man shall eat in safety,
Under his own vine, what he plants: and sing
The merry songs of peace to all his neighbours:

        *   *   *   *

So shall she leave her blessedness to one,
When heaven shall call her from this cloud of darkness,
Who from the sacred ashes of her honour
Shall starlike rise, as great in fame as she was,
And so stand fix'd: peace, plenty, love, truth, terror,
That were the servants to this chosen infant,
Shall then be his, and like a vine grow to him:
Wherever the bright sun of heaven shall shine
His honour and the greatness of his name
Shall be, and make new nations: he shall flourish,
And, like a mountain cedar, reach his branches
To all the plains about him: our children's children
Shall see this, and bless heaven.
  K. Hen.   Thou speakest wonders.

V. v. 43.

Cran. She shall be, to the happiness of England,
An aged princess; many days shall see her,
And yet no day without a deed to crown it.
Would I had known no more! but she must die,
She must, the saints must have her: yet a virgin,
A most unspotted lily shall she pass
To the ground, and all the world shall mourn her.

V. v. 57.

TROILUS AND CRESSIDA.

Pan. Well, I have told you enough of this : for my part,
I'll not meddle nor make no further.   He that will have a
cake out of the wheat, must needs tarry the grinding.

I. i. 13.

> I love her ;
> But, saying thus, instead of oil and balm,
> Thou lay'st in every gash that love hath given me
> The knife that made it.

I. i. 60.

Cres. And I'll spring up in his tears, an 'twere a nettle
against May.

I. ii. 190.

Cres. Ay, a minced man : and then to be baked with no
date in the pie,—for then the man's date's out.

I. ii. 277.

> Checks and disasters
> Grow in the veins of actions highest rear'd,
> As knots, by the conflux of meeting sap,
> Infect the sound pine and divert his grain
> Tortive and errant from his course of growth.

I. iii. 5.

> When the splitting wind
> Makes flexible the knees of knotted oaks,
> And flies fled under shade, why, then the thing of courage
> As roused with rage with rage doth sympathize,
> And with an accent tun'd in selfsame key
> Retorts to chiding fortune.

I. iii. 49.

> How could communities,
> Degrees in schools and brotherhoods in cities,
> Peaceful commerce from dividable shores,
> The primogenitive and due of birth,
> Prerogative of age, crowns, sceptres, laurels,
> But by degree, stand in authentic place ?

I. iii. 103.

Ajax. Toadstool, learn me the proclamation.
Ther. Dost thou think I have no sense, thou strikest me
thus ?

II. i. 22.

Ther. Hector shall have a great catch, if he knock out either of your brains : a' were as good crack a fusty nut with no kernel.

II. i. 109.

Tro. No, Pandarus : I stalk about her door,
Like a strange soul upon the Stygian banks
Staying for waftage.   O, be thou my Charon,
And give me swift transportance to those fields
Where I may wallow in the lily beds
Proposed for the deserver !

III. ii. 9.

Pan. Nay, I'll give my word for her too : our kindred, though they be long ere they are wooed, they are constant being won : they are burs, I can tell you ; they'll stick where they are thrown.

III. ii. 115.

Ther. How the devil Luxury, with his fat rump and potato finger, tickles these together !   Fry, lechery, fry !

V. ii. 55.

Ther. The parrot will not do more for an almond than he for a commodious drab.

V. ii. 193.

CORIOLANUS.

1st Cit. Let us kill him, and we'll have corn at our own price.

I. i. 10.

Men.   Though all at once cannot
See what I do deliver out to each,
Yet I can make my audit up, that all
From me do back receive the flour of all,
And leave me but the bran.   What say you to't ?

I. i. 145.

                  He that depends
Upon your favours swims with fins of lead
And hews down oaks with rushes.   Hang ye !   Trust ye ?

I. i. 183.

14—2

Men. For corn at their own rates; whereof, they say,
The city is well stored.

I. i. 193.

Mar.   They are dissolved: hang 'em!
They said they were an-hungry; sighed forth proverbs,
That hunger broke stone walls, that dogs must eat,
That meat was made for mouths, that the gods sent not
Corn for the rich men only: with these shreds
They vented their complainings.

I. i. 207.

Mar.   Nay, let them follow:
The Volsces have much corn; take these rats thither
To gnaw their garners.

I. i. 254.

To a cruel war I sent him; from whence he returned, his
brows bound with oak.

I. iii. 14.

                    Our gates,
Which yet seem shut, we have but pinn'd with rushes;
They'll open of themselves.   Hark you, far off!

I. iv. 16.

Auf. I am attended at the cypress grove: I pray you,
'Tis south the city mills—bring me word thither
How the world goes, that to the pace of it
I may spur on my journey.

I. x. 30.

You wear out a good wholesome forenoon in hearing a
cause between an orange-wife and a fosset-seller; and then
rejourn the controversy of three-pence to a second day of
audience.

II. i. 77.

Vol. On's brows: Menenius, he comes the third time home
with the oaken garland.

II. i. 137.

We have some old crab-trees here at home that will not
Be grafted to your relish.   Yet welcome, warriors:
We call a nettle but a nettle and
The faults of fools but folly.

II. i. 205.

He proved best man i' the field, and for his meed
Was brow-bound with the oak.

II. ii. 101.

1st Cit. And to make us no better thought of, a little help will serve ; for once, when we stood up about the corn, he himself stuck not to call us the many-headed multitude.

II. iii. 15.

Bru.   Call't not a plot:
The people cry you mock'd them, and of late,
When corn was given them gratis, you repined ;
Scandal'd the suppliants for the people, call'd them
Time-pleasers, flatterers, foes to nobleness.

III. i. 41.

Cor.   Tell me of corn !
This was my speech, and I will speak't again—
  Men. Not now, not now.
  1st Sen.   Not in this heat, sir, now.
  Cor. Now, as I live, I will.   My nobler friends,
I crave their pardons :
For the mutable, rank-scented many, let them
Regard me as I do not flatter, and
Therein behold themselves : I say again,
In soothing them, we nourish 'gainst our senate
The cockle of rebellion, insolence, sedition,
Which we ourselves have plough'd for, sow'd and scatter'd,
By mingling them with us, the honour'd number,
Who lack not virtue, no, nor power, but that
Which they have given to beggars.

III. i. 61.

  Cor. Whoever gave that counsel, to give forth
The corn o' the storehouse gratis, as 'twas used
Sometime in Greece,—
  Men.   Well, well, no more of that.
  Cor. Though there the people had more absolute power,
I say, they nourish'd disobedience, fed
The ruin of the state.
  Bru.   Why, shall the people give
One that speaks thus their voice ?
  Cor.   I'll give my reasons,
More worthier than their voices.   They know the corn
Was not our recompense, resting well assured
They ne'er did service for't: being press'd to the war,
Even when the navel of the state was touch'd,
They would not thread the gates.   This kind of service
Did not deserve corn gratis.   Being i' the war,
Their mutinies and revolts, wherein they show'd
Most valour, spoke not for them : the accusation
Which they have often made against the senate,

All cause unborn, could never be the motive
Of our so frank donation.

III. i. 114.

            Thy stout heart,
Now humble as the ripest mulberry
That will not hold the handling.

III. ii. 78.

   Cor.   Scratches with briers,
Scars to move laughter only.

III. iii. 52.

            Let me twine
Mine arms about that body, where against
My grained ash an hundred times hath broke,
And scarr'd the moon with splinters : here I clip
The anvil of my sword.

IV. v. 112.

         You that stood so much
Upon the voice of occupation and
The breath of garlic-eaters.

IV. vi. 96.

   Men.   For one poor grain or two !
I am one of those ; his mother, wife, his child,
And this brave fellow too, we are the grains :
You are the musty chaff, and you are smelt
Above the moon : we must be burnt for you.

V. i. 28.

   2nd Sen. The worthy fellow is our general : he is the rock,
the oak not to be wind-shaken.

V. ii. 116.

         Then let the mutinous winds
Strike the proud cedars 'gainst the fiery sun :
Murdering impossibility, to make
What cannot be, slight work.

V. iii. 59.

And bear the palm for having bravely shed
Thy wife and children's blood.

V. iii. 117.

To tear with thunder the wide cheeks o' the air,
And yet to charge thy sulphur with a bolt
That should but rive an oak.   Why dost not speak ?

V. iii. 151.

The tartness of his face sours ripe grapes : when he walks,
he moves like an engine, and the ground shrinks before his
treading : he is able to pierce a corslet with his eye.

V. iv. 18.

TITUS ANDRONICUS.

Cometh Andronicus, bound with laurel boughs,
To re-salute his country with his tears,
Tears of true joy for his return to Rome.
Thou great defender of this Capitol.

I. i. 74.

Tam. Have I not reason, think you, to look pale ?
These two have 'tic'd me hither to this place :
A barren detested vale you see it is ;
The trees, though summer, yet forlorn and lean,
O'ercome with moss and baleful mistletoe :
Here never shines the sun ; here nothing breeds,
Unless the nightly owl or fatal raven :
And when they show'd me this abhorred pit,
They told me, here, at dead time of the night,
A thousand fiends, a thousand hissing snakes,
Ten thousand swelling toads, as many urchins,
Would make such fearful and confused cries
As any mortal body hearing it,
Should straight fall mad, or else die suddenly.
No sooner had they told this hellish tale,
But straight they told me they would bind me here
Unto the body of a dismal yew,
And leave me to this miserable death.

II. iii. 91.

Dem. Stay, madam ; here is more belongs to her ;
First thrash the corn, then after burn the straw.

II. iii. 122.

Quin. What, art thou fall'n ?   What subtle hole is this,
Whose mouth is cover'd with rude-growing briers,
Upon whose leaves are drops of new-shed blood
As fresh as morning's dew distilled on flowers ?

II. iii. 198.

Sat. [*Reads*] " An if we miss to meet him handsomely—
Sweet huntsman, Bassianus 'tis we mean—
Do thou so much as dig the grave for him :
Thou know'st our meaning.   Look for thy reward
Among the nettles at the elder-tree

Which overshades the mouth of that same pit
Where we decreed to bury Bassianus.
Do this, and purchase us thy lasting friends."
O Tamora! was ever heard the like?
This is the pit, and this the elder-tree.
Look, sirs, if you can find the huntsman out
That should have murdered Bassianus here.

II. iii. 268.

O, had the monster seen those lily hands
Tremble, like aspen-leaves, upon a lute.

II. iv. 44.

When I did name her brothers, then fresh tears
Stood on her cheeks, as doth the honey-dew
Upon a gather'd lily almost wither'd.

III. i. 111.

Tit. He doth me wrong to feed me with delays.
I'll dive into the burning lake below,
And pull her out of Acheron by the heels.
Marcus, we are but shrubs, no cedars we,
No big-boned men framed of the Cyclops' size.

IV. iii. 42.

Sat. Is warlike Lucius general of the Goths?
These tidings nip me, and I hang the head
As flowers with frost or grass beat down with storms.

IV. iv. 69.

I will enchant the old Andronicus
With words more sweet, and yet more dangerous,
Than baits to fish, or honey-stalks to sheep,
When as the one is wounded with the bait,
The other rotted with delicious feed.

IV. iv. 89.

O, let me teach you how to knit again
This scatter'd corn into one mutual sheaf,
These broken limbs again into one body.

V. iii. 70.

ROMEO AND JULIET.

Where, underneath the grove of sycamore
That westward rooteth from the city's side,
So early walking did I see your son.

I. i. 128.

Rom. Your plaintain-leaf is excellent for that.

I. ii. 52

'Tis since the earthquake now eleven years ;
And she was wean'd,—I never shall forget it,—
Of all the days of the year, upon that day :
For I had then laid wormwood to my dug,
Sitting in the sun under the dove-house wall ;
My lord and you were then at Mantua :—
Nay, I do bear a brain :—but, as I said,
When it did taste the wormwood on the nipple
Of my dug and felt it bitter, pretty fool,
To see it tetchy and fall out with the dug !
' Shake ' quoth the dove-house : 'twas no need, I trow,
To bid me trudge.

I. iii. 23.

Rom. Is love a tender thing ? it is too rough,
Too rude, too boisterous, and it pricks like thorn.

I. iv. 25.

Ben. Come, knock and enter ; and no sooner in,
But every man betake him to his legs.
Rom. A torch for me : let wantons light of heart
Tickle the senseless rushes with their heels.

I. iv. 33.

Her chariot is an empty hazel-nut
Made by the joiner squirrel or old grub,
Time out of mind the fairies' coachmakers.

I. iv. 67.

Mer. If love be blind, love cannot hit the mark.
Now will he sit under a medlar-tree,
And wish his mistress were that kind of fruit
As maids call medlars, when they laugh alone.
O, Romeo, that she were, O, that she were
An open et cætera, thou a poperin pear !
Romeo, good-night : I'll to my truckle-bed ;
This field-bed is too cold for me to sleep :
Come, shall we go ?

II. i. 33.

O, be some other name !
What's in a name ? that which we call a rose
By any other name would smell as sweet.

II. ii. 42.

Rom. Lady, by yonder blessed moon I swear
That tips with silver all these fruit-tree tops.

II. ii. 107.

Now, ere the sun advance his burning eye,
The day to cheer and night's dank dew to dry,
I must up-fill this osier cage of ours
With baleful weeds and precious-juiced flowers
The earth that's nature's mother is her tomb.

II. iii. 5.

Mer. Nay, I am the very pink of courtesy.
Rom. Pink for flower.
Mer. Right.
Rom. Why, then, is my pump well flowered.
Mer. Well said: follow me this jest now till thou hast
worn out thy pump, that when the single sole of it is worn,
the jest may remain after the wearing sole singular.

II. iv. 61.

Mer. Thy wit is a very bitter sweeting: it is a most sharp
sauce.
Rom. And is it not well served in to a sweet goose?

II. iv. 83.

Nurse. . . . Doth not rosemary and Romeo begin both
with a letter?
Rom. Ay, nurse: what of that? both with an R.
Nurse. Ah, mocker! that's the dog's name; R is for the——
No; I know it begins with some other letter:—and she hath
the prettiest sententious of it, of you and rosemary, that it
would do you good to hear it.

II. iv. 219.

Thou wilt quarrel with a man for cracking nuts, having no
other reason but because thou hast hazel eyes.

III. i. 20.

I am peppered, I warrant, for this world.

III. i. 102.

Jul. Wilt thou be gone? it is not yet near day:
It was the nightingale, and not the lark,
That pierced the fearful hollow of thine ear;
Nightly she sings on yon pomegranate-tree:
Believe me, love, it was the nightingale.

III. v. 1.

The roses in thy lips and cheeks shall fade
To paly ashes, thy eyes' windows fall,
Like death, when he shuts up the day of life.

IV. i. 99.

What with loathsome smells,
And shrieks like mandrakes' torn out of the earth,
That living mortals, hearing them, run mad.

IV. iii. 46.

La. Cap. Hold, take these keys, and fetch more spices,
nurse.
Nurse. They call for dates and quinces in the pastry.

IV. iv. 1.

Dry up your tears, and stick your rosemary
On this fair corse ; and, as the custom is,
In all her best array bear her to church :
For though fond nature bids us all lament,
Yet nature's tears are reason's merriment.

IV. v. 79.

About his shelves
A beggarly account of empty boxes,
Green earthen pots, bladders and musty seeds,
Remnants of packthread and old cakes of roses,
Were thinly scatter'd, to make up a show.

V. i. 44.

Under yond yew-trees lay thee all along,
Holding thine ear close to the hollow ground.

V. iii. 3.

Bal. As I did sleep under this yew-tree here,
I dreamt my master and another fought,
And that my master slew him.

V. iii. 137.

TIMON OF ATHENS.

Alcib. Is this the balsam that the usuring senate
Pours into captains' wounds ?   Banishment !

III. v. 110.

. . . Rose-cheeked youth.

IV. iii. 87.

O, a root,—dear thanks !—
Dry up thy marrows, vines, and plough-torn leas ;
Whereof ingrateful man, with liquorish draughts
And morsels unctuous, greases his pure mind,
That from it all consideration slips !

IV. iii. 192.

Will these moss'd trees,
That have outlived the eagle, page thy heels,
And skip where thou point'st out?   Will the cold brook,
Candied with ice, caudle thy morning taste,
To cure thy o'er-night's surfeit!

IV. iii. 223.

That numberless upon me stuck as leaves
Do on the oak, have with one winter's brush
Fell from their boughs and left me open, bare
For every storm that blows: I, to bear this,
That never knew but better, is some burden.

IV. iii. 263.

Apem. There's a medlar for thee, eat it.
Tim. On what I hate I feed not.
Apem. Dost hate a medlar?
Tim. Ay, though it look like thee.
Apem. An thou hadst hated meddlers sooner, thou shouldst
have loved thyself better now.   What man didst thou ever
know unthrift that was beloved after his means?

IV. iii. 305.

Tim. Your greatest want is, you want much of meat.
Why should you want?   Behold, the earth hath roots;
Within this mile break forth a hundred springs;
The oaks bear mast, the briers scarlet hips;
The bounteous housewife, nature, on each bush
Lays her full mess before you.   Want? why want?
1st Ban. We cannot live on grass, on berries, water,
As beasts and birds and fishes.

IV. iii. 419.

Go, suck the subtle blood o' the grape,
Till the high fever seethe your blood to froth.

IV. iii. 432.

Pain. Nothing else: you shall see him a palm in Athens
again, and flourish with the highest.

V. i. 12.

1st Sen.   Noble and young,
When thy first griefs were but a mere conceit,
Ere thou hadst power or we had cause of fear,
We sent to thee, to give thy rages balm,
To wipe out our ingratitude with loves
Above their quantity.

V. iv. 14.

> Bring me into your city,
> And I will use the olive with my sword,
> Make war breed peace, make peace stint war, make each
> Prescribe to other as each other's leech.
> Let our drums strike.

V. iv. 81.

JULIUS CÆSAR.

And bear the palm alone.

I. ii. 131.

Casca. Are not you mov'd, when all the sway of earth
Shakes like a thing unfirm? O Cicero,
I have seen tempests when the scolding winds
Have riv'd the knotty oaks, and I have seen
The ambitious ocean swell and rage and foam,
To be exalted with the threatening clouds:
But never till to-night, never till now,
Did I go through a tempest dropping fire.

I. iii. 3.

MACBETH.

1st Witch. A sailor's wife had chestnuts in her lap,
And munch'd, and munch'd, and munch'd.

I. iii. 4.

Ban. Were such things here as we do speak about?
Or have we eaten on the insane root
That takes the reason prisoner?

I. iii. 83.

Sleep that knits up the ravell'd sleave of care,
The death of each day's life, sore labour's bath,
Balm of hurt minds, great nature's second course,
Chief nourisher in life's feast.

II. ii. 37.

I had thought to have let in some of all professions that go
the primrose way to the everlasting bonfire.

II. iii. 20.

3rd Witch. Scale of dragon, tooth of wolf,
Witches' mummy, maw and gulf
Of the ravin'd salt-sea shark,

Root of hemlock digg'd i' the dark,
Liver of blaspheming Jew,
Gall of goat, and slips of yew
Silver'd in the moon's eclipse,
Nose of Turk, and Tartar's lips.

IV. i. 22.

Macb. Go prick thy face, and over-red thy fear,
Thou lily-liver'd boy.   What soldiers, patch?
Death of thy soul! those linen cheeks of thine
Are counsellors to fear.   What soldiers, whey-face?

V. iii. 14.

Macb. What rhubarb, cyme, or what purgative drug
Would scour these English hence?   Hear'st thou of them?

V. iii. 55.

HAMLET.

A violet in the youth of primy nature,
Forward, not permanent, sweet, not lasting,
The perfume and suppliance of a minute;
No more.

I. iii. 7.

But, good my brother,
Do not, as some ungracious pastors do,
Show me the steep and thorny way to heaven;
Whiles, like a puff'd and reckless libertine,
Himself the primrose path of dalliance treads,
And recks not his own rede.

I. iii. 46.

Brief let me be.   Sleeping within mine orchard,
My custom always of the afternoon,
Upon my secure hour thy uncle stole,
With juice of cursed hebenon in a vial,
And in the porches of my ears did pour
The leperous distilment; whose effect
Holds such an enmity with blood of man
That quick as quicksilver it courses through
The natural gates and alleys of the body.

I. v. 59.

Ham. Slanders, sir: for the satirical rogue says here that
old men have gray beards, that their faces are wrinkled,
their eyes purging thick amber and plum-tree gum, and
that they have a plentiful lack of wit, together with most

weak hams: all which, sir, though I most powerfully
and potently believe, yet I hold it not honestly to have it
thus set down, for yourself, sir, should be old as I am, if
like a crab you could go backward.

II. ii. 198.

Ham. O God, I could be bounded in a nutshell and count
myself a king of infinite space, were it not that I have bad
dreams.

II. ii. 260.

The expectancy and rose of the fair state.

III. i. 160.

Ham. [*Aside*]   Wormwood, wormwood.

III. ii. 191.

Ham. Ay, sir but, " while the grass grows,"—the proverb
is something musty.

III. ii. 358.

Ham.   Such an act
That blurs the grace and blush of modesty,
Calls virtue hypocrite, takes off the rose.

III. iv. 40.

Like a mildew'd ear.

III. iv. 64.

. . . He keeps them, like an ape, in the corner of his jaw.
IV. ii. 17.

Hor. She speaks much of her father; says she hears
There's tricks i' the world ; and hems and beats her heart;
Spurns enviously at straws; speaks things in doubt.

IV. v. 4.

[*Singing.*]
He is dead and gone, lady,
   He is dead and gone;
At his head a grass-green turf,
   At his heels a stone.

IV. v. 29.

Larded with sweet flowers;
Which bewept to the grave did go
   With true-love showers.

IV. v. 37.

O heat, dry up my brains! tears seven times salt,
Burn out the sense and virtue of mine eye!
By heaven, thy madness shall be paid by weight,
Till our scale turn the beam. O rose of May!
Dear maid, kind sister, sweet Ophelia!
O heavens! is 't possible, a young maid's wits
Should be as mortal as an old man's life?
Nature is fine in love, and where 'tis fine,
It sends some precious instance of itself
After the thing it loves.

IV. v. 155.

Oph. There's rosemary, that's for remembrance; pray,
love, remember: and there is pansies, that's for thoughts.
Laer. A document in madness, thoughts and remembrance
fitted.
Oph. There's fennel for you, and columbines: there's rue
for you; and here's some for me: we may call it herb-grace
o' Sundays: O, you must wear your rue with a difference.
There's a daisy: I would give you some violets, but they
withered all when my father died.

IV. v. 175.

And will he not come again?
And will he not come again?
No, no, he is dead:
Go to thy death-bed:
He never will come again.

His beard was as white as snow,
All flaxen was his poll:
He is gone, he is gone,
And we cast away moan:
God ha' mercy on his soul!

IV. v. 190.

Queen. There is a willow grows aslant a brook,
That shows his hoar leaves in the glassy stream;
There with fantastic garlands did she come
Of crow-flowers, nettles, daisies, and long purples
That liberal shepherds give a grosser name,
But our cold maids do dead men's fingers call them:
There, on the pendent boughs her coronet weeds
Clambering to hang, an envious sliver broke;
When down her weedy trophies and herself
Fell in the weeping brook.

IV. vii. 167.

Laer.   Lay her i' the earth :
And from her fair and unpolluted flesh
May violets spring ! I tell thee, churlish priest,
A ministering angel shall my sister be,
When thou liest howling.

V. i. 261.

Ham. An earnest conjuration from the king,
As England was his faithful tributary,
As love between them like the palm might flourish,
As peace should still her wheaten garland wear,
And stand a comma 'tween their amities,
And many-such like 'As'es of great charge,
That, on the view and know of these contents,
Without debatement further, more or less,
He should the bearers put to sudden death
Not shriving-time allow'd.

V. ii. 38.

KING LEAR.

                          Now, our joy,
Although our last, not least ; to whose young love
The vines of France and milk of Burgundy
Strive to be interess'd.

I. i. 84.

France.   This is most strange,
That she, that even but now was your best object,
The argument of your praise, balm of your age,
The best, the dearest, should in this of trice of time
Commit a thing so monstrous, to dismantle
So many folds of favour.

I. i. 216.

              He that keeps nor crust nor crumb,
                  Weary of all, shall want some.
          That's a shealed peascod.

I. iv. 217.

Fool. Shalt see, thy other daughter will use thee kindly;
for though she's as like this as a crab's like an apple, yet I
can tell what I can tell.
Lear. Why, what canst thou tell, my boy ?
Fool. She will taste as like this as a crab does to a crab.
Thou canst tell why one's nose stands i' the middle on's
face ?

I. v. 13.

15

A lily-livered, action-taking knave.

II. ii. 18.

The country gives me proof and precedent
Of Bedlam beggars, who, with roaring voices,
Strike in their numb'd and mortified bare arms
Pins, wooden pricks, nails, sprigs of rosemary ;
And with this horrible object, from low farms,
Poor pelting villages, sheep-cotes, and mills,
Sometime with lunatic bans, sometime with prayers,
Enforce their charity.   Poor Turlygod ! poor Tom !
That's something yet : Edgar I nothing am.

II. iii. 13.

   Lear. Blow, winds, and crack your cheeks ! rage ! blow !
You cataracts and hurricanoes, spout
Till you have drench'd our steeples, drown'd the cocks !
You sulphurous and thought-executing fires,
Vaunt-couriers to oak-cleaving thunderbolts,
Singe my white head !   And thou all-shaking thunder,
Strike flat the thick rotundity o' the world !
Crack nature's moulds, all germens spill at once,
That make ingrateful man !

III. ii. 1.

   Edg. Still through the sharp hawthorn blows the wind.

III. iv. 102.

   Edg. This is the foul fiend Flibbertigibbet : he begins at
curfew, and walks to the first cock ; he gives the web and
the pin, squints the eye, and makes the hare-lip ; mildews the
white wheat, and hurts the poor creature of earth.

III. iv. 120.

   Edg. Sleepest or wakest thou, jolly shepherd ?
       Thy sheep be in the corn ;
      And for one blast of thy miniken mouth,
       Thy sheep shall take no harm.

III. vi. 43.

   Reg. Ingrateful fox ! 'tis he.
   Corn. Bind fast his corky arms.

III. vii. 27.

   3rd Serv. Go thou : I'll fetch some flax and whites of
      eggs
To apply to his bleeding face.   Now, heaven help him !

III. vii. 106.

Cor. Alack, 'tis he : why, he was met even now
As mad as the vex'd sea : singing aloud ;
Crown'd with rank fumiter and furrow weeds,
With burdocks, hemlock, nettles, cuckoo-flowers,
Darnel, and all the idle weeds that grow
In our sustaining corn.   A century send forth ;
Search every acre in the high-grown field,
And bring him to our eye.

IV. iv. 1.

Half way down
Hangs one that gathers samphire, dreadful trade !

IV. vi. 14.

Edg. Sweet marjoram.
Lear. Pass.
Glo. I know that voice.

IV. vi. 94.

Capt. I cannot draw a cart, nor eat dried oats ;
If it be man's work, I will do't.

V. iii. 38.

OTHELLO.

Iago. Virtue ! a fig ! 'tis in ourselves that we are thus or
thus. Our bodies are our gardens, to the which our wills are
gardeners ; so that if we will plant nettles, or sow lettuce,
set hyssop and weed up thyme, supply it with one gender of
herbs, or distract it with many, either to have it sterile with
idleness, or manured with industry, why, the power and
corrigible authority of this lies in our wills.

I. iii. 322.

The food that to him now is as luscious as locusts, shall be
to him shortly as bitter as coloquintida. She must change
for youth.

I. iii. 354.

Mon. Methinks the wind hath spoken loud at land ;
A fuller blast ne'er shook our battlements :
If it hath ruffian'd so upon the sea,
What ribs of oak, when mountains melt on them,
Can hold the mortise ? What shall we hear of this ?

II. i. 4.

15—2

Iago. Blessed fig's-end! the wine she drinks is made of grapes: if she had been blessed, she would never have loved the Moor. Blessed pudding! Didst thou not see her paddle with the palm of his hand? didst not mark that?

II. i. 256.

Iago.		Why, go to then;
She that, so young, could give out such a seeming,
To seel her father's eyes up close as oak
He thought 'twas witchcraft—but I am much to blame;
I humbly do beseech you of your pardon
For too much loving you.

III. iii. 208.

Iago. Nay, but be wise: yet we see nothing done;
She may be honest yet. Tell me but this,
Have you not sometimes seen a handkerchief
Spotted with strawberries in your wife's hand?

III. iii. 432.

Look, where he comes!

Enter OTHELLO.

			Not poppy, nor mandragora,
Nor all the drowsy syrups of the world,
Shall ever medicine thee to that sweet sleep
Which thou owedst yesterday.

III. iii. 330.

Des. My mother had a maid call'd Barbara:
She was in love, and he she lov'd prov'd mad
And did forsake her: she had a song of "willow";
An old thing 'twas, but it express'd her fortune,
And she died singing it: that song to-night
Will not go from my mind; I have much to do,
But to go hang my head all at one side,
And sing it like poor Barbara.

IV. iii 26.

The poor soul sat sighing by a sycamore tree,
	Sing all a green willow;
Her hand on her bosom, her head on her knee,
	Sing, willow, willow, willow:
The fresh streams ran by her, and murmur'd her moans;
	Sing willow, willow, willow;
Her salt tears fell from her, and soften'd the stones;—
Lay by these:—
	Sing willow, willow, willow;
Prithee, hie thee; he'll come anon:—
	Sing all a green willow must be my garland.

Let nobody blame him ; his scorn I approve,—
Nay, that's not next.—Hark ! who is't that knocks ?
  Emil. It's the wind.
  Des. [*Singing*]
I call'd my love false love ; but what said he then ?
  Sing willow, willow, willow :
If I court moe women, you'll couch with moe men.
IV. iii. 41.

        When I have pluck'd thy rose,
I cannot give it vital growth again,
It must needs wither : I'll smell it on the tree.
[*Kissing her.*
Ah, balmy breath, that dost almost persuade
Justice to break her sword !   One more, one more.
V. ii. 13.

  Emil.   What did thy song bode, lady ?
Hark, canst thou hear me ?   I will play the swan,
And die in music :   [*Singing*] Willow, willow, willow.—
Moor, she was chaste ; she lov'd thee, cruel Moor ;
So come my soul to bliss, as I speak true ;
So speaking as I think, I die, I die.
V. ii. 247.

Do you go back dismay'd ? 'tis a lost fear ;
Man but a rush against Othello's breast,
And he retires.   Where should Othello go ?
V. ii. 269.

        Of one whose subdu'd eyes,
Albeit unused to the melting mood,
Drop tears as fast as the Arabian trees
Their medicinal gum.
V. ii. 348.

ANTONY AND CLEOPATRA.

  Char. O excellent ! I love long life better than figs.
I. ii. 32.

And all the gods go with you ! upon your sword
Sit laurel victory ! and smooth success
Be strew'd before your feet !
I. iii. 99.

  Cleo. Give me to drink mandragora.
  Char.   Why, madam ?
  Cleo. That I might sleep out this great gap of time
My Antony is away.
I. v. 4.

Cleo.   My salad days
When I was green in judgment.

I. v. 73.

Pom.   You have made me offer
Of Sicily, Sardinia ; and I must
Rid all the sea of pirates ; then, to send
Measures of wheat to Rome ; this 'greed upon,
To part with unhack'd edges, and bear back
Our targes undinted.

II. vi. 34.

2nd Serv. Why, this it is to have a name in great men's
fellowship : I had as lief have a reed that will do me no
service as a partisan I could not heave.

II. vii. 12.

Come, thou monarch of the vine,
Plumpy Bacchus, with pink eyne !
In thy vats our cares be drown'd,
With thy grapes our hairs be crown'd :
  Cup us, till the world go round,
  Cup us, till the world go round !

II. vii. 120.

Eros. He's walking in the garden—thus ; and spurns
The rush that lies before him ; cries, "Fool Lepidus !"

III. v. 17.

Euph. I was of late as petty to his ends
As is the morn-dew on the myrtle-leaf
To his grand sea.

III. xii. 8.

Ant. To him again : tell him he wears the rose
Of youth upon him ; from which the world should note
Something particular ; his coin, ships, legions.

III. xiii. 20.

Cleo. What, no more ceremony ? See, my women !
Against the blown rose may they stop their nose,
That kneel'd unto the buds.

III. xiii. 38.

Eno.   What mean you, sir,
To give them this discomfort ? Look, they weep ;
And I, an ass, am onion-ey'd : for shame,
Transform us not to women.

IV. ii. 33.

Cæs. The time of universal peace is near :
Prove this a prosperous day, the three-nook'd world
Shall bear the olive freely.

IV. vi. 4.

Ant.   Where yond' pine does stand,
   *   *   *   *   *   *
Do we shake hands.   All come to this?   The hearts
That spaniel'd me at heels, to whom I gave
Their wishes, do discandy, melt their sweets
On blossoming Cæsar ; and this pine is bark'd,
That overtopp'd them all.

IV. xii. 1.

Guard.   Here is a rural fellow
That will not be denied your highness' presence :
He brings you figs.

V. ii. 233.

Immortal longings in me : now no more
The juice of Egypt's grape shall moist this lip.

V. ii. 284.

Char.   O, break ! O, break !
Cleo. As sweet as balm, as soft as air, as gentle.

V. ii. 313.

A simple countryman, that brought her figs.

V. ii. 342.

1st Guard. This is an aspic's trail ; and these fig-leaves
Have slime upon them, such as the aspic leaves
Upon the caves of Nile.

V. ii. 354.

CYMBELINE.

            So, so : well done, well done :
The violets, cowslips, and the primroses,
Bear to my closet.   Fare thee well, Pisanio ;
Think on my words.

I. v. 82.

                              Cytherea,
How bravely thou becom'st thy bed, fresh lily,
And whiter than the sheets !   That I might touch !
But kiss; one kiss !
                                        II. ii. 14.

                    On her left breast
A mole cinque-spotted, like the crimson drops
I' the bottom of a cowslip : here's a voucher,
Stronger than ever law could make : this secret
Will force him think I have pick'd the lock and ta'en
The treasure of her honour.
                                        II. ii. 36.

          Hark, hark ! the lark at heaven's gate sings,
              And Phœbus 'gins arise,
          His steeds to water at those springs
              On chaliced flowers that lies ;
          And winking Mary-buds begin
              To ope their golden eyes :
          With everything that pretty is,
              My lady sweet, arise,
                  Arise, arise !
                                        II. iii. 21.

                    Perchance he spoke not, but,
Like a full-acorn'd boar, a German one,
Cried " O !" and mounted ; found no opposition
But what he look'd for should oppose and she
Should from encounter guard.
                                        II. v. 15.

And let the stinking elder, grief, untwine,
His perishing root with the increasing vine !
                                        IV. ii. 59.

                    They are so gentle
As zephyrs blowing below the violet,
Not wagging his sweet head ;
                                        IV. ii. 171.

                    And yet as rough,
Their royal blood enchafed, as the rudest wind,
That by the top doth take the mountain pine.
                                        IV. ii. 171.

   Gui.   O sweetest, fairest lily !
My brother wears thee not the one half so well
As when thou grew'st thyself.
                                        IV. ii. 201.

Arv.   With fairest flowers
While summer lasts and I live here, Fidele,
I'll sweeten thy sad grave : thou shalt not lack
The flower that's like thy face, pale primrose, nor
The azured harebell, like thy veins, no, nor
The leaf of eglantine, whom not to slander,
Out-sweeten'd not thy breath : the ruddock would,
With charitable bill—O bill, sore-shaming
Those rich-left heirs that let their fathers lie
Without a monument !—bring thee all this ;
Yea, and furr'd moss besides, when flowers are none,
To winter-ground thy corse.

                                        IV. ii. 218.

    Arv.   Fear no more the frown o' the great ;
            Thou art past the tyrant's stroke ;
            Care no more to clothe and eat ;
            To thee the reed is as the oak :
            The sceptre, learning, physic, must
            All follow this, and come to dust.

                                        IV. ii. 264.

Luc.   Let us
Find out the prettiest daisied plot we can,
And make him with our pikes and partisans
A grave : come, arm him.

                                        IV. ii. 397.

    " When from a stately cedar shall be lopped branches,
which, being dead many years, shall after revive, be jointed
to the old stock, and freshly grow ; then shall Posthumus end
his miseries, Britain be fortunate and flourish in peace and
plenty."

                                        V. iv. 140.

    Sooth. The lofty cedar, royal Cymbeline,
Personates thee : and thy lopp'd branches point
Thy two sons forth ; who, by Belarius stol'n,
For many years thought dead, are now revived,
To the majestic cedar join'd ; whose issue
Promises Britain peace and plenty.

                                        V. v. 453.

PERICLES, PRINCE OF TYRE.

And these our ships, you happily may think,
Are like the Trojan horse was stuff'd within
With bloody veins, expecting overthrow,
Are stored with corn to make your needy bread,
And give them life whom hunger starved half dead.

I. iv. 92.

Cle.   Fear not, my lord, but think
Your grace, that fed my country with your corn,
For which the people's prayers still fall upon you,
Must in your child be thought on.

III. iii. 17.

Mar. No, I will rob Tellus of her weed,
To strew thy green with flowers : the yellows, blues,
The purple violets, and marigolds,
Shall as a carpet hang upon thy grave,
While summer days do last. Ay me! poor maid,
Born in a tempest, when my mother died,
This world to me is like a lasting storm,
Whirring me from my friends.

IV. i. 14.

A thornier piece of ground.

IV. vi. 153.

Boult. For flesh and blood, sir, white and red, you shall
see a rose ; and she were a rose, indeed, if she had but——

IV. vi. 37.

Bawd. She conjures : away with her! Would she had
never come within my doors! Marry, hang you! She's
born to undo us. Will you not go the way of women-kind ?
Marry, come up, my dish of chastity with rosemary and bays.

IV. vi. 155.

Gow.   And with her neeld composes
Nature's own shape, of bud, bird, branch, or berry,
That even her art sisters the natural roses ;
Her inkle, silk, twin with the rubied cherry.

V. i. 5.

VENUS AND ADONIS.

Even as the sun with purple-colour'd face
Had ta'en his last leave of the weeping morn,
Rose-cheek'd Adonis hied him to the chase.

L. 3.

" Thrice fairer than myself," thus she began,
" The field's chief flower, sweet above compare,
Stain to all nymphs, more lovely than a man,
More white and red than doves or roses are."

L. 7.

" Thus he that overruled, I oversway'd,
Leading him prisoner in a red-rose chain."

L. 109.

These blue-vein'd violets whereon we lean
Never can blab, nor know not what we mean.

L. 125.

" Witness this primrose bank whereon I lie ;
These forceless flowers like sturdy trees support me."

L. 151.

Narcissus so himself himself forsook,
And died to kiss his shadow in the brook.

L. 161.

Herbs for their smell, and sappy plants to bear ;
Things growing to themselves are growth's abuse :
Seeds spring from seeds and beauty breedeth beauty.

L. 165.

And when from thence he struggles to be gone,
She locks her lily fingers one in one.

L. 227.

" Within this limit is relief enough,
Sweet bottom-grass and high delightful plain,
Round rising hillocks brakes obscure and rough,
To shelter thee from tempest and from rain."

L. 236.

Full gently now she takes him by the hand,
A lily prison'd in a gaol of snow.

L. 361.

" Who wears a garment shapeless and unfinish'd
Who plucks the bud before one leaf put forth ?
If springing things be any jot diminish'd,
They wither in their prime, prove nothing worth."

L. 415.

Or as the berry breaks before it staineth.

L. 460.

For on the grass she lies as she were slain,
Till his breath breatheth life in her again.

L. 473.

The mellow plum doth fall, the green sticks fast,
Or being early pluck'd is sour to taste.

L. 527.

What though the rose have prickles, yet 'tis pluck'd.

L. 574.

            Whereat a sudden pale,
Like lawn being spread upon the blushing rose,
Usurps her cheeks.

L. 589.

Even as poor birds, deceived with painted grapes,
Do surfeit by the eye and pine the maw,
Even so she languisheth in her mishaps,
As those poor birds that helpless berries saw.

L. 601.

The thorny brambles and embracing bushes,
As fearful of him, part.

L. 629.

Each envious brier his weary legs doth scratch,
Each shadow makes him stop, each murmur stay.

L. 705.

The sun ariseth in his majesty ;
Who doth the world so gloriously behold
That cedar-tops and hills seem burnish'd gold.

L. 857.

This said, she hasteth to a myrtle grove.

L. 865.

And as she runs, the bushes in the way
Some catch her by the neck, some kiss her face,
Some twine about her thigh to make her stay.

L. 871.

" Hard-favour'd tyrant, ugly, meagre, lean,
Hateful divorce of love "—thus chides she Death—
" Grim-grinning ghost, earth's worm, what dost thou mean
To stifle beauty and to steal his breath,
Who when he lived, his breath and beauty set
Gloss on the rose, smell to the violet ?"

L. 931.

" Hadst thou but bid beware, then he had spoke,
And, hearing him, thy power had lost his power.
The Destinies well curse thee for this stroke;
They bid thee crop a weed, thou pluck'st a flower :
Love's golden arrow at him should have fled,
And not death's ebon dart, to strike him dead."

L. 943.

Whose wonted lily white
With purple tears, that his wound wept, was drench'd ;
No flower was nigh, no grass, herb, leaf, or weed,
But stole his blood and seem'd with him to bleed.

L. 1053.

Would bring him mulberries, and ripe-red cherries ;
He fed them with his sight, they him with berries.

L. 1103.

By this, the boy that by her side lay kill'd
Was melted like a vapour from her sight,
And in his blood that on the ground lay spill'd,
A purple flower sprung up, checquer'd with white,
Resembling well his pale cheeks and the blood
Which in round drops upon their whiteness stood.

L. 1165.

LUCRECE.

Their silent war of lilies and of roses,
Which Tarquin viewed in her fair face's field.

L. 71.

For one sweet grape who will the vine destroy ?
Or what fond beggar, but to touch the crown,
Would with the sceptre straight be strucken down ?

L. 215.

O how her fear did make her colour rise !
First red as roses that on lawn we lay,
Then white as lawn, the roses took away.

L. 257.

As corn o'ergrown by weeds, so heedful fear
Is almost chok'd by unresisted lust.
Away he steals with open listening ear,
Full of fell hope and full of fond mistrust ;
Both which, as servitors to the unjust,
So cross him with their opposite persuasion,
That now he vows a league, and now invasion.

L. 281.

And being lighted, by the light he spies
Lucretia's glove, wherein her needle sticks :
He takes it from the rushes where it lies,
And gripping it, the needle his finger pricks ;
As who should say, " This glove to wanton tricks
    Is not inured ; return again in haste ;
    Thou see't our mistress' ornaments are chaste."
                                                    L. 316.

Her lily hand her rosy cheek lies under,
Cozening the pillow of a lawful kiss.
                                                    L. 386.

Without the bed her other fair hand was,
On the green coverlet ; whose perfect white
Show'd like an April daisy on the grass,
With pearly sweat, resembling dew of night.
Her eyes, like marigolds, had sheath'd their light,
    And canopied in darkness sweetly lay,
    Till they might open to adorn the day.
                                                    L. 393.

Thus he replies : " The colour in thy face
That even for anger makes the lily pale,
And the red rose blush at her own disgrace,
Shall plead for me."
                                                    L. 477.

I see what crosses my attempt will bring ;
I know what thorns the growing rose defends ;
I think the honey guarded with a sting.
                                                    L. 491.

The lesser thing should not the greater hide ;
    The cedar stoops not to the base shrub's foot,
    But low shrubs wither at the cedar's root.
                                                    L. 664.

Thy secret pleasure turns to open shame,
Thy private feasting to a public fast,
Thy smoothing titles to a ragged name,
Thy sugar'd tongue to bitter wormwood taste :
Thy violent vanities can never last.
    How comes it then, vile Opportunity,
    Being so bad, such numbers seek for thee ?
                                                    L. 890.

To fill with worm-holes stately monuments,
To feed oblivion with decay of things,

To blot old books and alter their contents,
To pluck the quills from ancient ravens' wings,
To dry the old oak's sap and cherish springs,
  To spoil antiquities of hammer'd steel,
  And turn the giddy round of Fortune's wheel.

L. 946.

And whiles against a thorn thou bear'st thy part,
To keep thy sharp woes waking.

L. 1135.

My body or my soul, which was the dearer,
When the one pure, the other made divine?
Whose love of either to myself was nearer,
When both were kept for heaven and Collatine?
Ay me! the bark peel'd from the lofty pine,
  His leaves will wither and his sap decay;
  So must my soul, her bark being peel'd away.

L. 1163.

And, from the strand of Dardan, where they fought,
To Simois' reedy banks the red blood ran,
Whose waves to imitate the battle sought
With swelling ridges; and their ranks began
To break upon the galled shore, and then
  Retire again, till, meeting greater ranks,
  They join and shoot their foam at Simois' banks.

L. 1436.

SONNETS.

From fairest creatures we desire increase,
That thereby beauty's rose might never die,
But as the riper should by time decease,
His tender heir might bear his memory.

S. i.

When forty winters shall besiege thy brow,
And dig deep trenches in thy beauty's field,
Thy youth's proud livery, so gazed on now,
Will be a tatter'd weed, of small worth held.

S. ii.

When I behold the violet past prime,
And sable curls all silver'd o'er with white;
When lofty trees I see barren of leaves
Which erst from heat did canopy the herd,
And summer's green all girded up in sheaves
Born on the bier with white and bristly beard.

S. xii.

Shall I compare thee to a summer's day?
Thou art more lovely and more temperate:
Rough winds do shake the darling buds of May,
And summer's lease hath all too short a date.

S. xviii.

Let those who are in favour with their stars
Of public honour and proud titles boast,
Whilst I, whom fortune of such triumph bars,
Unlook'd for joy in that I honour most.
Great princes' favourites their fair leaves spread
But as the marigold at the sun's eye,
And in themselves their pride lies buried,
For at a frown they in their glory die.

S. xxv.

No more be grieved at that which thou hast done;
Roses have thorns, and silver fountains mud;
Clouds and eclipses stain both moon and sun,
And loathsome canker lives in sweetest bud.

S. xxxv.

O, how much more doth beauty beauteous seem
By that sweet ornament which truth doth give!
The rose looks fair, but fairer we it deem
For that sweet odour which doth in it live.
The canker-blooms have full as deep a dye
As the perfumed tincture of the roses,
Hang on such thorns and play as wantonly
When summer's breath their masked buds discloses:
They live unwoo'd, and unrespected fade,
Die to themselves.   Sweet roses do not so;
Of their sweet deaths are sweetest odours made.

S. liv.

Ah! wherefore with infection should he live,
And with his presence grace impiety,
That sin by him advantage should achieve
And lace itself with his society?
Why should false painting imitate his cheek,
And steal dead seeing of his living hue?
Why should poor beauty indirectly seek
Roses of shadow, since his rose is true?
Why should he live, now Nature bankrupt is,
Beggar'd of blood to blush through lively veins?

S. lxvii.

How like Eve's apple doth thy beauty grow,
If thy sweet virtue answer not thy show!

S. xciii.

For sweetest things turn sourest by their deeds ;
Lilies that fester smell far worse than weeds.

S. xciv.

How sweet and lovely dost thou make the shame
Which, like a canker in the fragrant rose,
Doth spot the beauty of thy budding name!
O, in what sweets dost thou thy sins enclose !

S. xcv.

From you have I been absent in the spring,
When proud-pied April dress'd in all his trim
Hath put a spirit of youth in everything,
That heavy Saturn laugh'd and leap'd with him.
Yet nor the lays of birds nor the sweet smell
Of different flowers in odour and in hue
Could make me any summer's story tell,
Or from their proud lap pluck them where they grew ;
Nor did I wonder at the lily's white,
Nor praise the deep vermilion in the rose ;
They were but sweet, but figures of delight,
Drawn after you, you pattern of all those.
    Yet seem'd it winter still, and, you away,
    As with your shadow I with these did play.

S. xcviii.

The forward violet thus did I chide :
Sweet thief, whence didst thou steal thy sweet that
    smells,
If not from my love's breath ?   The purple pride
Which on thy soft cheek for complexion dwells
In my love's veins thou hast too grossly dyed.
The lily I condemned for thy hand,
And buds of marjoram had stol'n thy hair :
The roses fearfully on thorns did stand,
One blushing shame, another white despair :
A third, nor red nor white, had stol'n of both,
And to his robbery had annex'd thy breath ;
But, for his theft, in pride of all his growth
A vengeful canker eat him up to death.
    More flowers I noted, yet I none could see
    But sweet or colour it had stol'n from thee.

S. xcix.

The mortal moon hath her eclipse endured
And the sad augurs mock their own presage ;
Incertainties now crown themselves assured,
And peace proclaims olives of endless age.

S. cvii

16

For nothing this wide universe I call,
Save thou, my rose ; in it thou art my all.

S. cix.

Love's not Time's fool, though rosy lips and cheeks
Within his bending sickle's compass come.

S. cxvi.

I have seen roses damask'd, red and white,
But no such roses see I in her cheeks ;
And in some perfumes is there more delight
Than in the breath that from my mistress reeks.

S. cxxx.

LOVER'S COMPLAINT.

When thou impressest, what are precepts worth
Of stale example ?   When thou wilt inflame,
How coldly those impediments stand forth
Of wealth, of filial fear, law, kindred, fame!
Love's arms are peace, 'gainst rule, 'gainst sense, 'gainst
    shame,
And sweetens, in the suffering pangs it bears,
The aloes of all forces, shocks, and fears.

L. 267.

THE PASSIONATE PILGRIM.

Those thoughts, to me like oaks, to thee like osiers
    bow'd.

L. 60.

When Cytherea, all in love forlorn,
A longing tarriance for Adonis made
Under an osier growing by a brook.

L 73

A lily pale, with damask dye to grace her.

L. 89.

Sweet rose, fair flower, untimely pluck'd, soon vaded.
Pluck'd in the bud, and vaded in the spring !

L. 131.

Venus, with young Adonis sitting by her
Under a myrtle shade.

L. 143.

SONNETS TO SUNDRY NOTES OF MUSIC.

There will I make thee a bed of roses,
With a thousand fragrant posies,
A cap of flowers, and a kirtle
Embroider'd all with leaves of myrtle

A belt of straw and ivy buds.

L. 361.

Sitting in a pleasant shade
Which a grove of myrtles made.

L. 375.

THE PHŒNIX AND THE TURTLE.

Let the bird of loudest lay,
On the sole Arabian tree.

L. 1.

THE END